WARREN BUFFETT

ON BUSINESS

PRINCIPLES FROM THE SAGE OF OMAHA

RICHARD J. CONNORS

WILEY

John Wiley & Sons, Inc.

Published by John Wiley & Sons, Inc., Hoboken, New Jersey.
Published simultaneously in Canada.

For general information on our other products and services, or technical support, please
contact our Customer Care Department within the United States at 800-762-2974,
outside the United States at 317-572-3993 or fax 317-572-4002.

Wiley also publishes its books in a variety of electronic formats. Some content that appears
in print may not be available in electronic books.

For more information about Wiley products, visit our web site at http://www.wiley.com.

Library of Congress Cataloging-in-Publication Data:

Connors, Richard J., 1940-
 Warren Buffett on business : principles from the sage of Omaha/Richard J. Connors.
  p. cm.
 Includes bibliographical references.
 ISBN 978-0-470-50230-3 (cloth)
 1. Management. 2. Buffett, Warren. 3. Berkshire Hathaway Inc.—Management.
I. Title.
 HD31.C6244 2010
 658—dc22
                                                              2009024946

Printed in the United States of America
10 9 8 7 6 5 4 3 2 1

To my father, a great investor, who would have loved to have met Warren Buffett

To my grandchildren, Bridget, Frankie, Richie, Patrick, Catherine, and Sean

I wish I knew what I know now when I was younger.
—ROD STEWART

The wisdom of the wise, and the experience of ages, may be preserved by quotation.
—ISAAC DISRAELI

Contents

Acknowledgments

Unknowingly, this book began in April 2006, when I wrote Judith Schwartz, the executive director of the Washington University in St. Louis Lifelong Learning Institute (LLI) proposing a course on Warren Buffett. Rather than throwing the letter away, she forwarded it to Harry Estill. After several planning meetings with Harry and Butch Sterbenz, the course was born. Thanks to Charlie Moore of the LLI for his encouragement and input. I thank them all for their interest and support and the LLI for its great facility, and its administrators and volunteers for their extraordinary contribution to the senior citizens in St. Louis.

I thank the many participants who have attended the course over the past three years. Their enthusiasm and participation were all A+. At the last class of each course, we feasted on Cherry Cokes, See's Candies, and Dairy Queen, all Warren's favorites. We had a lot of fun.

Thanks to Bob Shirrell, Alice Aslin, Bob Leggat and Bob Leonard for their early readings of the first draft. I am blessed to have signed up with John Wiley & Sons and its wonderful team, especially Debra Englander, Adrianna Johnson, Judy Howarth, and Mary Daniello. They had to work with a totally inexperienced rookie. Also, I thank Emma Harris who worked tirelessly to produce the initial electronic version of the manuscript and to Carrie Kizer, an assistant to Warren, who always promptly responded to my e-mails.

Last, and most importantly, I thank Warren for his time and extraordinary generous support over the past three years. Whenever I e-mailed him about my course or the book, I always received a quick response, usually the next day. He always had time for me, for which I will always be grateful.

Introduction

Most books written about Warren Buffett have focused on how he invests and how you can invest just like him. When I am asked "How can I invest like Warren Buffett?," my answer is simple and direct: Buy either Berkshire Class A or Class B stock. In his 1987 Berkshire stockholder letter, Buffett also advised, "If they want to participate in whatever Berkshire is buying they can always purchase Berkshire stock. But perhaps that is too simple."[1] Buffett also says that most individual investors should purchase stock index funds because they are very low cost and they outperform most professional investment managers. In January 2008, to prove his point, Buffett entered into a bet (each side put up roughly $320,000, with the final proceeds going to the winner's favorite charity) with Protege Partners, a fund-of-funds hedge fund, that their handpicked funds will not beat the S&P 500 index over the next 10 years. A principal of Protege said, "Fortunately, for us, we're betting against the S&P's performance, not Buffett's."[2]

For the past three years, I have presented a course on Buffett at the Washington University in St. Louis Lifelong Learning Institute. It all began in April 2006, when I sent a letter to Buffett telling him that I was going to present the course. Four days later, he wrote back encouraging me and supporting the course. I was very excited to receive his letter, but no more than the woman who framed it for display on my office wall. Since then, Buffett and I have regularly exchanged e-mails about the course. In January 2007, at his invitation, I traveled to Omaha and met him in his office. As busy as he is, he has always had time for me.

This book is different. It is not about how Buffett invests or how you can invest like him. Rather, it is about his business management principles and practices. It is about his way of communicating with and treating employees and shareholders fairly and honestly; responsible corporate governance; ethical behavior; patience and perseverance; admitting mistakes; having a passion for work; and having fun and a sense of humor. Can all this be learned from one man? In my view, yes. There are some people who are simply so unique, so very special, that no words can do them justice. His genius is in his character. His integrity is unsurpassed. His patience, discipline, and rationality are extraordinary.

The Buffett/Berkshire Hathaway model of managing a business, large or small, should be required reading for all business executives, entrepreneurs, and business school students. Shareholders, employees, and the public would all benefit by employing his management principles and by emulating his straightforward, genuine, and sincere behavior. His ideas and philosophy of life will last far beyond his own. When you strip it all away, effective business management—the Warren Buffett way—is remarkably obvious and simple. He describes his business principles as "simple, old, and few."[3]

In the words of Charlie Rose, "When we spend a year with someone in conversations in a variety of places, you learn what makes them tick. What do you come away with from conversations with Warren Buffett? It is his passion for his company, passion for his friends, passion for his work and a passion for living life. This is a man that has fun."[4]

This book is mainly a carefully selected compilation, by topic, in Buffett's own words from his Berkshire Hathaway shareholders letters, written over four decades (1977–2008). My most difficult task was deciding what *not* to include. I strongly urge you to read his letters in their entirety. They are freely available on the Berkshire Hathaway web site. Also, I recommend you read the *Intelligent Investor* by Benjamin Graham.

I hope this book will both educate and inspire you to be a better manager.

Chapter 1

Shareholders as Partners

Although our form is corporate, our attitude is partnership. Charlie Munger and I think of our shareholders as owners-partners, and ourselves as managing partners. . . . We do not view the company itself as the owner of our business assets but instead view the company as a conduit through which our shareholders own the assets.[1]

CEOs must embrace stewardship as a way of life and treat their owners as partners not patsies. It's time for CEOs to walk the walk.[2]

—WARREN BUFFETT

Charlie and I hope that you do not think of yourself as merely owning a piece of paper whose price wiggles around daily and that is a candidate for sale when some economic or political event makes you nervous. We hope you instead visualize yourself as a part owner of a business that you expect to stay with indefinitely, much as you might if you owned a farm or apartment house in partnership with members of your family. For our part, we do not view Berkshire shareholders as faceless members of an ever-shifting crowd, but rather as co-venturers who have entrusted their funds to us for what may well turn out to be the remainder of their lives.

The evidence suggests that most Berkshire shareholders have indeed embraced this long-term partnership concept. The annual percentage turnover in Berkshire's shares is a small fraction of that occurring in the stocks of other major American corporations, even when the shares I own are excluded from the calculation.

In effect, our shareholders behave in respect to their Berkshire stock much as Berkshire itself behaves in respect to companies in which it has an investment. As owners of, say, Coca-Cola or Gillette shares, we think of Berkshire as being a non-managing partner in two extraordinary businesses, in which we measure our success by the long-term progress of the companies rather than by the month-to-month movements of their stocks. In fact, we would not care in the least if several years went by in which there was no trading, or quotation of prices, in the stocks of those companies. If we have good long-term expectations, short-term price changes are meaningless for us except to the extent they offer us an opportunity to increase our ownership at an attractive price.

Charlie and I cannot promise you results. But we can guarantee that your financial fortunes will move in lockstep with ours for what-ever period of time you elect to be our partner. We have no interest in large salaries or options or other means of gaining an "edge" over you. We want to make money only when our partners do and in exactly the same proportion. Moreover, when I do something dumb, I want you to be able to derive some solace from the fact that my financial suffering is proportional to yours.[3]

■ ■ ■

At Berkshire, we believe that the company's money is the owners' money, just as it would be in a closely-held corporation, partnership, or sole proprietorship.[4]

■ ■ ■

What we promise you—along with more modest gains—is that during your ownership of Berkshire, you will fare just as Charlie and I do. If you suffer, we will suffer; if we prosper, so will you. And we will not break this bond by introducing compensation arrangements that give us a greater participation in the upside than the downside.

We further promise you that our personal fortunes will remain overwhelmingly concentrated in Berkshire shares: We will not ask you to invest with us and then put our own money elsewhere. In addition, Berkshire dominates both the investment portfolios of most members of our families and of a great many friends who belonged to partnerships that Charlie and I ran in the 1960s. We could not be more motivated to do our best.[5]

■ ■ ■

Though our primary goal is to maximize the amount that our shareholders, in total, reap from their ownership of Berkshire, we wish also to minimize the benefits going to some shareholders at the expense of others. These are goals we would have were we managing a family partnership, and we believe they make equal sense for the manager of a public company. In a partnership, fairness requires that partnership interests be valued equitably when partners enter or exit; in a public company, fairness prevails when market price and intrinsic value are in sync. Obviously, they won't always meet that ideal, but a manager—by his policies and communications—can do much to foster equity.[6]

Chapter 2

Corporate Culture

Why Don't More Companies and Investors Copy Berkshire Hathaway? It's a good question. Our approach has worked for us. Look at the fun we, our managers and our shareholders are having. More people should copy us. It's not difficult, but it looks difficult because it's unconventional—it isn't the way things are normally done. We have low overhead, don't have quarterly goals and budgets or a standard personnel system, and our investing is much more concentrated than is the average. It's simple and common sense.[1]

—CHARLIE MUNGER

The priority is that all of us continue to zealously guard Berkshire's reputation. We can't be perfect but we can try to be. . . . We can afford to lose money—even a lot of money. But we can't afford to lose reputation—even a shred of reputation. We must continue to measure every act against not only what is legal but also what we would be happy to have written about on the front page of a national newspaper in an article written by an unfriendly but intelligent reporter.[2]

—WARREN BUFFETT

I think we have a very good culture virtually everyplace in Berkshire. I hope it's everyplace. This is what we are looking for, and it's more a question of culture than controls. If you have a good culture, I think you can make the rules pretty simple.[3]

—WARREN BUFFETT

Give Warren a Call

Our long-avowed goal is to be the "buyer of choice" for businesses—particularly those built and owned by families. The way to achieve this goal is to deserve it. That means we must keep our promises; avoid leveraging up acquired businesses; grant unusual autonomy to our managers; and hold the purchased companies through thick and thin (though we prefer thick and thicker).

Our record matches our rhetoric. Most buyers competing against us, however, follow a different path. For them, acquisitions are "merchandise." Before the ink dries on their purchase contracts, these operators are contemplating "exit strategies." We have a decided advantage, therefore, when we encounter sellers who truly care about the future of their businesses.

Some years back our competitors were known as "leveraged-buyout operators." But LBO became a bad name. So in Orwellian fashion, the buyout firms decided to change their moniker. What they did not change, though, were the essential ingredients of their previous operations, including their cherished fee structures and love of leverage.

Their new label became "private equity," a name that turns the facts upside-down: A purchase of a business by these firms almost invariably results in dramatic *reductions* in the equity portion of the acquiree's capital structure compared to that previously existing. A number of these acquirees, purchased only two to three years ago, are now in mortal danger because of the debt piled on them by their private-equity buyers. Much of the bank debt is selling below 70¢ on the dollar, and the public debt has taken a far greater beating. The private equity firms, it should be noted, are not rushing in to inject the equity their wards now desperately need. Instead, they're keeping their remaining funds *very* private.[4]

■ ■ ■

If we fail, we will have no excuses. Charlie and I operate in an ideal environment. To begin with, we are supported by an incredible group of

Allocating scarce investment capital, in the face of business risks and uncertainties.

men and women who run our operating units. If there were a Corporate Cooperstown, its roster would surely include many of our CEOs. Any shortfall in Berkshire's results will not be caused by our managers.

Additionally, we enjoy a rare sort of managerial freedom. Most companies are saddled with institutional constraints. A company's history, for example, may commit it to an industry that now offers limited opportunity. A more common problem is a shareholder constituency that pressures its manager to dance to Wall Street's tune. Many CEOs resist, but others give in and adopt operating and capital allocation policies far different from those they would choose if left to themselves.

At Berkshire, neither history nor the demands of owners impede intelligent decision-making. When Charlie and I make mistakes, they are—in tennis parlance—unforced errors.[5]

■ ■ ■

Very few CEOs of public companies operate under a similar mandate, mainly because they have owners who focus on short-term prospects and reported earnings. Berkshire, however, has a shareholder base— which it will have for decades to come—that has the longest investment horizon to be found in the public-company universe. Indeed, a majority of our shares are held by investors who expect to die still holding them. We can therefore ask our CEOs to manage for maximum long-term value, rather than for next quarter's earnings. We certainly don't ignore the current results of our businesses—in most cases, they are of great importance—but we *never* want them to be achieved at the expense of our building ever-greater competitive strengths.[6]

■ ■ ■

We find it meaningful when an owner *cares* about whom he sells to. We like to do business with someone who loves his company, not just the money that a sale will bring him (though we certainly understand why he likes that as well). When this emotional attachment exists, it signals that important qualities will likely be found within the business: honest accounting, pride of product, respect for customers, and a loyal group of associates having a strong sense of direction. The reverse is apt to be true, also. When an owner auctions off his business, exhibiting a total lack of interest in what follows, you will frequently find that it has been dressed up for sale, particularly when the seller is a "financial owner." And if owners behave with little regard for their business and its people, their conduct will often contaminate attitudes and practices throughout the company.

When a business masterpiece has been created by a lifetime—or several lifetimes—of unstinting care and exceptional talent, it should be important to the owner what corporation is entrusted to carry on its history. Charlie and I believe Berkshire provides an almost unique home. We take our obligations to the people who created a business very seriously, and Berkshire's ownership structure ensures that we can fulfill our promises.

How much better it is for the "painter" of a business Rembrandt to personally select its permanent home than to have a trust officer or uninterested heirs auction it off. Throughout the years we have had great experiences with those who recognize that truth and apply it to their business creations. We'll leave the auctions to others.[7]

■ ■ ■

I think there's more chance of our corporate culture being maintained intact for many decades than any company I can think of. We have a board that's bought into it entirely. They're big owners themselves in almost every case. They've seen it work. We've got 70 managers at 76 businesses out there. They have come to us because of that culture. They've seen it work, too. You've had it communicated through annual reports, at annual meetings. I think it's as strong a culture as you could possibly have. I think that anybody that tried to fool with it would not be around here very long and the fact is that I would come back and haunt them, too.[8]

■ ■ ■

They would not have sold to anybody but us. It's that simple because they know what they're getting. They know what museum they're going into. They know that their picture is going to hang there and not get stuck in the basement, and they know that we're not going to come in and tell somebody to paint over it.[9]

■ ■ ■

We will not engage in unfriendly takeovers. We can promise complete confidentiality and a very fast answer—customarily within five minutes—as to whether we're interested. (With Brown, we didn't even need to take five.) We prefer to buy for cash, but will consider issuing stock when we receive as much in intrinsic business value as we give.[10]

■ ■ ■

Unlike many business buyers, Berkshire has no "exit strategy." We buy to keep. We do, though, have an entrance strategy, looking for businesses in this country or abroad that meet our six criteria and are available at a price that will produce a reasonable return. If you have a business that fits, give me a call. Like a hopeful teenage girl, I'll be waiting by the phone.[11]

■ ■ ■

Sometimes your associates will say "Everybody else is doing it." This rationale is almost always a bad one if it is the main justification for a business action. It is totally unacceptable when evaluating a moral decision. Whenever somebody offers that phrase as a rationale, in effect they are saying that they can't come up with a *good* reason. If anyone offers this explanation, tell them to try using it with a reporter or a judge and see how far it gets them.[12]

■ ■ ■

Our culture is very old-fashioned, like Ben Franklin's or Andrew Carnegie's. Can you imagine Carnegie hiring consultants? It's amazing how well this approach still works. A lot of the businesses we buy are kind of cranky and old-fashioned like us.

For many of our shareholders, our stock is all they own, and we're acutely aware of that. Our culture (of conservatism) runs pretty deep. This is an amazingly sound place. We are more disaster-resistant than most other places. We haven't pushed it as hard as other people would have pushed it.[13]

Some Thoughts on Selling Your Business*

Dear _____:

Here are a few thoughts pursuant to our conversation of the other day.

Most business owners spend the better part of their lifetimes building their businesses. By experience built upon endless repetition, they sharpen their skills in merchandising, purchasing, personnel selection, etc. It's a learning process, and mistakes made in one year often contribute to competence and success in succeeding years.

In contrast, owner-managers sell their business only once—frequently in an emotionally charged atmosphere with a multitude of pressures coming from different directions. Often, much of the pressure comes from brokers whose compensation is contingent upon consummation of a sale, regardless of its consequences for both buyer and seller. The fact that the decision is so important, both financially and personally, to the owner can make the process more, rather than less, prone to error. And, mistakes made in the once-in-a-lifetime sale of a business are not reversible.

---

*This is an edited version of a letter I sent some years ago to a man who had indicated that he might want to sell his family business. I present it here because it is a message I would like to convey to other prospective sellers. —W.E.B.

Price is very important, but often is not the most critical aspect of the sale. You and your family have an extraordinary business—one of a kind in your field—and any buyer is going to recognize that. It's also a business that is going to get more valuable as the years go by. So if you decide not to sell now, you are very likely to realize more money later on. With that knowledge you can deal from strength and take the time required to select the buyer you want.

If you should decide to sell, I think Berkshire Hathaway offers some advantages that most other buyers do not. Practically all of these buyers will fall into one of two categories:

(1) A company located elsewhere but operating in your business or in a business somewhat akin to yours. Such a buyer—no matter what promises are made—will usually have managers who feel they know how to run your business operations and, sooner or later, will want to apply some hands-on "help." If the acquiring company is much larger, it often will have squads of managers, recruited over the years in part by promises that they will get to run future acquisitions. They will have their own way of doing things and, even though your business record undoubtedly will be far better than theirs, human nature will at some point cause them to believe that their methods of operating are superior. You and your family probably have friends who have sold their businesses to larger companies, and I suspect that their experiences will confirm the tendency of parent companies to take over the running of their subsidiaries, particularly when the parent knows the industry, or thinks it does.

(2) A financial maneuverer, invariably operating with large amounts of borrowed money, who plans to resell either to the public or to another corporation as soon as the time is favorable. Frequently, this buyer's major contribution will be to change accounting methods so that earnings can be presented in the most favorable light just prior to his bailing out. I'm enclosing a recent article that describes this sort of transaction, which is becoming much more frequent because of a rising stock market and the great supply of funds available for such transactions.

If the sole motive of the present owners is to cash their chips and put the business behind them—and plenty of sellers fall in this category—either type of buyer that I've just described is satisfactory. But if the sellers' business represents the creative work of a lifetime and forms an integral part of their personality and sense of being, buyers of either type have serious flaws.

Berkshire is another kind of buyer—a rather unusual one. We buy to keep, but we don't have, and don't expect to have, operating people in our parent organization. All of the businesses we own are run autonomously to an extraordinary degree. In most cases, the managers of important businesses we have owned for many years have not been to Omaha or even met each other. When we buy a business, the sellers go on running it just as they did before the sale; we adapt to their methods rather than vice versa.

We have no one—family, recently recruited MBAs, etc.— to whom we have promised a chance to run businesses we have bought from owner-managers. And we won't have.

You know of some of our past purchases. I'm enclosing a list of everyone from whom we have ever bought a business, and I invite you to check with them as to our performance versus our promises. You should be particularly interested in checking with the few whose businesses did not do well in order to ascertain how we behaved under difficult conditions.

ˋAny buyer will tell you that he needs you personally—and if he has any brains, he most certainly does need you. But a great many buyers, for the reasons mentioned above, don't match their subsequent actions to their earlier words. We will behave exactly as promised, both because we have so promised, and because we need to in order to achieve the best business results.

This need explains why we would want the operating members of your family to retain a 20% interest in the business. We need 80% to consolidate earnings for tax purposes, which is a step important to us. It is equally important to us that the family members who run the business remain as owners. Very simply, we would not want to buy unless we felt key members of present management would stay on as our partners. Contracts cannot guarantee your continued interest; we would simply rely on your word.

The areas I get involved in are capital allocation and selection and compensation of the top man. Other personnel decisions, operating strategies, etc. are his bailiwick. Some Berkshire managers talk over some of their decisions with me; some don't. It depends upon their personalities and, to an extent, upon their own personal relationship with me.

If you should decide to do business with Berkshire, we would pay in cash. Your business would not be used as collateral for any loan by Berkshire. There would be no brokers involved.

Furthermore, there would be no chance that a deal would be announced and that the buyer would then back off or start suggesting adjustments (with apologies, of course, and with an explanation that banks, lawyers, boards of directors, etc. were to be blamed). And finally, you would know exactly with whom you are dealing. You would not have one executive negotiate the deal only to have someone else in charge a few years later, or have the president regretfully tell you that his board of directors required this change or that (or possibly required sale of your business to finance some new interest of the parent's).

It's only fair to tell you that you would be no richer after the sale than now. The ownership of your business already makes you wealthy and soundly invested. A sale would change the form of your wealth, but it wouldn't change its amount. If you sell, you will have exchanged a 100%-owned valuable asset that you understand for another valuable asset—cash—that will probably be invested in small pieces (stocks) of other businesses that you understand less well. There is often a sound reason to sell but, if the transaction is a fair one, the reason is not so that the seller can become wealthier.

I will not pester you; if you have any possible interest in selling, I would appreciate your call. I would be extraordinarily proud to have Berkshire, along with the key members of your family, own _____; I believe we would do very well financially; and I believe you would have just as much fun running the business over the next 20 years as you have had during the past 20.

Sincerely,

Warren E. Buffett[14]

Chapter 3

Corporate Governance

*If able but greedy managers overreach and try to dip too deeply
into the shareholders' pockets, directors must slap their hands.*[1]
—WARREN BUFFETT

Accountability and Stewardship

True independence—meaning the willingness to challenge a forceful
CEO when something is wrong or foolish—is an enormously valuable
trait in a director. It is also rare. The place to look for it is among high-
grade people whose interests are in line with those of rank-and-file
shareholders—*and are in line in a very big way.*

We've made that search at Berkshire. We now have eleven directors and *each* of them, combined with members of their families,
owns more than $4 million of Berkshire stock. Moreover, all have
held major stakes in Berkshire for many years. In the case of six of the
eleven, family ownership amounts to at least hundreds of millions and
dates back at least three decades. All eleven directors purchased their
holdings in the market just as you did; we've never passed out options
or restricted shares. Charlie and I love such honest-to-God ownership.
After all, who ever washes a rental car? In addition, director fees at
Berkshire are nominal (as my son, Howard, periodically reminds me).
Thus, the upside from Berkshire for all eleven is proportionately the
same as the upside for any Berkshire shareholder. And it always will be.

The downside for Berkshire directors is actually worse than yours
because we carry *no* directors and officers liability insurance. Therefore,

if something really catastrophic happens on our directors' watch, they are exposed to losses that will far exceed yours.

The bottom line for our directors: You win, they win big; you lose, they lose big. Our approach might be called owner-capitalism. We know of no better way to engender true independence. (This structure does not guarantee perfect behavior, however: I've sat on boards of companies in which Berkshire had huge stakes and remained silent as questionable proposals were rubber-stamped.)

In addition to being independent, directors should have business savvy, a shareholder orientation and a genuine interest in the company. The rarest of these qualities is business savvy—and if it is lacking, the other two are of little help. Many people who are smart, articulate and admired have no real understanding of business. That's no sin; they may shine elsewhere. But they don't belong on corporate boards. Similarly, I would be useless on a medical or scientific board (though I would likely be welcomed by a chairman who wanted to run things his way). My name would dress up the list of directors, but I wouldn't know enough to critically evaluate proposals. Moreover, to cloak my ignorance, I would keep my mouth shut (if you can imagine that). In effect, I could be replaced, without loss, by a potted plant.

Last year, as we moved to change our board, I asked for self-nominations from shareholders who believed they had the requisite qualities to be a Berkshire director. Despite the lack of either liability insurance or meaningful compensation, we received more than twenty applications. Most were good, coming from owner-oriented individuals having family holdings of Berkshire worth well over $1 million. After considering them, Charlie and I—with the concurrence of our incumbent directors—asked four shareholders who did not nominate themselves to join the board: David Gottesman, Charlotte Guyman, Don Keough and Tom Murphy. These four people are all friends of mine, and I know their strengths well. They bring an extraordinary amount of business talent to Berkshire's board.[2]

■ ■ ■

Both the ability and fidelity of managers have long needed monitoring. Indeed, nearly 2,000 years ago, Jesus Christ addressed this subject, speaking (Luke 16:2) approvingly of "a certain rich man" who told his manager, "Give an account of thy stewardship; for thou mayest no longer be steward."

Accountability and stewardship withered in the last decade, becoming qualities deemed of little importance by those caught up in the Great Bubble. As stock prices went up, the behavioral norms of managers went down. By the late '90s, as a result, CEOs who traveled the high road did not encounter heavy traffic.

Most CEOs, it should be noted, are men and women you would be happy to have as trustees for our children's assets or as next-door neighbors. Too many of these people, however, have in recent years behaved badly at the office, fudging numbers and drawing obscene pay for mediocre business achievements. These otherwise decent people simply followed the career path of Mae West: "I was Snow White but I drifted."

In theory, corporate boards should have prevented this deterioration of conduct. I last wrote about the responsibilities of directors in the 1993 annual report. (We will send you a copy of this discussion on request, or you may read it on the Internet in the Corporate Governance section of the 1993 letter.) There, I said that directors "should behave as if there was a single absentee owner, whose long-term interest they should try to further in all proper ways." This means that directors must get rid of a manager who is mediocre or worse, no matter how likable he may be. Directors must react as did the chorus-girl bride of an 85-year-old multimillionaire when he asked whether she would love him if he lost his money. "Of course," the young beauty replied, "I would miss you, but I would still love you."

In the 1993 annual report, I also said directors had another job: "If able but greedy managers overreach and try to dip too deeply into the shareholders' pockets, directors must slap their hands." Since I wrote that, over-reaching has become common but few hands have been slapped.

Why have intelligent and decent directors failed so miserably? The answer lies not in inadequate laws—it's always been clear that directors are obligated to represent the interests of shareholders—but rather in what I'd call "boardroom atmosphere."[3]

■ ■ ■

It's almost impossible, for example, in a boardroom populated by well-mannered people, to raise the question of whether the CEO should be replaced. It's equally awkward to question a proposed acquisition that has been endorsed by the CEO, particularly when his inside staff and outside advisors are present and unanimously support his decision. (They wouldn't be in the room if they didn't.) Finally, when the compensation committee—armed, as always, with support from a high-paid consultant—reports on a megagrant of options to the CEO, it would be like belching at the dinner table for a director to suggest that the committee reconsider.

These "social" difficulties argue for outside directors regularly meeting without the CEO—a reform that is being instituted and that I enthusiastically endorse. I doubt, however, that most of the other new governance rules and recommendations will provide benefits commensurate with the monetary and other costs they impose.

The current cry is for "independent" directors. It is certainly true that it is desirable to have directors who think and speak independently—but they must also be business-savvy, interested and shareholder oriented.

In my 1993 commentary, those are the three qualities I described as essential. Over a span of 40 years, I have been on 19 public-company boards (excluding Berkshire's) and have interacted with perhaps 250 directors. Most of them were "independent" as defined by today's rules. But the great majority of these directors lacked at least one of the three qualities I value. As a result, their contribution to shareholder well-being was minimal at best and, too often, negative. These people, decent and intelligent though they were, simply did not know enough about business and/or care enough about shareholders to question foolish acquisitions or egregious compensation. My own behavior, I must ruefully add, frequently fell short as well: Too often I was silent when management made proposals that I judged to be counter to the interests of shareholders. In those cases, collegiality trumped independence.[4]

■■■

Rules that have been proposed and that are almost certain to go into effect will require changes in Berkshire's board, obliging us to add directors who meet the codified requirements for "independence."

Doing so, we will add a test that we believe is important, but far from determinative, in fostering independence: We will select directors who have huge and true ownership interests (that is, stock that they or their family have *purchased*, not been given by Berkshire or received via options), expecting those interests to influence their actions to a degree that dwarfs other considerations such as prestige and board fees.

That gets to an often-overlooked point about directors' compensation, which at public companies averages perhaps $50,000 annually. It baffles me how the many directors who look to these dollars for perhaps 20% or more of their annual income can be considered independent when Ron Olson, for example, who is on our board, may be deemed not independent because he receives a tiny percentage of his very large income from Berkshire legal fees. As the investment company saga suggests, a director whose moderate income is heavily dependent on directors' fees—and who hopes mightily to be invited to join other boards in order to earn more fees—is highly unlikely to offend a CEO or fellow directors, who in a major way will determine his reputation in corporate circles. If regulators believe that "significant" money taints independence (and it certainly can), they have overlooked a massive class of possible offenders.

At Berkshire, wanting our fees to be meaningless to our directors, we pay them only a pittance. Additionally, not wanting to insulate our directors from any corporate disaster we might have, we don't provide them with officers' and directors' liability insurance (an unorthodoxy that, not so incidentally, has saved our shareholders many millions of dollars over the years). Basically, we want the behavior of our directors to be driven by the effect their decisions will have on their family's net worth, not by their compensation. That's the equation for Charlie and me as managers, and we think it's the right one for Berkshire directors as well.

To find new directors, we will look through our shareholders list for people who directly, or in their family, have had large Berkshire holdings—in the millions of dollars—for a long time. Individuals making that cut should automatically meet two of our tests, namely that they be interested in Berkshire and shareholder-oriented. In our third test, we will look for business savvy, a competence that is far from commonplace.

Finally, we will continue to have members of the Buffett family on the board. They are not there to run the business after I die, nor will they then receive compensation of any kind. Their purpose is to ensure, for both our shareholders and managers, that Berkshire's special culture will be nurtured when I'm succeeded by other CEOs.

Any change we make in the composition of our board will not alter the way Charlie and I run Berkshire. We will continue to emphasize substance over form in our work and waste as little time as possible during board meetings in show-and-tell and perfunctory activities. The most important job of our board is likely to be the selection of successors to Charlie and me, and that is a matter upon which it will focus.

The board we have had up to now has overseen a shareholder-oriented business, consistently run in accord with the economic principles set forth on pages 68–74 of the Owner's Manual (which I urge all new shareholders to read).

Our goal is to obtain new directors who are equally devoted to those principles.[5]

■ ■ ■

I can't resist mentioning that Jesus understood the calibration of independence far more clearly than do the protesting institutions. In Matthew 6:21, he observed: "For where your treasure is, there will your heart be also." Even to an institutional investor, $8 billion should qualify as "treasure" that dwarfs any profits Berkshire might earn on its routine transactions with Coke.

Measured by the biblical standard, the Berkshire board is a model: (a) *every* director is a member of a family owning at least $4 million of stock; (b) *none* of these shares were acquired from Berkshire via options or grants; (c) *no* directors receive committee, consulting or board fees from the company that are more than a tiny portion of their annual income; and (d) although we have a standard corporate indemnity arrangement, we carry no liability insurance for directors.

At Berkshire, board members travel the same road as shareholders.[6]

■ ■ ■

Berkshire's board has fully discussed each of the three CEO candidates and has unanimously agreed on the person who should succeed me if a replacement were needed today. The directors stay updated on this subject and could alter their view as circumstances change—new managerial stars may emerge and present ones will age. The important point is that the directors know now—and will always know in the future—exactly what they will do when the need arises.

The other question that must be addressed is whether the Board will be prepared to make a change if that need should arise not from my death but rather from my decay, particularly if this decay is accompanied by my delusionally thinking that I am reaching new peaks of managerial brilliance. That problem would not be unique to me. Charlie and I have faced this situation from time to time at Berkshire's subsidiaries. Humans age at greatly varying rates—but sooner or later their talents and vigor decline. Some managers remain effective well into their 80s—Charlie is a wonder at 82—and others noticeably fade in their 60s. When their abilities ebb, so usually do their powers of self-assessment. Someone else often needs to blow the whistle.

When that time comes for me, our board will have to step up to the job. From a financial standpoint, its members are unusually motivated to do so. I know of no other board in the country in which the financial interests of directors are so completely aligned with those of shareholders. Few boards even come close. On a personal level, however, it is extraordinarily difficult for most people to tell someone, particularly a friend, that he or she is no longer capable.

If I become a candidate for that message, however, our board will be doing me a favor by delivering it. *Every* share of Berkshire that I own is destined to go to philanthropies, and I want society to reap the maximum good from these gifts and bequests. It would be a tragedy if the philanthropic potential of my holdings was diminished because my associates shirked their responsibility to (tenderly, I hope) show me the door. But don't worry about this. We have an outstanding group of directors, and they will always do what's right for shareholders.[7]

■ ■ ■

In selecting a new director, we were guided by our long-standing criteria, which are that board members be owner-oriented, business-savvy, interested and truly independent. I say "truly" because many directors who are now deemed independent by various authorities and observers are far from that, relying heavily as they do on directors' fees to maintain their standard of living. These payments, which come in many forms, often range between $150,000 and $250,000 annually, compensation that may approach or even exceed all other income of the "independent" director. And—surprise, surprise—director compensation has soared in recent years, pushed up by recommendations from corporate America's favorite consultant, Ratchet, Ratchet, and Bingo. (The name may be phony, but the action it conveys is not.)

Charlie and I believe our four criteria are essential if directors are to do their job—which, by law, is to faithfully represent *owners*. Yet these criteria are usually ignored. Instead, consultants and CEOs seeking board candidates will often say, "We're looking for a woman," or "a Hispanic," or "someone from abroad," or what have you. It sometimes sounds as if the mission is to stock Noah's ark. Over the years I've been queried many times about potential directors and have yet to hear *anyone* ask, "Does he think like an intelligent owner?"

The questions I instead get would sound ridiculous to someone seeking candidates for, say, a football team, or an arbitration panel or a military command. In those cases, the selectors would look for people who had the specific talents and attitudes that were required for a specialized job. At Berkshire, we are in the specialized activity of running a business well, and therefore we seek *business* judgment.[8]

■ ■ ■

The primary job of our directors is to select my successor, either upon my death or disability, or when I begin to lose my marbles. (David Ogilvy had it right when he said: "Develop your eccentricities when young. That way, when you get older, people won't think you are going gaga." Charlie's family and mine feel that we overreacted to David's advice.)

At our directors' meetings we cover the usual run of housekeeping matters. But the real discussion—both with me in the room and absent—centers on the strengths and weaknesses of the four internal candidates to replace me.

Our board knows that the ultimate scorecard on its performance will be determined by the record of my successor. He or she will need to maintain Berkshire's culture, allocate capital and keep a group of America's best managers happy in their jobs. This isn't the toughest task in the world—the train is already moving at a good clip down the track—and I'm totally comfortable about it being done well by any of the four candidates we have identified. I have more than 99% of my net worth in Berkshire and will be happy to have my wife or foundation (depending on the order in which she and I die) continue this concentration.[9]

■ ■ ■

Two post-bubble governance reforms have been particularly useful at Berkshire, and I fault myself for not putting them in place many years ago. The first involves regular meetings of directors without the CEO present. I've sat on 19 boards, and on many occasions this process would have led to dubious plans being examined more thoroughly. In a few cases, CEO changes that were needed would also have been made more promptly. There is no downside to this process, and there are many possible benefits.

The second reform concerns the "whistleblower line," an arrangement through which employees can send information to me and the board's audit committee without fear of reprisal. Berkshire's extreme decentralization makes this system particularly valuable both to me and the committee. (In a sprawling "city" of 180,000—Berkshire's current employee count—not every sparrow that falls will be noticed at headquarters.) Most of the complaints we have received are of "the guy next to me has bad breath" variety, but on occasion I have learned of important problems at our subsidiaries that I otherwise would have missed. The issues raised are usually not of a type discoverable by audit, but relate instead to personnel and business practices. Berkshire would be more valuable today if I had put in a whistleblower line decades ago.

Charlie and I love the idea of shareholders thinking and behaving like owners. Sometimes that requires them to be proactive. And in this arena, large institutional owners should lead the way.

So far, however, the moves made by institutions have been less than awe-inspiring. Usually, they've focused on minutiae and ignored the three questions that truly count. First, does the company have the right CEO? Second, is he/she overreaching in terms of compensation? Third, are proposed acquisitions more likely to create or destroy per-share value?

On such questions, the interests of the CEO may well differ from those of the shareholders. Directors, moreover, sometimes lack the knowledge or gumption to overrule the CEO. Therefore, it's vital that large owners focus on these three questions and speak up when necessary.

Instead many simply follow a "checklist" approach to the issue du jour. Last year I was on the receiving end of a judgment reached in that manner. Several institutional shareholders and their advisors decided I lacked "independence" in my role as a director of Coca-Cola. One group wanted me removed from the board and another simply wanted me booted from the audit committee.[10]

■ ■ ■

The acid test for reform will be CEO compensation. Managers will cheerfully agree to board "diversity," attest to SEC filings and adopt meaningless proposals relating to process. What many will fight, however, is a hard look at their own pay and perks.

Directors should not serve on compensation committees unless they are *themselves* capable of negotiating on behalf of owners. They should explain both how they think about pay and how they measure performance. Dealing with shareholders' money, moreover, they should behave as they would were it their own.

In the 1890s, Samuel Gompers described the goal of organized labor as "More!" In the 1990s, America's CEOs adopted his battle cry. The upshot is that CEOs have often amassed riches while their shareholders have experienced financial disasters.

Directors should stop such piracy. There's nothing wrong with paying well for truly exceptional business performance. But, for anything short of that, it's time for directors to shout "Less!" It would be a travesty if the bloated pay of recent years became a baseline for future compensation. Compensation committees should go back to the drawing boards.[11]

The Audit Committee

Audit committees can't audit. Only a company's outside auditor can determine whether the earnings that a management purports to have made are suspect. Reforms that ignore this reality and that instead focus on the structure and charter of the audit committee will accomplish little. As we've discussed, far too many managers have fudged their company's numbers in recent years, using both accounting and operational techniques that are typically legal but that nevertheless materially mislead investors. Frequently, auditors knew about these deceptions. Too often, however, they remained silent. The key job of the audit committee is simply to get the auditors to divulge what they know.

To do this job, the committee must make sure that the auditors worry more about misleading its members than about offending management. In recent years auditors have not felt that way. They have instead generally viewed the CEO, rather than the shareholders or directors, as their client. That has been a natural result of day-to-day working relationships and also of the auditors' understanding that, no matter what the book says, the CEO and CFO pay their fees and determine whether they are retained for both auditing and other work. The rules that have been recently instituted won't materially change this reality. What *will* break this cozy relationship is audit committees unequivocally putting auditors on the spot, making them understand they will become liable for major monetary penalties if they don't come forth with what they know or suspect.

In my opinion, audit committees can accomplish this goal by asking four questions of auditors, the answers to which should be recorded and reported to shareholders. These questions are:

1. If the auditor were solely responsible for preparation of the company's financial statements, would they have in any way been prepared differently from the manner selected by management? This question should cover both material and nonmaterial differences. If the auditor would have done something differently, both management's argument and the auditor's response should be disclosed. The audit committee should then evaluate the facts.

2. If the auditor were an investor, would he have received—in plain English—the information essential to his understanding the company's financial performance during the reporting period?

3. Is the company following the same internal audit procedure that would be followed if the auditor himself were CEO? If not, what are the differences and why?

4. Is the auditor aware of any actions—either accounting or operational—that have had the purpose and effect of moving revenues or expenses from one reporting period to another?

If the audit committee asks these questions, its composition—the focus of most reforms—is of minor importance. In addition, the procedure will save time and expense. When auditors are put on the spot, they will do their duty. If they are not put on the spot . . . well, we have seen the results of that.

The questions we have enumerated should be asked at least a week before an earnings report is released to the public. That timing will allow differences between the auditors and management to be aired with the committee and resolved. If the timing is tighter—if an earnings release is imminent when auditors and committee interact—the committee will feel pressure to rubberstamp the prepared figures. Haste is the enemy of accuracy. My thinking, in fact, is that the SEC's recent shortening of reporting deadlines will hurt the quality of information that shareholders receive. Charlie and I believe that rule is a mistake and should be rescinded.

The primary advantage of our four questions is that they will act as a prophylactic. Once the auditors know that the audit committee will require them to affirmatively endorse, rather than merely acquiesce to, management's actions, they will resist misdoings early in the process, well before specious figures become embedded in the company's books. Fear of the plaintiff's bar will see to that.[12]

Chapter 4

Berkshire Managers

Our managers have produced extraordinary results by doing rather ordinary things—but doing them exceptionally well. Our managers protect their franchises, they control costs, they search for new products and markets that build their existing strengths and they don't get diverted. They work exceptionally hard at the details of their businesses, and it shows.[1]

—WARREN BUFFETT

So when I buy a business, I am usually buying the manager with them, because I don't know how to run the business. So when someone comes along that wants to sell their business, I have to look at them in the eye and I have to decide whether they love the money or love the business. It's okay to love the money, but they have to love the business.[2]

—WARREN BUFFETT

Our prototype for occupational fervor is the Catholic tailor who used his small savings of many years to finance a pilgrimage to the Vatican. When he returned, his parish held a special meeting to get his first-hand account of the pope. "Tell us," said the eager faithful, "just what sort of fellow is he?" Our hero wasted no words: "He's a 44 medium."[3]

—WARREN BUFFETT

We intend to continue our practice of working only with people whom we like and admire. This policy not only maximizes our chances for good results, it also ensures us an extraordinarily good time. On the other hand, working with people who cause your stomach to churn seems much like marrying for money—probably a bad idea under any circumstances, but absolute madness if you are already rich.[4]

■ ■ ■

My managerial model is Eddie Bennett, who was a batboy. In 1919, at age 19, Eddie began his work with the Chicago White Sox, who that year went to the World Series. The next year, Eddie switched to the Brooklyn Dodgers, and they, too, won their league title. Our hero, however, smelled trouble. Changing boroughs, he joined the Yankees in 1921, and they promptly won their first pennant in history. Now Eddie settled in, shrewdly seeing what was coming. In the next seven years, the Yankees won five American League titles.

What does this have to do with management? It's simple—to be a winner, work with winners. In 1927, for example, Eddie received $700 for the 1/8th World Series share voted him by the legendary Yankee team of Ruth and Gehrig. This sum, which Eddie earned by working only four days (because New York swept the Series) was roughly equal to the full-year pay then earned by batboys who worked with ordinary associates.

Eddie understood that how he lugged bats was unimportant; what counted instead was hooking up with the cream of those on the playing field. I've learned from Eddie. At Berkshire, I regularly hand bats to many of the heaviest hitters in American business.[5]

■ ■ ■

Usually the manager came with the companies we bought, having demonstrated their talents throughout careers that spanned a wide variety of business circumstances. They were managerial stars long before they knew us, and our main contribution has been to not get in their way. This approach seems elementary: if my job were to manage a golf team—and if Jack Nicklaus or Arnold Palmer were playing for me—neither would get a lot of directives from me about how to swing.[6]

■ ■ ■

This means no second-guessing by Charlie and me. We avoid the attitude of the alumnus whose message to the football coach is "I'm 100% with you—win or tie." Our basic goal as an owner is to behave with our managers as we like our owners to behave with us.[7]

■ ■ ■

When we were due to close the purchase at Charlie's office, Jack was late. Finally arriving, he explained that he had been driving around looking for a parking meter with some unexpired time. That was a magic moment for me. I knew then that Jack was going to be my kind of manager.[8]

■ ■ ■

Second thing, they want applause. I want applause. I like it when people say that's a good job. Our managers are just the same way. Our managers have a lot of money, most of them, and they want to be treated fairly and they don't want to be taken advantage of. They want to paint their own painting. They love that, and they get that at Berkshire like no other place and they want applause and when they get applause from me they are getting applause from a knowledgeable observer. It is not uninformed applause. That keeps them and we have had remarkable success in keeping managers over the years.[9]

"How Do You Know When You're Dealing with an Honest Person?"

Well, it's a great question, and I would say this. If you—if we get 100 possible sellers to us of businesses, I don't think I can make a correct judgment on all of the 100. But I only have to be right on the ones I make an affirmative judgment on. So I think I can be right a high percentage of time on the six or eight that I might pick out from there, and I think I can sort of pick out the obvious thieves, you know, of the six and eight. But in between, I think, I can't grade everybody in that 100. And—but we have had—I mean, when we bought the Furniture Mart from the Blumkin family, I'd seen them operate for 20 or 30 years. I knew them personally. There wasn't any doubt in my mind whatsoever that they would work harder and more—you know, for me than they had when they owned it all themselves. And we've had good luck in that. But, we've not batted 100 percent. Every now and then I make a mistake.[10]

■ ■ ■

Charlie and I know that the right players will make almost any team manager look good. We subscribe to the philosophy of Ogilvy & Mather's founding genius, David Ogilvy: "If each of us hires people who are smaller than we are, we shall become a company of dwarfs. But, if each of us hires people who are bigger than we are, we shall become a company of giants."[11]

■ ■ ■

Charlie and I try to behave with our managers just as we attempt to behave with Berkshire shareholders, treating both groups as we would wish to be treated, if our positions were reversed. Though "working" means nothing to me financially, I love doing it at Berkshire for some simple reasons: It gives me a sense of achievement, a freedom to act as I see fit and an opportunity to interact daily with people I like and trust. Why should our managers—accomplished artists at what they do—see things differently?[12]

Chapter 5

Communication

We will be candid in our reporting to you, emphasizing the pluses and minuses important in appraising business value. The guideline is to tell you the business facts that we would want to know if our positions were reversed. We give you no less. Moreover, as a company with a major communications business, it would be inexcusable for us to apply lesser standards of accuracy, balance and incisiveness when reporting on others. We also believe candor benefits us as managers. The CEO who misleads others in public may eventually mislead himself in private[1]

—WARREN BUFFETT

Full Disclosure—Both the Good *and* the Bad

It's called an annual report. It's not called the annual sales document. It's not called the annual, you know, tribute to management's aspirations or anything. It's called the annual report.

I really have a mental picture of my sisters in mind and it's Dear Doris and Birdie. And I envision them as people who have a very significant part of their net worth in the company, who are bright but who have been away for a year and who are not business specialists.

And once a year I tell them what's going on. And then, at the end, I take the Dear Birdie and Doris out and put in the shareholders of Berkshire Hathaway. I think that should be the mental approach.[2]

■■■

At Berkshire, full reporting means giving you the information that we would wish you to give to us if our positions were reversed. What Charlie and I would want under that circumstance would be all the important facts about current operations as well as the CEO's frank view of the long-term economic characteristics of the business. We would expect both a lot of financial details and a discussion of any significant data we would need to interpret what was presented.

When Charlie and I read reports, we have no interest in pictures of personnel, plants or products.

References to EBITDA make us shudder—does management think the tooth fairy pays for capital expenditures? We're very suspicious of accounting methodology that is vague or unclear, since too often that means management wishes to hide something. And we don't want to read messages that a public relations department or consultant has turned out. Instead, we expect a company's CEO to explain in his or her own words what's happening.

For us, fair reporting means getting information to our 300,000 "partners" simultaneously, or as close to that mark as possible. We therefore put our annual and quarterly financials on the Internet between the close of the market on a Friday and the following morning. By our doing that, shareholders and other interested investors have timely access to these important releases and also have a reasonable amount of time to digest the information they include before the markets open on Monday.[3]

■ ■ ■

But when you do receive a communication from us, it will come from the fellow you are paying to run the business. Your Chairman has a firm belief that owners are entitled to hear directly from the CEO as to what is going on and how he evaluates the business, currently and prospectively. You would demand that in a private company; you should expect no less in a public company. A once-a-year report for stewardship should not be turned over to a staff specialist or public relations consultant who is unlikely to be in a position to talk frankly on a manager-to-owner basis.

In large part, companies obtain the shareholder constituency that they seek and deserve. If they focus their thinking and communications on short-term results or short-term stock market consequences they will, in large part, attract shareholders who focus on the same factors. And if they are cynical in their treatment of investors, eventually that cynicism is highly likely to be returned by the investment community.[4]

■ ■ ■

The future returns of Berkshire . . . won't be as good in the future as they have been in the past. (This is true of all large, successful companies.) The only difference is that we will tell you.[5]

■ ■ ■

After all, CEOs seldom tell their shareholders that they have assembled a bunch of turkeys to run things. Their reluctance to do so makes for some strange annual reports. Oftentimes, in his shareholders' letter, a CEO will go on for pages detailing corporate performance that is woefully inadequate. He will nonetheless end with a warm paragraph describing his managerial comrades as "our most precious asset." Such comments sometimes make you wonder what the other assets can possibly be.[6]

■ ■ ■

The financial consequences of these boners are regularly dumped into massive restructuring charges or write-offs that are casually waved off as "nonrecurring." Managements just love these. Indeed, in recent years it has seemed that no earnings statement is complete without them. The origins of these charges, though, are never explored. When it comes to corporate blunders, CEOs invoke the concept of the Virgin Birth.[7]

■ ■ ■

A column entitled "Today's Rumors," however, would not equate with the self-image of the many news organizations that think themselves above such stuff. These members of the media would feel that publishing such acknowledged fluff would be akin to L'Osservatore Romano initiating a gossip column. But rumors are what these organizations often publish and broadcast, whatever euphemism they duck behind. At a minimum, readers deserve honest terminology—a warning label that will protect their financial health in the same way that smokers whose physical health is at risk are given a warning.[8]

■ ■ ■

During all of the story's iterations, I never heard or read the word "rumor." Apparently reporters and editors, who generally pride themselves on their careful use of language, just can't bring themselves to attach this word to their accounts. But what description would fit more precisely? Certainly not the usual "sources say" or "it has been reported."[9]

■ ■ ■

In contrast, we include no narrative with our quarterly reports. Our owners and managers both have very long time-horizons in regard to this business, and it is difficult to say anything new or meaningful each quarter about events of long-term significance.[10]

■ ■ ■

I have another caveat to mention about last year's results. If you've been a reader of financial reports in recent years, you've seen a flood of "pro-forma" earnings statements—tabulations in which managers invariably show "earnings" far in excess of those allowed by their auditors. In these presentations, the CEO tells his owners "don't count this, don't count that—just count what makes earnings fat." Often, a forget-all-this-bad-stuff message is delivered year after year without management so much as blushing.[11]

■ ■ ■

Three suggestions for investors: First, beware of companies displaying weak accounting. If a company still does not expense options, or if its pension assumptions are fanciful, watch out. When managements take the low road in aspects that are visible, it is likely they are following a similar path behind the scenes. There is seldom just one cockroach in the kitchen.

Trumpeting EBITDA (earnings before interest, taxes, depreciation and amortization) is a particularly pernicious practice. Doing so implies that depreciation is not truly an expense, given that it is a "non-cash" charge. That's nonsense. In truth, depreciation is a particularly unattractive expense because the cash outlay it represents is paid up front, before the asset acquired has delivered any benefits to the business. Imagine, if you will, that at the beginning of this year a company paid all of its employees for the next ten years of their service (in the way they would lay out cash for a fixed asset to be useful for ten years). In the following nine years, compensation would be a "non-cash" expense—a reduction of a prepaid compensation asset established this year. Would anyone care to argue that the recording of the expense in years two through ten would be simply a bookkeeping formality?

Second, unintelligible footnotes usually indicate untrustworthy management. If you can't understand a footnote or other managerial explanation, it's usually because the CEO doesn't want you to. Enron's descriptions of certain transactions still baffle me.

Finally, be suspicious of companies that trumpet earnings projections and growth expectations.

Businesses seldom operate in a tranquil, no-surprise environment, and earnings simply don't advance smoothly (except, of course, in the offering books of investment bankers).

Charlie and I not only don't know today what our businesses will earn next year—we don't even know what they will earn next quarter. We are suspicious of those CEOs who regularly claim they do know the future—and we become downright incredulous if they consistently reach their declared targets. Managers that always promise to "make the numbers" will at some point be tempted to make up the numbers.[12]

■ ■ ■

We will be communicating with you in several ways. Through the annual report, I try to give all shareholders as much value-defining information as can be conveyed in a document kept to reasonable length. We also try to convey a liberal quantity of condensed but important information in the quarterly reports we post on the Internet, though I don't write those (one recital a year is enough). Still another important occasion for communication is our Annual Meeting, at which Charlie and I are delighted to spend five hours or more answering questions about Berkshire. But there is one way we can't communicate: on a one-on-one basis. That isn't feasible given Berkshire's many thousands of owners.

In all of our communications, we try to make sure that no single shareholder gets an edge: We do not follow the usual practice of giving earnings "guidance" or other information of value to analysts or large shareholders. Our goal is to have all of our owners updated at the same time.[13]

■ ■ ■

As managers, Charlie and I want to give our owners the financial information and commentary we would wish to receive if our roles were reversed. To do this with both clarity and reasonable brevity becomes more difficult as Berkshire's scope widens. Some of our businesses have vastly different economic characteristics from others, which means that our consolidated statements, with their jumble of figures, make useful analysis almost impossible.

On the following pages, therefore, we will present some balance sheet and earnings figures from our four major categories of businesses along with commentary about each. We particularly want you to understand the limited circumstances under which we will use debt, given that we typically shun it. We will not, however, inundate you with data that has no real value in estimating Berkshire's intrinsic value. Doing so would tend to obfuscate the facts that count.[14]

■ ■ ■

The Annual Meeting

Our annual meeting will be on May 21, 1985, in Omaha, and I hope that you attend. Many annual meetings are a waste of time, both for shareholders and for management. Sometimes that is true because management is reluctant to open up on matters of business substance. More often a nonproductive session is the fault of shareholder participants who are more concerned about their own moment on stage than they are about the affairs of the corporation. What should be a forum for business discussion becomes a forum for theatrics, spleen-venting and advocacy of issues. (The deal is irresistible: for the price of one share you get to tell a captive audience your ideas as to how the world should be.) Under such circumstances, the quality of the meeting often deteriorates from year to year as the antics of those interested in themselves discourage attendance by those interested in the business.

Berkshire's meetings are a different story. The number of shareholders attending grows a bit each year and we have yet to experience a silly question or an ego-inspired commentary. Instead, we get a wide variety of thoughtful questions about the business. Because the annual meeting is the time and place for these, Charlie and I are happy to answer them all, no matter how long it takes. (We cannot, however, respond to written or phoned questions at other times of the year; one-person-at-a-time reporting is a poor use of management time in a company with 3,000 shareholders.) The only business matters that are off limits at the annual meeting are those about which candor might cost our company real money. Our activities in securities would be the main example.[15]

When it comes to our Annual Meetings, Charlie and I are managerial oddballs: We thoroughly enjoy the event. So come join us on Monday, May 6th. At Berkshire, we have no investor relations department and don't use financial analysts as a channel for disseminating information, earnings "guidance," or the like. Instead, we prefer direct manager-to-owner communication and believe that the Annual Meeting is the ideal place for this interchange of ideas. Talking to you there is efficient for us and also democratic in that all present simultaneously hear what we have to say.[16]

■ ■ ■

Charlie and I are extraordinarily lucky. We were born in America; had terrific parents who saw that we got good educations; have enjoyed wonderful families and great health; and came equipped with a "business" gene that allows us to prosper in a manner hugely disproportionate to other people who contribute as much or more to our society's well-being. Moreover, we have long had jobs that we love, in which we are helped every day in countless ways by talented and cheerful associates. No wonder we tap dance to work. But nothing is more fun for us than getting together with our shareholder-partners at Berkshire's annual meeting. So join us on May 5th at the Qwest for our annual Woodstock for Capitalists. We'll see you there.[17]

■ ■ ■

Last year the first question at the annual meeting was asked by 11-year-old Nicholas Kenner, a third-generation shareholder from New York City. Nicholas plays rough: "How come the stock is down?" he fired at me. My answer was not memorable.

We hope that other business engagements won't keep Nicholas away from this year's meeting. If he attends, he will be offered the chance to again ask the first question; Charlie and I want to tackle him while we're fresh. This year, however, it's Charlie's turn to answer.[18]

■■■

Nicholas Kenner nailed me—again—at last year's meeting, pointing out that I had said in the 1990 annual report that he was 11 in May 1990, when actually he was 9. So, asked Nicholas rather caustically: "If you can't get that straight, how do I know the numbers in the back (the financials) are correct?" I'm still searching for a snappy response. Nicholas will be at this year's meeting—he spurned my offer of a trip to Disney World on that day—so join us to watch a continuation of this lopsided battle of wits.[19]

■■■

Charlie Munger: You have to remember the annual meeting of Berkshire has evolved unlike any in the history of the world. No capitalist enterprise has ever had an annual shareholders meeting anything like the one we have.[20]

Chapter 6

Acquisition of Nebraska Furniture Mart

"The Amazing Mrs. B"

Sell cheap and tell the truth.[1]

—ROSE BLUMKIN

I'd rather wrestle grizzlies than compete with Mrs. B and her progeny.[2]

—WARREN BUFFETT

A Business Story Like No Other

Charlie Rose: In 1983 you purchased Nebraska Furniture Mart for $60 million. Tell me about her.

Warren Buffett: This is a woman who walked out of Russia, got on a peanut boat and landed in Seattle with a tag around her neck. She couldn't speak a word of English. The Red Cross got her out of Fort Dodge, Iowa. That's what the tag said. She couldn't learn the language. She moved to Omaha because there were more Russian Jews there who she could talk with. Her oldest daughter started school. She came home and taught her words that she learned. She took 16 years to save $500 so she could start this company. Selling used clothing, she brought her siblings and her mother and father over at $50 a crack. In 1937, for $500, she went in business competing against people with all kinds of advantages in every way and she killed them.

Charlie Rose: How was she able to kill them?

Warren Buffett: She cared and she was smart. She knew her limitations of her knowledge and she was confident in the circle of her competence. She didn't get outside of it and she took care of her customers. She sold cheap and it took her a long time but she built the largest home furnishing store in the country in a town like Omaha, a town of 700,000 people.

Charlie Rose: How did you come to buy it?

Warren Buffett: She was my kind of woman and I bought it when she was 89 and she worked 'til she was 103. There was a period where she left for a couple of years. If you went over to visit her house, as I did, a very nice house, you would go in and on her sofas, lamps and bed; there would be little green tags hanging on them. They made her feel like she was at the store. She was a remarkable woman, and Charlie, she could not read or write and I think every business school should study her.

Charlie Rose: What would they learn?

Buffett: They would learn the essence of business. They would learn that taking care of customers is what it is all about. Taking care of them. I mean by that, giving them good deals, which nobody would touch. She did and working like crazy she was there day after day. She had a passion for it. The truth is, if you took the Fortune 500 CEO's and I gave you the first draft pick on 10 of them, and I put them in competition with her; she would win.[3]

■ ■ ■

About 67 years ago Mrs. Blumkin, then 23, talked her way past a border guard to leave Russia for America. She had no formal education, not even at the grammar school level, and knew no English. After some years in this country, she learned the language when her older daughter taught her, every evening, the words she had learned in school during the day.

In 1937, after many years of selling used clothing, Mrs. Blumkin had saved $500 with which to realize her dream of opening a furniture store. Upon seeing the American Furniture Mart in Chicago—then the center of the nation's wholesale furniture activity—she decided to christen her dream Nebraska Furniture Mart.

She met every obstacle you would expect (and a few you wouldn't) when a business endowed with only $500 and no locational or product advantage goes up against rich, long-entrenched competition. At one early point, when her tiny resources ran out, "Mrs. B" (a personal trademark now as well recognized in Greater Omaha as Coca-Cola or Sanka) coped in a way not taught at business schools: she simply sold the furniture and appliances from her home in order to pay creditors precisely as promised.

Omaha retailers began to recognize that Mrs. B would offer customers far better deals than they had been giving, and they pressured furniture and carpet manufacturers not to sell to her. But by various strategies she obtained merchandise and cut prices sharply. Mrs. B was then hauled into court for violation of Fair Trade laws. She not only won all the cases, but received invaluable publicity. At the end of one case, after demonstrating to the court that she could profitably sell carpet at a huge discount from the prevailing price, she sold the judge $1,400 worth of carpet.

Today Nebraska Furniture Mart generates over $100 million of sales annually out of one 200,000 square-foot store. No other home furnishings store in the country comes close to that volume. That single store also sells more furniture, carpets, and appliances than do all Omaha competitors combined.

One question I always ask myself in appraising a business is how I would like, assuming I had ample capital and skilled personnel, to compete with it. I'd rather wrestle grizzlies than compete with Mrs. B and her progeny. They buy brilliantly, they operate at expense ratios competitors don't even dream about, and they then pass on to their customers much of the savings. It's the ideal business—one built upon exceptional value to the customer that in turn translates into exceptional economics for its owners.

Mrs. B is wise as well as smart and, for far-sighted family reasons, was willing to sell the business last year. I had admired both the family and the business for decades, and a deal was quickly made. But Mrs. B, now 90, is not one to go home and risk, as she puts it, "losing her marbles." She remains Chairman and is on the sales floor seven days a week. Carpet sales are her specialty. She personally sells quantities that would be a good departmental total for other carpet retailers.

We purchased 90% of the business—leaving 10% with members of the family who are involved in management—and have optioned 10% to certain key young family managers.

And what managers they are. Geneticists should do handsprings over the Blumkin family. Louie Blumkin, Mrs. B's son, has been President of Nebraska Furniture Mart for many years and is widely regarded as the shrewdest buyer of furniture and appliances in the country. Louie says he had the best teacher, and Mrs. B says she had the best student. They're both right. Louie and his three sons all have the Blumkin business ability, work ethic, and, most important, character. On top of that, they are really nice people. We are delighted to be in partnership with them.[4]

■■■

Last year I introduced you to Mrs. B (Rose Blumkin) and her family. I told you they were terrific, and I understated the case. After another year of observing their remarkable talents and character, I can honestly say that I never have seen a managerial group that either functions or behaves better than the Blumkin family.

Mrs. B, Chairman of the Board, is now 91, and recently was quoted in the local newspaper as saying, "I come home to eat and sleep, and that's about it. I can't wait until it gets daylight so I can get back to the business." Mrs. B is at the store seven days a week, from opening to close, and probably makes more decisions in a day than most CEOs do in a year (better ones, too).

In May Mrs. B was granted an Honorary Doctorate in Commercial Science by New York University. (She's a "fast track" student: not one day in her life was spent in a school room prior to her receipt of the doctorate.) Previous recipients of honorary degrees in business from NYU include Clifton Garvin, Jr., CEO of Exxon Corp.; Walter Wriston, then CEO of Citicorp; Frank Cary, then CEO of IBM; Tom Murphy, then CEO of General Motors; and, most recently, Paul Volcker. (They are in good company.)

The Blumkin blood did not run thin. Louie, Mrs. B's son, and his three boys, Ron, Irv, and Steve, all contribute in full measure to NFM's amazing success. The younger generation has attended the best business school of them all—that conducted by Mrs. B and Louie—and their training is evident in their performance.[5]

Mrs. B, chairman of Nebraska Furniture Mart, continues at age 93 to outsell and out-hustle any manager I've ever seen. She's at the store seven days a week, from opening to close. Competing with her represents a triumph of courage over judgment.

It's easy to overlook what I consider to be the critical lesson of the Mrs. B saga: at 93, Omaha-based Board Chairmen have yet to reach their peak. Please file this fact away to consult before you mark your ballot at the 2024 annual meeting of Berkshire.[6]

■ ■ ■

Agatha Christie, whose husband was an archaeologist, said that was the perfect profession for one's spouse: "The older you become, the more interested they are in you." It is students of business management, not archaeologists, who should be interested in Mrs. B (Rose Blumkin), the 94-year-old chairman of Nebraska Furniture Mart.

Fifty years ago Mrs. B started the business with $500, and today NFM is far and away the largest home furnishings store in the country. Mrs. B continues to work seven days a week at the job from the opening of each business day until the close. She buys, she sells, she manages—and she runs rings around the competition. It's clear to me that she's gathering speed and may well reach her full potential in another five or ten years. Therefore, I've persuaded the Board to scrap our mandatory retirement-at-100 policy. (And it's about time: With every passing year, this policy has seemed sillier to me.)[7]

■ ■ ■

Ask Mrs. B the secret of her astonishingly low carpet prices. She will confide to you—as she does to everyone—how she does it: "I can sell so cheap 'cause I work for this dummy who doesn't know anything about carpet."[8]

■ ■ ■

Mrs. B—Rose Blumkin—had her 100th birthday on December 3, 1993. (The candles cost more than the cake.) That was a day on which the store was scheduled to be open in the evening. Mrs. B, who works seven days a week, for however many hours the store operates, found the proper decision quite obvious: She simply postponed her party until an evening when the store was closed.

Mrs. B's story is well-known but worth telling again. She came to the United States 77 years ago, unable to speak English and devoid of formal schooling. In 1937, she founded the Nebraska Furniture Mart with $500. Last year the store had sales of $200 million, a larger amount by far than that recorded by any other home furnishings store in the United States. Our part in all of this began ten years ago when Mrs. B sold control of the business to Berkshire Hathaway, a deal we completed without obtaining audited financial statements, checking real estate records, or getting any warranties. In short, her word was good enough for us.

Naturally, I was delighted to attend Mrs. B's birthday party. After all, she's promised to attend *my* 100th.[9]

■ ■ ■

I have been asked by a number of people just what secrets the Blumkins bring to their business. These are not very esoteric. All members of the family: (1) apply themselves with an enthusiasm and energy that would make Ben Franklin and Horatio Alger look like dropouts;

(2) define with extraordinary realism their area of special competence and act decisively on all matters within it; (3) ignore even the most enticing propositions falling outside of that area of competence; and (4) unfailingly behave in a high grade manner with everyone they deal with. (Mrs. B boils it down to sell cheap and tell the truth.)

Our evaluation of the integrity of Mrs. B and her family was demonstrated when we purchased 90% of the business: NFM had never had an audit and we did not request one; we did not take an inventory nor verify the receivables; we did not check property titles. We gave Mrs. B a check for $55 million and she gave us her word. That made an even exchange.[10]

■ ■ ■

I am a moderate in my views about retirement compared to Rose Blumkin, better known as Mrs. B. At 99, she continues to work seven days a week. And about her, I have some particularly good news.

You will remember that after her family sold 90% of Nebraska Furniture Mart (NFM) to Berkshire in 1983, Mrs. B continued to be Chairman and run the carpet operation. In 1989, however, she left because of a managerial disagreement and opened up her own operation next door in a large building that she had owned for several years. In her new business, she ran the carpet section but leased out other home-furnishings departments.

At the end of last year, Mrs. B decided to sell her building and land to NFM. She'll continue, however, to run her carpet business at its current location (no sense slowing down just when you're hitting full stride). NFM will set up shop alongside her, in that same building, thereby making a major addition to its furniture business.

I am delighted that Mrs. B has again linked up with us. Her business story has no parallel and I have always been a fan of hers, whether she was a partner or a competitor. But believe me, partner is better.

This time around, Mrs. B graciously offered to sign a non-compete agreement—and I, having been incautious on this point when she was 89, snapped at the deal. Mrs. B belongs in the *Guinness Book of World*

Records on many counts. Signing a non–compete at 99 merely adds one more.[11]

■ ■ ■

NFM was founded by Rose Blumkin ("Mrs. B") in 1937 with $500. She worked until she was 103 (hmmm . . . not a bad idea). One piece of wisdom she imparted to the generations following her was, "If you have the lowest price, customers will find you at the bottom of a river." Our store serving greater Kansas City, which is located in one of the area's more sparsely populated parts, has proved Mrs. B's point. Though we have more than 25 acres of parking, the lot has at times overflowed.

"Victory," President Kennedy told us after the Bay of Pigs disaster, "has a thousand fathers, but defeat is an orphan." At NFM, we knew we had a winner a month after the boffo opening in Kansas City, when our new store attracted an unexpected paternity claim. A speaker there, referring to the Blumkin family, asserted, "They had enough confidence and the policies of the Administration were working such that they were able to provide work for 1,000 of our fellow citizens." The proud papa at the podium? President George W. Bush.[12]

Chapter 7

Acquisition of GEICO

"The Security I Like Best"

What is the single best investment on a large scale that you have made?[1]

—CHARLIE ROSE

GEICO—twice, three times in my life. It was a good investment when I was 20 years of age when I put three-fourths of my net worth in GEICO and that caused my net worth to double or something like that. That was great at the time. In 1976, the company got in trouble and what we bought turned out to be half of the company for $40 million. Then, in 1995, we bought the other half for $2.3 billion and that was a good deal. It's been a triple play.[2]

—WARREN BUFFETT

Right after year-end, we completed the purchase of 100% of GEICO, the seventh largest auto insurer in the United States, with about 3.7 million cars insured. I've had a 45-year association with GEICO, and though the story has been told before, it's worth a short recap here.

I attended Columbia University's business school in 1950–51, not because I cared about the degree it offered, but because I wanted to study under Ben Graham, then teaching there. The time I spent in

Ben's classes was a personal high, and quickly induced me to learn all I could about my hero. I turned first to *Who's Who in America,* finding there, among other things, that Ben was Chairman of Government Employees Insurance Company, to me an unknown company in an unfamiliar industry.

A librarian next referred me to Best's Fire and Casualty insurance manual, where I learned that GEICO was based in Washington, DC. So on a Saturday in January, 1951, I took the train to Washington and headed for GEICO's downtown headquarters. To my dismay, the building was closed, but I pounded on the door until a custodian appeared. I asked this puzzled fellow if there was anyone in the office I could talk to, and he said he'd seen one man working on the sixth floor.

And thus I met Lorimer Davidson, Assistant to the President, who was later to become CEO. Though my only credentials were that I was a student of Graham's, "Davy" graciously spent four hours or so showering me with both kindness and instruction. No one has ever received a better half-day course in how the insurance industry functions nor in the factors that enable one company to excel over others. As Davy made clear, GEICO's method of selling—direct marketing—gave it an enormous cost advantage over competitors that sold through agents, a form of distribution so ingrained in the business of these insurers that it was impossible for them to give it up. After my session with Davy, I was more excited about GEICO than I have ever been about a stock.

When I finished at Columbia some months later and returned to Omaha to sell securities, I naturally focused almost exclusively on GEICO. My first sales call—on my Aunt Alice, who always supported me 100%—was successful. But I was then a skinny, unpolished 20-year-old who looked about 17, and my pitch usually failed. Undaunted, I wrote a short report late in 1951 about GEICO for "The Security I Like Best" column in the *Commercial and Financial Chronicle,* a leading financial publication of the time. More important, I bought stock for my own account.

You may think this odd, but I have kept copies of every tax return I filed, starting with the return for 1944. Checking back, I find that I purchased GEICO shares on four occasions during 1951, the last purchase being made on September 26. This pattern of persistence suggests to me that my tendency toward self-intoxication was developed early. I probably came back on that September day from unsuccessfully trying to sell some prospect and decided—despite my already having more than 50% of my net worth in GEICO—to load up further. In any event, I accumulated 350 shares of GEICO during the year, at a cost of $10,282. At year-end, this holding was worth $13,125, more than 65% of my net worth.

You can see why GEICO was my first business love. Furthermore, just to complete this stroll down memory lane, I should add that I earned most of the funds I used to buy GEICO shares by delivering *The Washington Post*, the chief product of a company that much later made it possible for Berkshire to turn $10 million into $500 million.

Alas, I sold my entire GEICO position in 1952 for $15,259, primarily to switch into Western Insurance Securities. This act of infidelity can partially be excused by the fact that Western was selling for slightly more than one times its current earnings, a p/e ratio that for some reason caught my eye. But in the next 20 years, the GEICO stock I sold grew in value to about $1.3 million, which taught me a lesson about the inadvisability of selling a stake in an identifiably-wonderful company.

In the early 1970's, after Davy retired, the executives running GEICO made some serious errors in estimating their claims costs, a mistake that led the company to underprice its policies—and that almost caused it to go bankrupt. The company was saved only because Jack Byrne came in as CEO in 1976 and took drastic remedial measures.

Because I believed both in Jack and in GEICO's fundamental competitive strength, Berkshire purchased a large interest in the company during the second half of 1976, and also made smaller purchases later. By year-end 1980, we had put $45.7 million into GEICO and owned 33.3% of its shares. During the next 15 years, we did not make further purchases. Our interest in the company, nonetheless, grew to about 50% because it was a big repurchaser of its own shares.

Then, in 1995, we agreed to pay $2.3 billion for the half of the company we didn't own. That is a steep price. But it gives us full ownership of a growing enterprise whose business remains exceptional for precisely the same reasons that prevailed in 1951. In addition, GEICO has two extraordinary managers: Tony Nicely, who runs the insurance side of the operation, and Lou Simpson, who runs investments.

Tony, 52, has been with GEICO for 34 years. There's no one I would rather have managing GEICO's insurance operation. He has brains, energy, integrity and focus. If we're lucky, he'll stay another 34 years.

Lou runs investments just as ably. Between 1980 and 1995, the equities under Lou's management returned an average of 22.8% annually vs. 15.7% for the S&P. Lou takes the same conservative, concentrated approach to investments that we do at Berkshire, and it is an enormous plus for us to have him on board. One point that goes beyond Lou's GEICO work: His presence on the scene assures us that Berkshire would have an extraordinary professional immediately available to handle its investments if something were to happen to Charlie and me.

GEICO, of course, must continue both to attract good policyholders and keep them happy. It must also reserve and price properly. But the ultimate key to the company's success is its rock-bottom operating costs, which virtually no competitor can match. In 1995, moreover, Tony and his management team pushed underwriting and loss adjustment expenses down further to 23.6% of premiums, nearly one percentage point below 1994's ratio. In business, I look for economic castles protected by unbreachable "moats." Thanks to Tony and his management team, GEICO's moat widened in 1995.

Finally, let me bring you up to date on Davy. He's now 93 and remains my friend and teacher. He continues to pay close attention to GEICO and has always been there when the company's CEOs—Jack Byrne, Bill Snyder and Tony—have needed him. Our acquisition of 100% of GEICO caused Davy to incur a large tax. Characteristically, he still warmly supported the transaction.

Davy has been one of my heroes for the 45 years I've known him, and he's never let me down. You should understand that Berkshire would not be where it is today if Davy had not been so generous with his time on a cold Saturday in 1951. I've often thanked him privately, but it is fitting that I use this report to thank him on behalf of Berkshire's shareholders.[3]

■ ■ ■

I believe the GEICO story demonstrates the benefits of Berkshire's approach. Charlie and I haven't taught Tony a thing—and never will—but we *have* created an environment that allows him to apply all of his talents to what's important. He does not have to devote his time or energy to board meetings, press interviews, presentations by investment bankers or talks with financial analysts. Furthermore, he need never spend a moment thinking about financing, credit ratings or "Street" expectations for earnings per share. Because of our ownership structure, he also knows that this operational framework will endure for decades to come. In this environment of freedom, both Tony and his company can convert their almost limitless potential into matching achievements.[4]

Reprinted from

The COMMERCIAL *and* FINANCIAL CHRONICLE

Thursday, December 6, 1951

The Security I Like Best

WARREN E. BUFFETT
Buffett-Falk & Co., Omaha, Nebr.

Government Employees Insurance Co.

Full employment, boomtime profits and record dividend payments do not set the stage for depressed security prices. Most industries have been riding this wave of prosperity during the past five years with few ripples to disturb the tide.

The auto insurance business has not shared in the boom. After the staggering losses of the immediate postwar period, the situation began to right itself in 1949. In 1950, stock casualty companies again took it on the chin with underwriting experience the second worst in 15 years. The recent earnings reports of casualty companies, particularly those with the bulk of writings in auto lines, have diverted bull market enthusiasm from their stocks. On the basis of normal earning power and asset factors, many of these stocks appear undervalued.

Warren E. Buffett

The nature of the industry is such as to ease cyclical bumps. Auto insurance is regarded as a necessity by the majority of purchasers. Contracts must be renewed yearly at rates based upon experience. The lag of rates behind costs, although detrimental in a period of rising prices as has characterized the 1945-1951 period, should prove beneficial if deflationary forces should be set in action.

Other industry advantages include lack of inventory, collection, labor and raw material problems. The hazard of product obsolescence and related equipment obsolescence is also absent.

Government Employees Insurance Corporation was organized in the mid-30's to provide complete auto insurance on a nationwide basis to an eligible class including: (1) Federal, State and municipal government employees; (2) active and reserve commissioned officers and the first three pay grades of non-commissioned officers of the Armed Forces; (3) veterans who were eligible when on active duty; (4) former policyholders; (5) faculty members of universities, colleges and schools; (6) government contractor employees engaged in defense work exclusively, and (7) stockholders.

The company has no agents or branch offices. As a result, policyholders receive standard auto insurance policies at premium discounts running as high as 30% off manual rates. Claims are handled promptly through approximately 500 representatives throughout the country.

The term "growth company" has been applied with abandon during the past few years to companies whose sales increases represented little more than inflation of prices and general easing of business competition. GEICO qualifies as a legitimate growth company based upon the following record:

Year—	Premiums Written	Policy-holders
1936___	$103,696.31	3,754
1940___	768,057.86	25,514
1945___	1,638,562.09	51,697
1950___	8,016,975.79	143,944

Of course the investor of today does not profit from yesterday's growth. In GEICO's case, there is reason to believe the major portion of growth lies ahead. Prior to 1950, the company was only licensed in 15 of 50 jurisdictions including D. C. and Hawaii. At the beginning of the year there were less than 3,000 policyholders in New York State. Yet 25% saved on an insurance bill of $125 in New York should look bigger to the prospect than the 25% saved on the $50 rate in more sparsely settled regions.

As cost competition increases in importance during times of recession, GEICO's rate attraction should become even more effective in diverting business from the brother-in-law. With insurance rates moving higher due to inflation, the 25% spread in rates becomes wider in terms of dollars and cents.

There is no pressure from agents to accept questionable applicants or renew poor risks. In States where the rate structure is inadequate, new promotion may be halted.

Probably the biggest attraction of GEICO is the profit margin advantage it enjoys. The ratio of underwriting profit to premiums earned in 1949 was 27.5% for GEICO as compared to 6.7% for the 135 stock casualty and surety companies summarized by Best's. As experience turned for the worse in 1950, Best's aggregate's profit margin dropped to 3.0% and GEICO's dropped to 18.0%. GEICO does not write all casualty lines; however, bodily injury and property damage, both important lines for GEICO, were among the least profitable lines. GEICO also does a large amount of collision writing, which was a profitable line in 1950.

During the first half of 1951, practically all insurers operated in the red on casualty lines with bodily injury and property damage among the most unprofitable. Whereas GEICO's profit margin was cut to slightly above 9%, Massachusett's Bonding & Insurance showed a 16% loss, New Amsterdam Casualty an 8% loss, Standard Accident Insurance a 9% loss, etc.

Because of the rapid growth of GEICO, cash dividends have had to remain low. Stock dividends and a 25-for-1 split increased the outstanding shares from 3,000 on June 1, 1948, to 250,000 on Nov. 10, 1951. Valuable rights to subscribe to stock of affiliated companies have also been issued.

Benjamin Graham has been Chairman of the Board since his investment trust acquired and distributed a large block of the stock in 1948. Leo Goodwin, who has guided GEICO's growth since inception, is the able President. At the end of 1950, the 10 members of the Board of Directors owned approximately one-third of the outstanding stock.

Earnings in 1950 amounted to $3.92 as contrasted to $4.71 on the smaller amount of business in 1949. These figures include no allowance for the increase in the unearned premium reserve which was substantial in both years. Earnings in 1951 will be lower than 1950, but the wave of rate increases during the past summer should evidence themselves in 1952 earnings. Investment income quadrupled between 1947 and 1950, reflecting the growth of the company's assets.

At the present price of about eight times the earnings of 1950, a poor year for the industry, it appears that no price is being paid for the tremendous growth potential of the company.

This is part of a continuous forum appearing in the "Chronicle," in which each week, a different group of experts in the investment and advisory field from all sections of the country participate and give their reasons for favoring a particular security.

Source: Warren E. Buffett, "The Security I Like Best," *Commercial and Financial Chronicle* (December 6, 1951).

Chapter 8

Acquisition of General Reinsurance

2002–2006

…Gen Re had accumulated an aggregation of risks that would have been fatal had, say, terrorists detonated several large-scale nuclear bombs in an attack on the U.S. A disaster of that scope was highly improbable, of course, but it is up to insurers to limit their risks in a manner that leaves their finances rock solid if the "impossible" happens. Indeed, had Gen Re remained independent, the World Trade Center attack alone would have threatened the company's existence.[1]

—WARREN BUFFETT

I f our insurance operations are to generate low-cost float over time, they must: (a) underwrite with unwavering discipline; (b) reserve conservatively; and (c) avoid an aggregation of exposures that would allow a supposedly "impossible" incident to threaten their solvency. All of our major insurance businesses, with one exception, have regularly met those tests.

The exception is General Re, and there was much to do at that company last year to get it up to snuff. I'm delighted to report that under Joe Brandon's leadership, and with yeoman assistance by Tad Montross, enormous progress has been made on each of the fronts described.

When I agreed in 1998 to merge Berkshire with Gen Re, I thought that company stuck to the three rules I've enumerated. I had studied the operation for decades and had observed underwriting discipline that was consistent and reserving that was conservative. At merger time, I detected no slippage in Gen Re's standards.

I was dead wrong. Gen Re's culture and practices had substantially changed and unbeknownst to management—and to me—the company was grossly mispricing its current business.[2]

■ ■ ■

Gen Re's financial strength, unmatched among reinsurers even as we started 2003, further improved during the year. Many of the company's competitors suffered credit downgrades last year, leaving Gen Re, and its sister operation at National Indemnity, as the only AAA rated companies among the world's major reinsurers.

When insurers purchase reinsurance, they buy only a promise—one whose validity may not be tested for decades—and there are no promises in the reinsurance world equaling those offered by Gen Re and National Indemnity. Furthermore, unlike most reinsurers, we retain virtually all of the risks we assume. Therefore, our ability to pay is not dependent on the ability or willingness of others to reimburse us. This *independent* financial strength could be enormously important when the industry experiences the mega-catastrophe it surely will.[3]

■ ■ ■

A far less pleasant unwinding operation is taking place at Gen Re Securities, the trading and derivatives operation we inherited when we purchased General Reinsurance. When we began to liquidate Gen Re Securities in early 2002, it had 23,218 outstanding tickets with 884 counterparties (some having names I couldn't pronounce, much less creditworthiness I could evaluate). Since then, the unit's managers have been skillful and diligent in unwinding positions. Yet, at year-end—nearly two years later—we still had 7,580 tickets outstanding with 453 counterparties. (As the country song laments, "How can I miss you if you won't go away?")

The shrinking of this business has been costly. We've had pre-tax losses of $173 million in 2002 and $99 million in 2003. These losses, it should be noted, came from a portfolio of contracts that—in full compliance with GAAP—had been regularly marked-to-market with standard allowances for future credit-loss and administrative costs. Moreover, our liquidation has taken place both in a benign market—we've had no credit losses of significance—and in an orderly manner. This is just the opposite of what might be expected if a financial crisis forced a number of derivatives dealers to cease operations simultaneously.

If our derivatives experience—and the Freddie Mac shenanigans of mind-blowing size and audacity that were revealed last year—makes you suspicious of accounting in this arena, consider yourself wised up. No matter how financially sophisticated you are, you can't possibly learn from reading the disclosure documents of a derivatives-intensive company what risks lurk in its positions. Indeed, the more you know about derivatives, the less you will feel you can learn from the disclosures normally proffered you. In Darwin's words, "Ignorance more frequently begets confidence than does knowledge."[4]

■ ■ ■

And now it's confession time: I'm sure I could have saved you $100 million or so, pre-tax, if I had acted more promptly to shut down Gen Re Securities. Both Charlie and I knew at the time of the General Reinsurance merger that its derivatives business was unattractive. Reported profits struck us as illusory, and we felt that the business carried sizable risks that could not effectively be measured or limited. Moreover, we knew that any major problems the operation might experience would likely correlate with troubles in the financial or insurance world that would affect Berkshire elsewhere. In other words, if the derivatives business were ever to need shoring up, it would commandeer the capital and credit of Berkshire at just the time we could otherwise deploy those resources to huge advantage.

(A historical note: We had just such an experience in 1974 when we were the victim of a major insurance fraud. We could not determine for some time how much the fraud would ultimately cost us and therefore kept more funds in cash-equivalents than we normally would have. Absent this precaution, we would have made larger purchases of stocks that were then extraordinarily cheap.)

Charlie would have moved swiftly to close down Gen Re Securities—no question about that. I, however, dithered. As a consequence, our shareholders are paying a far higher price than was necessary to exit this business.[5]

■ ■ ■

The wind-down of Gen Re Securities continues. We decided to exit this derivative operation three years ago, but getting out is easier said than done. Though derivative instruments are purported to be highly liquid—and though we have had the benefit of a benign market while liquidating ours—we still had 2,890 contracts outstanding at year-end, down from 23,218 at the peak. Like Hell, derivative trading is easy to enter but difficult to leave. (Other similarities come to mind as well.)

Gen Re's derivative contracts have always been required to be marked to market, and I believe the company's management conscientiously tried to make realistic "marks." The market prices of derivatives, however, can be very fuzzy in a world in which settlement of a transaction is sometimes decades away and often involves multiple variables as well. In the interim the marks influence the managerial and trading bonuses that are paid annually. It's small wonder that phantom profits are often recorded.

Investors should understand that in all types of financial institutions, rapid growth sometimes masks major underlying problems (and occasionally fraud). The real test of the earning power of a derivatives operation is what it achieves after operating for an extended period in a no-growth mode. You only learn who has been swimming naked when the tide goes out.[6]

■ ■ ■

We lost $104 million pre-tax last year in our continuing attempt to exit Gen Re's derivative operation. Our aggregate losses since we began this endeavor total $404 million.

Originally we had 23,218 contracts outstanding. By the start of 2005 we were down to 2,890. You might expect that our losses would have been stemmed by this point, but the blood has kept flowing. Reducing our inventory to 741 contracts last year cost us the $104 million mentioned above. Remember that the rationale for establishing this unit in 1990 was Gen Re's wish to meet the needs of insurance clients. Yet one of the contracts we liquidated in 2005 had a term of 100 years! It's difficult to imagine what "need" such a contract could fulfill except, perhaps, the need of a compensation-conscious trader to have a long-dated contract on his books. Long contracts, or alternatively those with multiple variables, are the most difficult to mark to market (the standard procedure used in accounting for derivatives) and provide the most opportunity for "imagination" when traders are estimating their value. Small wonder that traders promote them.

A business in which huge amounts of compensation flow from assumed numbers is obviously fraught with danger. When two traders execute a transaction that has several, sometimes esoteric, variables and a far-off settlement date, their respective firms must subsequently value these contracts whenever they calculate their earnings. A given contract may be valued at one price by Firm A and at another by Firm B. You can bet that the valuation differences—and I'm personally familiar with several that were *huge*—tend to be tilted in a direction favoring higher earnings at each firm. It's a strange world in which two parties can carry out a paper transaction that each can promptly report as profitable.

I dwell on our experience in derivatives each year for two reasons. One is personal and unpleasant. The hard fact is that I have cost you a lot of money by not moving immediately to close down Gen Re's trading operation. Both Charlie and I knew at the time of the Gen Re purchase that it was a problem and told its management that we wanted to exit the business. It was my responsibility to make sure that happened. Rather than address the situation head on, however, I wasted several years while we attempted to sell the operation. That was a doomed endeavor because no realistic solution could have extricated us from the maze of liabilities that was going to exist for decades. Our obligations were particularly worrisome because their potential to explode could not be measured. Moreover, if severe trouble occurred, we knew it was likely to correlate with problems elsewhere in financial markets.

The second reason I regularly describe our problems in this area lies in the hope that our experiences may prove instructive for managers, auditors, and regulators. In a sense, we are a canary in this business coal mine and should sing a song of warning as we expire. The number and value of derivative contracts outstanding in the world continues to mushroom and is now a multiple of what existed in 1998, the last time that financial chaos erupted.

Our experience should be particularly sobering because we were a better-than-average candidate to exit gracefully. Gen Re was a relatively minor operator in the derivatives field. It has had the good fortune to unwind its supposedly liquid positions in a benign market, all the while free of financial or other pressures that might have forced it to conduct the liquidation in a less-than-efficient manner. Our accounting in the past was conventional and actually thought to be conservative. Additionally, we know of no bad behavior by anyone involved.

It could be a different story for others in the future. Imagine, if you will, one or more firms (troubles often spread) with positions that are many multiples of ours attempting to liquidate in chaotic markets and under extreme, and well-publicized, pressures. This is a scenario to which much attention should be given now rather than after the fact. The time to have considered—and improved—the reliability of New Orleans' levees was *before* Katrina.

When we finally wind up Gen Re Securities, my feelings about its departure will be akin to those expressed in a country song, "My wife ran away with my best friend, and I sure miss him a lot."[7]

■ ■ ■

You will be happy to hear—and I'm even happier—that this will be my last discussion of the losses at Gen Re's derivative operation. When we started to wind this business down early in 2002, we had 23,218 contracts outstanding. Now we have 197. Our cumulative pre-tax loss from this operation totals $409 million, but only $5 million occurred in 2006. Charlie says that if we had properly classified the $409 million on our 2001 balance sheet, it would have been labeled "Good Until Reached For." In any event, a Shakespearean thought—slightly modified—seems appropriate for the tombstone of this derivative business: "All's well that ends."[8]

Derivatives

Derivatives are dangerous. They have dramatically increased the leverage and risks in our financial system. They have made it almost impossible for investors to understand and analyze our largest commercial banks and investment banks. They allowed Fannie Mae and Freddie Mac to engage in massive misstatements of earnings for years. So indecipherable were Freddie and Fannie that their federal regulator, OFHEO, whose more than 100 employees had no job except the oversight of these two institutions, totally missed their cooking of the books.

Indeed, recent events demonstrate that certain big-name CEOs (or former CEOs) at major financial institutions were simply incapable of managing a business with a huge, complex book of derivatives. Include Charlie and me in this hapless group: When Berkshire purchased General Re in 1998, we knew we could not get our minds around its book of 23,218 derivatives contracts, made with 884 counterparties (many of which we had never heard of). So we decided to close up shop. Though we were under no pressure and were operating in benign markets as we exited, it took us five years and more than $400 million in losses to largely complete the task. Upon leaving, our feelings about the business mirrored a line in a country song: "I liked you better before I got to know you so well."

Improved "transparency"—a favorite remedy of politicians, commentators and financial regulators for averting future train wrecks—won't cure the problems that derivatives pose. I know of no reporting mechanism that would come close to describing and measuring the risks in a huge and complex portfolio of derivatives. Auditors can't audit these contracts, and regulators can't regulate them. When I read the pages of "disclosure" in 10-Ks of companies that are entangled with these instruments, all I end up knowing is that I *don't* know what is going on in their portfolios (and then I reach for some aspirin).

A normal stock or bond trade is completed in a few days with one party getting its cash, the other its securities. Counterparty risk therefore quickly disappears, which means credit problems can't accumulate. This rapid settlement process is key to maintaining the integrity of markets. That, in fact, is a reason for NYSE and NASDAQ *shortening* the settlement period from five days to three days in 1995.

Derivatives contracts, in contrast, often go unsettled for years, or even decades, with counterparties building up huge claims against each other. "Paper" assets and liabilities—often hard to quantify—become important parts of financial statements though these items will not be validated for many years. Additionally, a frightening web of mutual dependence develops among huge financial institutions. Receivables and payables by the billions become concentrated in the hands of a few large dealers who are apt to be highly leveraged in other ways as well. Participants seeking to dodge troubles face the same problem as someone seeking to avoid venereal disease: It's not just whom *you* sleep with, but also whom *they* are sleeping with.

Sleeping around, to continue our metaphor, can actually be useful for large derivatives dealers because it assures them government aid if trouble hits. In other words, only companies having problems that can infect the entire neighborhood—I won't mention names—are certain to become a concern of the state (an outcome, I'm sad to say, that is proper). From this irritating reality comes *The First Law of Corporate Survival* for ambitious CEOs who pile on leverage and run large and unfathomable derivatives books: Modest incompetence simply won't do; it's mindboggling screw-ups that are required.

Considering the ruin I've pictured, you may wonder why Berkshire is a party to 251 derivatives contracts (other than those used for operational purposes at MidAmerican and the few left over at Gen Re). The answer is simple: I believe each contract we own was mispriced at inception, sometimes dramatically so. I both initiated these positions and monitor them, a set of responsibilities consistent with my belief that the CEO of any large financial organization *must* be the Chief Risk Officer as well. If we lose money on our derivatives, it will be my fault.

Our derivatives dealings require our counterparties to make payments to us when contracts are initiated. Berkshire therefore always holds the money, which leaves us assuming no meaningful counterparty risk. As of year-end, the payments made to us less losses we have paid—our derivatives "float," so to speak—totaled $8.1 billion. This float is similar to insurance float: If we break even on an underlying transaction, we will have enjoyed the use of free money for a long time. Our expectation, though it is far from a sure thing, is that we will do better than break even and that the substantial investment income we earn on the funds will be frosting on the cake.[9]

■ ■ ■

Charlie and I are of one mind in how we feel about derivatives and the trading activities that go with them: We view them as time bombs, both for the parties that deal in them and the economic system.

Having delivered that thought, which I'll get back to, let me retreat to explaining derivatives, though the explanation must be general because the word covers an extraordinarily wide range of financial contracts. Essentially, these instruments call for money to change hands at some future date, with the amount to be determined by one or more reference items, such as interest rates, stock prices or currency values. If, for example, you are either long or short an S&P 500 futures contract, you are a party to a very simple derivatives transaction—with your gain or loss *derived* from movements in the index. Derivatives contracts are of varying duration (running sometimes to 20 or more years) and their value is often tied to several variables.

Unless derivatives contracts are collateralized or guaranteed, their ultimate value also depends on the creditworthiness of the counterparties to them. In the meantime, though, before a contract is settled, the counterparties record profits and losses—often huge in amount—in their current earnings statements without so much as a penny changing hands.

The range of derivatives contracts is limited only by the imagination of man (or sometimes, so it seems, madmen). At Enron, for example, newsprint and broadband derivatives, due to be settled many years in the future, were put on the books. Or say you want to write a contract speculating on the number of twins to be born in Nebraska in 2020. No problem—at a price, you will easily find an obliging counterparty.

When we purchased Gen Re, it came with General Re Securities, a derivatives dealer that Charlie and I didn't want, judging it to be dangerous. We failed in our attempts to sell the operation, however, and are now terminating it.

But closing down a derivatives business is easier said than done. It will be a great many years before we are totally out of this operation (though we reduce our exposure daily). In fact, the reinsurance and derivatives businesses are similar: Like Hell, both are easy to enter and almost impossible to exit. In either industry, once you write a contract—which may require a large payment decades later—you are usually stuck with it. True, there are methods by which the risk can be laid off with others. But most strategies of that kind leave you with residual liability.

Another commonality of reinsurance and derivatives is that both generate reported earnings that are often wildly overstated. That's true because today's earnings are in a significant way based on estimates whose inaccuracy may not be exposed for many years.

Errors will usually be honest, reflecting only the human tendency to take an optimistic view of one's commitments. But the parties to derivatives also have enormous incentives to cheat in accounting for them. Those who trade derivatives are usually paid (in whole or part) on "earnings" calculated by mark-to-market accounting. But often there is no real market (think about our contract involving twins) and mark-to-model's utilized. This substitution can bring on large-scale mischief. As a general rule, contracts involving multiple reference items and distant settlement dates increase the opportunities for counterparties to use fanciful assumptions. In the twins scenario, for example, the two parties to the contract might well use differing models allowing *both* to show substantial profits for many years. In extreme cases, mark-to-model degenerates into what I would call mark-to-myth.

Of course, both internal and outside auditors review the numbers, but that's no easy job. For example, General Re Securities at year-end (after ten months of winding down its operation) had 14,384 contracts outstanding, involving 672 counterparties around the world. Each contract had a plus or minus value derived from one or more reference items, including some of mind-boggling complexity. Valuing a portfolio like that, expert auditors could easily and honestly have widely varying opinions.

The valuation problem is far from academic: In recent years, some huge-scale frauds and near-frauds have been facilitated by derivatives trades. In the energy and electric utility sectors, for example, companies used derivatives and trading activities to report great "earnings"—until the roof fell in when they actually tried to convert the derivatives-related receivables on their balance sheets into cash. "Mark-to-market" then turned out to be truly "mark-to-myth."

I can assure you that the marking errors in the derivatives business have not been symmetrical. Almost invariably, they have favored either the trader who was eyeing a multimillion-dollar bonus or the CEO who wanted to report impressive "earnings" (or both). The bonuses were paid, and the CEO profited from his options. Only much later did shareholders learn that the reported earnings were a sham.

Another problem about derivatives is that they can exacerbate trouble that a corporation has run into for completely unrelated reasons. This pile-on effect occurs because many derivatives contracts require that a company suffering a credit downgrade immediately supply collateral to counterparties. Imagine, then, that a company is downgraded because of general adversity and that its derivatives instantly kick in with *their* requirement, imposing an unexpected and enormous demand for cash collateral on the company. The need to meet this demand can then throw the company into a liquidity crisis that may, in some cases, trigger still more downgrades. It all becomes a spiral that can lead to a corporate meltdown.

Derivatives also create a daisy-chain risk that is akin to the risk run by insurers or reinsurers that lay off much of their business with others. In both cases, huge receivables from many counterparties tend to build up over time. (At Gen Re Securities, we still have $6.5 billion of receivables, though we've been in a liquidation mode for nearly a year.) A participant may see himself as prudent, believing his large credit exposures to be diversified and therefore not dangerous. Under certain circumstances, though, an exogenous event that causes the receivable from Company A to go bad will also affect those from Companies B through Z. History teaches us that a crisis often causes problems to correlate in a manner undreamed of in more tranquil times.

In banking, the recognition of a "linkage" problem was one of the reasons for the formation of the Federal Reserve System. Before the Fed was established, the failure of weak banks would sometimes put sudden and unanticipated liquidity demands on previously-strong banks, causing them to fail in turn. The Fed now insulates the strong from the troubles of the weak. But there is no central bank assigned to the job of preventing the dominoes toppling in insurance or derivatives. In these industries, firms that are fundamentally solid can become troubled simply because of the travails of other firms further down the chain. When a "chain reaction" threat exists within an industry, it pays to minimize links of any kind. That's how we conduct our reinsurance business, and it's one reason we are exiting derivatives.

Many people argue that derivatives reduce systemic problems, in that participants who can't bear certain risks are able to transfer them to stronger hands. These people believe that derivatives act to stabilize the economy, facilitate trade, and eliminate bumps for individual participants. And, on a micro level, what they say is often true. Indeed, at Berkshire, I sometimes engage in large-scale derivatives transactions in order to facilitate certain investment strategies.

Charlie and I believe, however, that the macro picture is dangerous and getting more so. Large amounts of risk, particularly credit risk, have become concentrated in the hands of relatively few derivatives dealers, who in addition trade extensively with one other. The troubles of one could quickly infect the others. On top of that, these dealers are owed huge amounts by non-dealer counterparties. Some of these counterparties, as I've mentioned, are linked in ways that could cause them to contemporaneously run into a problem because of a single event (such as the implosion of the telecom industry or the precipitous decline in the value of merchant power projects). Linkage, when it suddenly surfaces, can trigger serious systemic problems.

Indeed, in 1998, the leveraged and derivatives-heavy activities of a single hedge fund, Long-Term Capital Management, caused the Federal Reserve anxieties so severe that it hastily orchestrated a rescue effort. In later Congressional testimony, Fed officials acknowledged that, had they not intervened, the outstanding trades of LTCM—a firm unknown to the general public and employing only a few hundred people—could well have posed a serious threat to the stability of American markets. In other words, the Fed acted because its leaders were fearful of what might have happened to other financial institutions had the LTCM domino toppled. And this affair, though it paralyzed many parts of the fixed-income market for weeks, was far from a worst-case scenario.

One of the derivatives instruments that LTCM used was total-return swaps—contracts that facilitate 100% leverage in various markets, including stocks. For example, Party A to a contract, usually a bank, puts up all of the money for the purchase of a stock while Party B, without putting up any capital, agrees that at a future date it will receive any gain or pay any loss that the bank realizes.

Total-return swaps of this type make a joke of margin requirements. Beyond that, other types of derivatives severely curtail the ability of regulators to curb leverage and generally get their arms around the risk profiles of banks, insurers and other financial institutions. Similarly, even experienced investors and analysts encounter major problems in analyzing the financial condition of firms that are heavily involved with derivatives contracts. When Charlie and I finish reading the long footnotes detailing the derivatives activities of major banks, the only thing we understand is that we *don't* understand how much risk the institution is running.

The derivatives genie is now well out of the bottle, and these instruments will almost certainly multiply in variety and number until some event makes their toxicity clear. Knowledge of how dangerous they are has already permeated the electricity and gas businesses, in which the eruption of major troubles caused the use of derivatives to diminish dramatically. Elsewhere, however, the derivatives business continues to expand unchecked. Central banks and governments have so far found no effective way to control, or even monitor, the risks posed by these contracts.

Charlie and I believe Berkshire should be a fortress of financial strength—for the sake of our owners, creditors, policyholders and employees. We try to be alert to any sort of mega-catastrophe risk, and that posture may make us unduly apprehensive about the burgeoning quantities of long-term derivatives contracts and the massive amount of uncollateralized receivables that are growing alongside. In our view, however, derivatives are financial weapons of mass destruction, carrying dangers that, while now latent, are potentially lethal.[10]

Chapter 9

The Assessment and Management of Risk

Charlie and I detest taking even small risks unless we feel we are being adequately compensated for doing so. About as far as we will go down that path is occasionally eat cottage cheese a day after the expiration on the carton.[1]

—WARREN BUFFETT

What counts in this business is underwriting discipline. The winners are those that unfailingly stick to three key principles:

1. They accept only those risks that they are able to properly evaluate (staying within their circle of competence) and that, after they have evaluated all relevant factors including remote loss scenarios, carry the expectancy of profit. These insurers ignore market-share considerations and are sanguine about losing business to competitors that are offering foolish prices or policy conditions.
2. They limit the business they accept in a manner that guarantees they will suffer no aggregation of losses from a single event or from related events that will threaten their solvency. They ceaselessly search for possible correlation among seemingly unrelated risks.
3. They avoid business involving moral risk: No matter what the rate, trying to write good contracts with bad people doesn't work.

While most policyholders and clients are honorable and ethical, doing business with the few exceptions is usually expensive, sometimes extraordinarily so.[2]

■ ■ ■

In this operation, we sell policies that insurance and reinsurance companies buy to protect themselves from the effects of mega-catastrophes. Since truly major catastrophes are rare occurrences, our super-cat business can be expected to show large profits in most years—and to record huge loss occasionally. In other words, the attractiveness of our super-cat business will take a great many years to measure. *What you must understand, however, is that a truly terrible year in the super-cat business is not a possibility—it's a certainty. The only question is when it will come.*

In our super-cat operation, our customers are insurers that are exposed to major earnings volatility and that wish to reduce it. The product we sell—for what we hope is an appropriate price—is our willingness to shift that volatility to our own books. Gyrations in Berkshire's earnings don't bother us in the least: Charlie and I would much rather earn a lumpy 15% over time than a smooth 12%. (After all, our earnings swing wildly on a daily and weekly basis—why should we demand that smoothness accompany each orbit that the earth makes of the sun?) We are most comfortable with that thinking, however, when we have shareholder/partners who can also accept volatility, and that's why we regularly repeat our cautions.[3]

■ ■ ■

A few facts about our exposure to California earthquakes—our largest risk—seem in order.

So what are the true odds of our having to make a payout during the policy's term? We don't know—nor do we think computer models will help us, since we believe the precision they project is a chimera. In fact, such models can lull decision-makers into a false sense of security and thereby increase their chances of making a really huge mistake.

We've already seen such debacles in both insurance and investments. Witness "portfolio insurance," whose destructive effects in the 1987 market crash led one wag to observe that it was the computers that should have been jumping out of windows.

Even if perfection in assessing risks is unattainable, insurers can underwrite sensibly. After all, you need not know a man's precise age to know that he is old enough to vote nor know his exact weight to recognize his need to diet. In insurance, it is essential to remember that virtually all surprises are unpleasant, and with that in mind we try to price our super-cat exposures so that about 90% of total premiums end up being eventually paid out in losses and expenses. Over time, we will find out how smart our pricing has been, but that will not be quickly. The super-cat business is just like the investment business in that it often takes a long time to find out whether you knew what you were doing.

In this respect, as in others, we try to "reverse engineer" our future at Berkshire, bearing in mind Charlie's dictum: "All I want to know is where I'm going to die so I'll never go there." (Inverting really works: Try singing country western songs backwards and you will quickly regain your house, your car and your wife.) If we can't tolerate a possible consequence, remote though it may be, we steer clear of planting its seeds. That is why we don't borrow big amounts and why we make sure that our super-cat business losses, large though the maximums may sound, will not put a major dent in Berkshire's intrinsic value.[4]

■ ■ ■

At Berkshire, it should be noted, we have for some years been willing to assume more risk than any other insurer has *knowingly* taken on. That's still the case. We are perfectly willing to lose $2 billion to $2½ billion in a single event (as we did on September 11th) if we have been paid properly for assuming the risk that caused the loss (which on that occasion we weren't).[5]

■ ■ ■

We want to emphasize, however, that we assume risks in Ajit's operation that are huge—*far* larger than those retained by any other insurer in the world. Therefore, a single event could cause a major swing in Ajit's results in any given quarter or year. That bothers us not at all: As long as we are paid appropriately, we love taking on short-term volatility that others wish to shed. At Berkshire, we would rather earn a lumpy 15% over time than a smooth 12%.[6]

■ ■ ■

Were a true mega-catastrophe to occur in the next decade or two—and that's a real possibility—some reinsurers would not survive. The largest insured loss to date is the World Trade Center disaster, which cost the insurance industry an estimated $35 billion. Hurricane Andrew cost insurers about $15.5 billion in 1992 (though that loss would be far higher in today's dollars). Both events rocked the insurance and reinsurance world. But a $100 billion event, or even a larger catastrophe, remains a possibility if either a particularly severe earthquake or hurricane hits just the wrong place. Four significant hurricanes struck Florida during 2004, causing an aggregate of $25 billion or so in insured losses. Two of these—Charley and Ivan—could have done at least three times the damage they did had they entered the U.S. not far from their actual landing points.

Many insurers regard a $100 billion industry loss as "unthinkable" and won't even plan for it. But at Berkshire, we are fully prepared. Our share of the loss would probably be 3% to 5%, and earnings from our investments and other businesses would comfortably exceed that cost. When "the day after" arrives, Berkshire's checks will clear.[7]

■ ■ ■

It's an open question whether atmospheric, oceanic or other causal factors have dramatically changed the frequency or intensity of hurricanes. Recent experience is worrisome. We know, for instance, that in the 100 years before 2004, about 59 hurricanes of Category 3 strength, or greater, hit the Southeastern and Gulf Coast states, and that only three of these were Category 5s. We further know that in 2004 there were three Category 3 storms that hammered those areas and that these were followed by four more in 2005, one of them, Katrina, the most destructive hurricane in industry history. Moreover, there were three Category 5s near the coast last year that fortunately weakened before landfall.

Was this onslaught of more frequent and more intense storms merely an anomaly? Or was it caused by changes in climate, water temperature or other variables we don't fully understand? And could these factors be developing in a manner that will soon produce disasters dwarfing Katrina?

Joe, Ajit and I don't know the answer to these all-important questions. What we do know is that our ignorance means we must follow the course prescribed by Pascal in his famous wager about the existence of God. As you may recall, he concluded that since he didn't know the answer, his personal gain/loss ratio dictated an affirmative conclusion.

So guided, we've concluded that we should now write mega-cat policies only at prices far higher than prevailed last year—and then only with an aggregate exposure that would not cause us distress if shifts in some important variable produce far more costly storms in the near future. To a lesser degree, we felt this way after 2004—and cut back our writings when prices didn't move. Now our caution has intensified. If prices seem appropriate, however, we continue to have both the ability and the appetite to be the largest writer of mega-cat coverage in the world.[8]

■ ■ ■

Don't think, however, that we have lost our taste for risk. We remain prepared to lose $6 billion in a single event, *if* we have been paid appropriately for assuming that risk. We are not willing, though, to take on even very small exposures at prices that don't reflect our evaluation of loss probabilities. Appropriate prices don't guarantee profits in any given year, but inappropriate prices most certainly guarantee eventual losses. Rates have recently fallen because a flood of capital has entered the super-cat field. We have therefore sharply reduced our wind exposures. Our behavior here parallels that which we employ in financial markets: Be fearful when others are greedy, and be greedy when others are fearful.[9]

■ ■ ■

When we can't find anything exciting in which to invest, our "default" position is U.S. Treasuries, both bills and repos. No matter how low the yields on these instruments go, we never "reach" for a little more income by dropping our credit standards or by extending maturities. Charlie and I detest taking even small risks unless we feel we are being adequately compensated for doing so. About as far as we will go down that path is to occasionally eat cottage cheese a day after the expiration date on the carton.[10]

Chapter 10

Executive Compensation

In recent years compensation committees too often have been tail-wagging puppy dogs meekly following recommendations by consultants, a breed not known for allegiance to faceless shareholders who pay their fees. (If you can't tell whose side someone is on, they are not on yours.) True, each committee is required by the SEC to state its reasoning about pay in the proxy. But words are usually boilerplate written by the company's lawyers or its human-relations department.

There's nothing wrong with paying well for truly exceptional performance. But, for anything short of that, it's time for directors to shout "less!" It would be a travesty if the bloated pay of recent years became a baseline for future compensation. Compensation committees should go back to the drawing boards.[1]

—WARREN BUFFETT

I have been the Typhoid Mary of compensation committees.[2]

—WARREN BUFFETT

Let me pause for a brief confession. In criticizing comp committee behavior, I don't speak as a true insider. Though I have served as a director of twenty public companies, only one CEO has put me on his comp committee. Hmmm....[3]

—WARREN BUFFETT

At Berkshire, after all, I am a one-man compensation committee who determines the salaries and incentives for the CEOs of around 40 significant operating businesses.

How much time does this aspect of my job take? Virtually none. How many CEOs have voluntarily left us for other jobs in our 42-year history? Precisely none.

Berkshire employs many different incentive arrangements, with their terms depending on such elements as the economic potential or capital intensity of a CEO's business. Whatever the compensation arrangement, though, I try to keep it both simple and fair.

When we use incentives—and these can be large—they are always tied to the operating results for which a given CEO has authority. We issue no lottery tickets that carry payoffs unrelated to business performance. If a CEO bats .300, he gets paid for being a .300 hitter, even if circumstances outside of his control cause Berkshire to perform poorly. And if he bats .150, he doesn't get a payoff just because the successes of others have enabled Berkshire to prosper mightily. An example: We now own $61 billion of equities at Berkshire, whose value can easily rise or fall by 10% in a given year. Why in the world should the pay of our operating executives be affected by such $6 billion swings, however important the gain or loss may be for shareholders?

You've read loads about CEOs who have received astronomical compensation for mediocre results. Much less well-advertised is the fact that America's CEOs also generally live the good life. Many, it should be emphasized, are exceptionally able, and almost all work far more than 40 hours a week. But they are usually treated like royalty in the process. (And we're certainly going to keep it that way at Berkshire. Though Charlie still favors sackcloth and ashes, I prefer to be spoiled rotten. Berkshire owns The Pampered Chef; our wonderful office group has made me The Pampered Chief.)

CEO perks at one company are quickly copied elsewhere. "All the other kids have one" may seem a thought too juvenile to use as a rationale in the boardroom. But consultants employ precisely this argument, phrased more elegantly of course, when they make recommendations to comp committees.

Irrational and excessive comp practices will not be materially changed by disclosure or by "independent" comp committee members. Indeed, I think it's likely that the reason I was rejected for service on so many comp committees was that I was regarded as *too* independent. Compensation reform will only occur if the largest institutional shareholders—it would only take a few—demand a *fresh* look at the whole system. The consultants' present drill of deftly selecting "peer" companies to compare with their clients will only perpetuate present excesses.[4]

■■■

At Berkshire, we want to have compensation policies that are both easy to understand and in sync with what we wish our associates to accomplish.[5]

■■■

In setting compensation, we like to hold out the promise of large carrots, but make sure their delivery is tied directly to results in the area that a manager controls. When capital invested in an operation is significant, we also both charge managers a high rate for incremental capital they employ and credit them at an equally high rate for capital they release.

The product of this money's-not-free approach is definitely visible at Scott Fetzer. If Ralph can employ incremental funds at good returns, it pays him to do so: His bonus increases when earnings on additional capital exceed a meaningful hurdle charge. But our bonus calculation is symmetrical: If incremental investment yields sub-standard returns, the shortfall is costly to Ralph as well as to Berkshire. The consequence of this two-way arrangement is that it pays Ralph—and pays him well—to send to Omaha any cash he can't advantageously use in his business.

It has become fashionable at public companies to describe almost every compensation plan as aligning the interests of management with those of shareholders. In our book, alignment means being a partner in both directions, not just on the upside. Many "alignment" plans flunk this basic test, being artful forms of "heads I win, tails you lose."

A common form of misalignment occurs in the typical stock option arrangement, which does not periodically increase the option price to compensate for the fact that retained earnings are building up the wealth of the company. Indeed, the combination of a ten-year option, a low dividend payout, and compound interest can provide lush gains to a manager who has done no more than tread water in his job. A cynic might even note that when payments to owners are held down, the profit to the option-holding manager increases. I have yet to see this vital point spelled out in a proxy statement asking shareholders to approve an option plan.

In all instances, we pursue rationality. Arrangements that pay off in capricious ways, unrelated to a manager's personal accomplishments, may well be welcomed by certain managers. Who, after all, refuses a free lottery ticket? But such arrangements are wasteful to the company and cause the manager to lose focus on what should be his real areas of concern. Additionally, irrational behavior at the parent may well encourage imitative behavior at subsidiaries.[6]

■ ■ ■

At Berkshire, however, we use an incentive compensation system that rewards key managers for meeting targets in their own bailiwicks. If See's does well, that does not produce incentive compensation at the News—nor vice versa. Neither do we look at the price of Berkshire stock when we write bonus checks. We believe good unit performance should be rewarded whether Berkshire stock rises, falls, or stays even. Similarly, we think average performance should earn no special rewards even if our stock should soar. "Performance," furthermore, is defined in different ways depending upon the underlying economics of the business: in some our managers enjoy tailwinds not of their own making, in others they fight unavoidable headwinds.

The rewards that go with this system can be large. At our various business units, top managers sometimes receive incentive bonuses of five times their base salary, or more, and it would appear possible that one manager's bonus could top $2 million in 1986. (I hope so.) We do not put a cap on bonuses, and the potential for rewards is not hierarchical. The manager of a relatively small unit can earn far more than the manager of a larger unit if results indicate he should. We believe, further, that such factors as seniority and age should not affect incentive compensation (though they sometimes influence basic compensation). A 20-year-old who can hit .300 is as valuable to us as a 40-year-old performing as well.[7]

■ ■ ■

But when CEOs (or their representatives) have met with compensation committees, too often one side—the CEO's—has cared far more than the other about what bargain is struck. A CEO, for example, will always regard the difference between receiving options for 100,000 shares or for 500,000 as monumental. To a comp committee, however, the difference may seem unimportant—particularly if, as has been the case at most companies, neither grant will have any effect on reported earnings. Under these conditions, the negotiation often has a "play-money" quality.

Overreaching by CEOs greatly accelerated in the 1990s as compensation packages gained by the most avaricious—a title for which there was vigorous competition—were promptly replicated elsewhere. The couriers for this epidemic of greed were usually consultants and human relations departments, which had no trouble perceiving who buttered their bread. As one compensation consultant commented: "There are two classes of clients you don't want to offend—actual and potential."[8]

■ ■ ■

Getting fired can produce a particularly bountiful payday for a CEO. Indeed, he can "earn" more in that single day, while cleaning out his desk, than an American worker earns in a lifetime of cleaning toilets. Forget the old maxim about nothing succeeding like success: Today, in the executive suite, the all-too-prevalent rule is that nothing succeeds like *failure*.

Huge severance payments, lavish perks and outsized payments for ho-hum performance often occur because comp committees have become slaves to comparative data. The drill is simple: Three or so directors—*not chosen by chance*—are bombarded for a few hours before a board meeting with pay statistics that perpetually ratchet upward. Additionally, the committee is told about new perks that other managers are receiving. In this manner, outlandish "goodies" are showered upon CEOs simply because of a corporate version of the argument we all used when children: "But, Mom, all the other kids have one." When comp committees follow this "logic," yesterday's most egregious excess becomes today's baseline.

Comp committees should adopt the attitude of Hank Greenberg, the Detroit slugger and a boyhood hero of mine. Hank's son, Steve, at one time was a player's agent. Representing an outfielder in negotiations with a major league club, Steve sounded out his dad about the size of the signing bonus he should ask for. Hank, a true pay-for-performance guy, got straight to the point, "What did he hit last year?" When Steve answered ".246," Hank's comeback was immediate: "Ask for a uniform."[9]

■ ■ ■

Most managers talk the talk but don't walk the walk, choosing instead to employ compensation systems that are long on carrots but short on sticks (and that almost invariably treat equity capital as if it were cost-free).[10]

Chapter 11

Time Management

We both insist on a lot of time being available almost everyday to just sit and think. That is very uncommon in American business. We read and think. So Warren and I do more reading and thinking and less doing than most people in business. We do that because we like that kind of life.[1]

—CHARLIE MUNGER

I have learned an incredible amount from Warren, some of them are things you can express, like really looking at the time on your calendar, valuing as much free time as possible. I love when Warren gets out his calendar.[2]

—BILL GATES

Charlie Rose: Warren Buffett has constructed a life which enables him to do what he loves in a way that is comfortable and totally productive for him. We talked about how he lives his life over dinner at Gorat's, his favorite steakhouse in Omaha. Give me a sense. Walk through a day with me.

Warren Buffett: Day, you wouldn't believe today. I come down, and well, I usually read the papers at home. I get up around 6:45 A.M.

Charlie Rose: Are they papers or on-line?

Warren Buffett: Mostly papers, but I do click on-line for some things.

Charlie Rose: You have your favorites listed.

Warren Buffett: Yeah, I even have the Charlie Rose Show listed. I want to see who's going to be on there. Really, I do. So I get up around 6:45 A.M., but I get in the office around 9:00 A.M. or 8:00 A.M., depends on what's going on, I have no schedule to speak of. Here is my date book, just take a look.

Charlie Rose: This isn't jam packed with appointments.

Warren Buffett: Eight o'clock, nine o'clock. I just don't do it. I don't want to live that way.

Charlie Rose: You decided that a long time ago.

Warren Buffett: A long, long time ago. I decided that when I was delivering papers when I was a kid. I knew what I enjoyed and what I didn't enjoy. I enjoyed delivering papers. I don't want to head IBM or General Motors.

Charlie Rose: Why not?

Warren Buffett: Your life is so taken up by things that you really don't have a choice about. I really just don't want to do it.

Charlie Rose: You get in around 9:45 A.M.

Warren Buffett: I read five newspapers a day. I read all kinds of annual reports, magazines, 10Ks 10Qs and so I'd say I spend 75% to 80% of the day reading. I spend the rest of the day on the phone, buying or selling stocks, foreign currencies, but that doesn't take much time. We are not doing that on a broad scale, and then I go home and play bridge or read some more.

Charlie Rose: You go home around 5:30 P.M. to 6:00 P.M.

Warren Buffett: Although there is no set time, I don't like to be structured.

Charlie Rose: You could go home at 3:00 P.M., or if you want to, go home at 7:00 P.M.

Warren Buffett: Exactly.

Charlie Rose: You could read more.

Warren Buffett: Yea, usually, or play bridge now and then.

Charlie Rose: On-line?

Warren Buffett: I would pay $5 million a year for the ability to play on-line bridge 12 hours a week. It's worth it to me. If I compare it to the cost of a second home, that would mean nothing to me. If I deliver 12 hours of enjoyment playing bridge with my sister in Carmel, or whomever, doing it in a few seconds, clicking it on, I would pay it. They can't figure it out, so I'm paying about $95 a year.

Charlie Rose: So, principal enjoyment is playing bridge and friends.

Warren Buffett: And the bridge and the friends intersect, of course. This Saturday I'll play with Bill at 10:00 P.M. my time, 8:00 P.M. his time. We'll play a couple of hours. His name is "Challenger" but he doesn't spell it right. He spells it "Chalengr." I got a look at the spelling.

Charlie Rose: What's your name?

Warren Buffett: T-Bone.

Charlie Rose: Your name is "T-Bone," he's "Challenger" and you both get on-line and play a couple of hours. You always win?

Warren Buffett: No, I'd tell you so, but you'd check with him and there you go. . . .[3]

■ ■ ■

Warren's oldest son, Howard, eventually came to understand his father's time management process: "My father couldn't run a lawn-mower . . . I never saw him cut the grass, trim a hedge, or wash a car. I remember that used to be irritating; and only when I got older and understood the value of time did I realize why he did things the way he did. His time is so valuable.[4]

■ ■ ■

"It's not a plus to get terribly well known. As you can see [waving toward the small suite that makes up Berkshire Hathaway headquarters], we are not equipped to handle tons of inquiries. We get letters from people all over who want advice on investments. I don't like to be hard-nosed, but there's also no way I can do it and get my job done."[5]

■ ■ ■

A shareholder once asked Buffett how he spent his days. Warren said he mostly read and talked on the telephone. "That's what I do, Charlie, what do you do?"

"That [question] reminds me very much of a friend of mine in World War II in a group that had nothing to do," replied Munger. "A general once went up to my friend's boss, we'll call him Captain Glotz. He said 'Captain Glotz, What do you do?' His boss said, 'Not a damn thing.'

"The General got madder and madder and turned to my friend and said, 'What do you do?'

"My friend said, 'I help Captain Glotz.' That's the best way to describe what I do at Berkshire."[6]

■ ■ ■

Though in the public spotlight, Buffett was standing guard over a still uncommonly private life. So unlike the modern CEO, he did block out his time in advance, preferring to keep it unencumbered. When Bill Graham (a son of Kay) asked when he might stop by, Buffett replied, "Come *any* time, I don't have a schedule." Richard Simmons, president of the Washington Post Co., was amazed by the quiet in Buffett's emerald green sanctum. He did not have an electronic calculator, a stock terminal, or a computer. "I am a computer," he noted to an interviewer. When Buffett was in his office, Simmons said, "Nothing seems to happen, except Bill Scott (Buffett's trader) pokes his head in to say, 'Ten million dollars at 125 1/8th: yes or no?' The phone doesn't ring much. Buffett has so much more *time* than the average CEO." His day was a veritable stream of unstructured hours and cherry colas. He would sit at the redwood horseshoe desk and read for hours, joined to the world by a telephone (which he answered himself) and three private lines: to Salomon Brothers, Smith Barney, and Goldman Sachs.[7]

■ ■ ■

Well, I just use the Nancy Reagan policy, I just say no.[8]

Chapter 12

How to Manage a Crisis

Warren Buffett's Wild Ride at Salomon

Warren Buffett's Wild Ride at Salomon: A harrowing bizarre tale of misdeeds and mistakes that pushed Salomon to the brink and produced the "most important day" in Warren Buffett's life.[1]
—CAROL LOOMIS

Background

In 1987, Berkshire Hathaway purchased, for $700 million, Salomon Brothers redeemable preferred stock and, in effect, became the company's largest shareholder.

In December 1990 and February 1991, managing director Paul W. Mozer, a 34-year-old bond trader, made U.S. Treasury securities trades above the legal limit for any one institution, as well as secret and unauthorized trades in Salomon client accounts, which were then transferred to Salomon's books.

Salomon's chairman (John Gutfreund), president (Thomas Strauss) and in-house counsel (Donald Feuerstein) admitted knowing of these violations for four months without telling Salomon's board of directors or Buffett.

■ ■ ■

At the center of this experience was a single day—what he has called "the most important day of my life." Sunday, August 18, 1991—in which the U.S. Treasury first banned Salomon from bidding in government securities auctions and then, because of Buffett's efforts, rescinded the ban. In the four hours of suspense between the two actions, Buffett struggled passionately to ward off a tragedy he saw threatening to unfold. In Buffett's opinion, the ban put Salomon, the company now being priced at $9 billion, in sure danger of immediately filing for bankruptcy. Even more important, he believed on that day, as he does now, that the collapse of Salomon would have shaken the world's financial system to the core.[2]

■ ■ ■

Following is an account of how Buffett saved Salomon from the brink of collapse and restored the confidence of regulators, shareholders, and employees.

Contrition

"Gutfreund's silence regarding Mozer was 'inexplicable and inexcusable.'"[3]

"We did wrong. We're going to show how we did wrong. We've signed the charge sheet."[4]

"I would like to start by apologizing for the acts that have brought us here. The Nation has a right to expect its rules and laws will be obeyed. At Salomon, certain of these were broken."[5]

"I want employees to ask themselves whether they are willing to have any contemplated act appear on the front page of their local paper the next day, to be read by their spouses, children and friends. . . . If they follow this test, they need not fear my other message to them: Lose money for the firm, and I will be understanding; lose a shred of reputation for the firm, and I will be ruthless."[6]

Full Disclosure

"Charlie insisted that they get the whole truth out. We didn't know what would happen."[7]

"We would give them everything we had as fast as we could get it. In the end, they decided not to indict. We built the confidence that the new leadership would clean the place up, that they were not rotten to the core, not involved in the problems."[8]

"Call us anytime someone doesn't give you what you want. You'll have a new person to deal with within twenty minutes."[9]

On September 4, 1991, Buffett presented to a subcommittee of the House Committee on Energy and Commerce a 52 page report on Salomon's internal investigation.

A Second Job

In 1989 when I—a happy consumer of five cans of Cherry Coke daily—announced our purchase of $1 billion worth of Coca-Cola stock, I described the move as a rather extreme example of putting our money where my mouth was. On August 18 of last year, when I was elected Interim Chairman of Salomon Inc, it was a different story: I put my mouth where our money was.

You've all read of the events that led to my appointment. My decision to take the job carried with it an implicit but important message: Berkshire's operating managers are so outstanding that I knew I could materially reduce the time I was spending at the company and yet remain confident that its economic progress would not skip a beat. The Blumkins, the Friedman family, Mike Goldberg, the Heldmans, Chuck Huggins, Stan Lipsey, Ralph Schey and Frank Rooney (CEO of H.H. Brown, our latest acquisition, which I will describe later) are all masters of their operations and need no help from me. My job is merely to treat them right and to allocate the capital they generate. Neither function is impeded by my work at Salomon.

The role that Charlie and I play in the success of our operating units can be illustrated by a story about George Mira, the one-time quarterback of the University of Miami, and his coach, Andy Gustafson. Playing Florida and near its goal line, Mira dropped back to pass. He spotted an open receiver but found his right shoulder in the unshakable grasp of a Florida linebacker. The right-handed Mira thereupon switched the ball to his other hand and threw the only left-handed pass of his life—for a touchdown. As the crowd erupted, Gustafson calmly turned to a reporter and declared: "Now that's what I call coaching."

Given the managerial stars we have at our operating units, Berkshire's performance is not affected if Charlie or I slip away from time to time. You should note, however, the "interim" in my Salomon title. Berkshire is my first love and one that will never fade: At the Harvard Business School last year, a student asked me when I planned to retire and I replied, "About five to ten years after I die."[10]

A Plan of Action

Change in Leadership

Mozer is fired. Gutfreund and Strauss resign.

On August 18, Buffett is elected to be the interim, unsalaried chairman.

Buffett appoints Deryck Maughan as Chief Operating Officer.

Buffett demands resignation of Donald Feuerstein, and replaces him with Robert Denham, Buffett's lawyer on Berkshire matters for fifteen years. Denham is named Chairman of Salomon.

A Letter and Report to the Shareholders of Salomon

To the Shareholders of Salomon Inc:

In this report, I want not only to tell you about Salomon Inc's third-quarter results but also to give you my thinking as to where the company must head.

From announcements we have made and from the media you have learned about the events that led to my appointment as interim Chairman of Salomon Inc on August 18. We have since continued to investigate Salomon's past actions in the Government securities market and in other areas as well. Our conclusion so far: A few Salomon employees behaved egregiously—a fact that will prove costly to you as shareholders—but the misconduct and misjudgments were limited to those few. In short, I believe that we had an extremely serious problem, but not a pervasive one.

Controls and Compliance

Since August 18, we have installed rules and procedures at Salomon Brothers Inc, our securities subsidiary, that we think set a standard for the industry. In addition, we have begun to monitor what goes on in Salomon Brothers in new ways—for example, by setting up a Compliance Committee of the Board—and expect in that area also to be a leader. Even so, an atmosphere encouraging exemplary behavior is probably even more important than rules, necessary though these are. During my tenure as Chairman, I will consider myself the firm's chief compliance officer and I have asked all 9,000 of Salomon's employees to assist me in that effort. I have also urged them to be guided by a test that goes beyond rules: Contemplating any business act, an employee should ask himself whether he would be willing to see it immediately described by an informed and critical reporter on the front page of his local paper, there to be read by his spouse, children and friends. At Salomon we simply want no part of any activities that pass legal tests but that we, as citizens, would find offensive.

Operating Results

Ordinary operations during the third quarter produced excellent profits, in large part because of exceptionally favorable trends in the fixed-income markets. I need to alert you, however, to two major adjustments that affected the bottom line, one negatively, one positively.

In the first instance, we have set up a pre-tax legal reserve of $200 million for potential settlements, judgments, penalties, fines, litigation expense and other related costs. In the second instance, the compensation expense we have recorded for Salomon Brothers is about $110 million less than what might normally be expected. Because certain legal costs may not be deductible for tax purposes, different tax rates apply to the two unusual items. Their combined effect, therefore, was a reduction in net income of about $75 million.

Legal Costs

I would like to elaborate on each of these unusual items, beginning with legal costs. No one can now estimate with any degree of certainty what the eventual direct costs of Salomon's past misdeeds and misjudgments will be to the company. (There are also very important secondary costs, such as loss of business and increased funding costs; but, as I shall detail later, there may additionally be secondary benefits, perhaps substantial.) Whatever these costs are, however, our large equity base— $4 billion—virtually insures that they will not be crippling.

We will pay any fines or penalties with dispatch and we will also try to settle valid legal claims promptly. However, we will litigate invalid or inflated claims, of which there will be many, to whatever extent necessary. That is, we will make appropriate amends for past conduct but we will be no one's patsy.

Accounting rules require that we review the size of our reserve with our auditors and counsel. That has been done and—based on the limited amount of information presently available—they agree with the present estimate. We will make upward or downward adjustments to the reserve as information and events clarify the situation.

Compensation

Most of you have read articles about the high levels of compensation at Salomon Brothers. Some of you have also read discussions of incentive compensation that I have written in the Berkshire Hathaway annual report. In those, I have said that I believe a rational incentive compensation plan to be an excellent way to reward managers, and I have also embraced the concept of truly extraordinary pay for extraordinary managerial performance. I continue to subscribe to those views. But the problem at Salomon Brothers has been a compensation plan that was irrational in certain crucial respects.

One irrationality has been compensation levels that overall have been too high in relation to overall results. For example, last year the securities unit earned about 10% oil equity capital—far tinder the average earned by American business—yet 106 individuals who worked for the unit earned $1 million or more. Many of these people performed exceedingly well and clearly deserved their pay. But the overall result made no sense: Though 1990 operating profits before compensation were flat versus 1989, pay jumped by more than $120 million. And that, of course, meant earnings for shareholders fell by the same amount.

In Salomon Brothers' business, which combines leverage with earnings volatility, it is particularly necessary and appropriate that the financial equation applying personally to managers be comparable to that applying to the ordinary shareholder. We wish to see the unit's managers become wealthy through ownership, not by simply free-riding on the ownership of others, I think in fact that ownership can in time bring our best managers substantial wealth, perhaps in amounts well beyond what they now think possible.

To avoid dilution, the trustee of the EPP purchases stock for the plan in the market and at some point in the future, the company may itself elect to make stock repurchases to reduce the shares outstanding. Within a relatively few years Salomon Inc.'s key employees could own 25% or more of the business, purchased with their own compensation. The better job each employee does for the company, the more stock he or she will own.

Our pay-for-performance philosophy will undoubtedly cause some managers to leave. But very importantly, this same philosophy may induce the top performers to stay, since these people may identify themselves as .350 hitters about to be paid appropriately instead of seeing their just rewards partially assigned to lesser performers. Indeed, I am pleased to report that certain of our very best managers have already asked that the EPP be modified to allow them to substantially increase the proportion of their earnings that can be invested through the plan.

Were an abnormal number of people to leave the firm, the results would not necessarily be bad. Other men and women who share our thinking and values would then be given added responsibilities and opportunities. In the end we must have people to match our principles, not the reverse.

Our goal is going to be that stated many decades ago by J.P. Morgan, who wished to see his bank transact "first-class business—in a first-class way." We will judge ourselves in fact not only by the business we do, but also by the business we decline to do. As is the case at all large organizations, there will be mistakes at Salomon and even failures, but to the best of our ability we will acknowledge our errors quickly and correct them with equal promptness.

The best decision I have made since assuming my post was my appointment of Deryck Maughan as Chief Operating Officer of Salomon Brothers Inc. He, along with the management of Phibro, join me in a pledge to make Salomon Inc a company that produces superior results for clients, employees and owners.

Warren Buffett
Interim Chairman[11]

The Salomon Interlude

Last June, I stepped down as Interim Chairman of Salomon Inc after ten months in the job. You can tell from Berkshire's 1991–92 results that the company didn't miss me while I was gone. But the reverse isn't true: I missed Berkshire and am delighted to be back full-time. There is no job in the world that is more fun than running Berkshire and I count myself lucky to be where I am.

The Salomon post, though far from fun, was interesting and worthwhile: In Fortune's annual survey of America's Most Admired Corporations, conducted last September, Salomon ranked second among 311 companies in the degree to which it improved its reputation. Additionally, Salomon Brothers, the securities subsidiary of Salomon Inc, reported record pre-tax earnings last year—34% above the previous high.

Many people helped in the resolution of Salomon's problems and the righting of the firm, but a few clearly deserve special mention. It is no exaggeration to say that without the combined efforts of Salomon executives Deryck Maughan, Bob Denham, Don Howard, and John MacFarlane, the firm very probably would not have survived. In their work, these men were tireless, effective, supportive and selfless, and I will forever be grateful to them.

Salomon's lead lawyer in its Government matters, Ron Olson of Munger, Tolles & Olson, was also key to our success in getting through this trouble. The firm's problems were not only severe, but complex. At least five authorities—the SEC, the Federal Reserve Bank of New York, the U.S. Treasury, the U.S. Attorney for the Southern District of New York, and the Antitrust Division of the Department of Justice—had important concerns about Salomon. If we were to resolve our problems in a coordinated and prompt manner, we needed a lawyer with exceptional legal, business and human skills. Ron had them all.[12]

■ ■ ■

Our two laggards, meanwhile, have come to life in a very major way. In a transaction that finally rewarded its long-suffering shareholders, Salomon recently merged into Travelers Group. All of Berkshire's shareholders—including me, very personally—owe a huge debt to Deryck Maughan and Bob Denham for, first, playing key roles in saving Salomon from extinction following its 1991 scandal and, second, restoring the vitality of the company to a level that made it an attractive acquisition for Travelers. I have often said that I wish to work with executives that I like, trust and admire. No two fit that description better than Deryck and Bob.[13]

■ ■ ■

Berkshire's final results from its Salomon investment won't be tallied for some time, but it is safe to say that they will be far better than I anticipated two years ago. Looking back, I think of my Salomon experience as having been both fascinating and instructional, though for a time in 1991–92 I felt like the drama critic who wrote: "I would have enjoyed the play except that I had an unfortunate seat. It faced the stage."[14]

Lessons Learned According to Charlie Munger

"Smart, hard-working people aren't exempted from the professional disaster of overconfidence. Often, they just go aground in the more difficult voyages they choose, relying on their self-appraisals that they have superior talents and methods."[15]

"When the final chapter is written, the behavior evinced by Salomon in other similar cases, people will be smart enough to realize this is the response we want—super prompt—even if it means cashiering some people who may not deserve it."[16]

"*Face* your big troubles. Don't sweep them under the rug."[17]

"Warren and I will never stop criticizing some aspect of investment banking culture. It's hard to have people floating around in a miasma of billions without an occasional regrettable act."[18]

Lessons Learned According to Buffett

A reluctance to face up immediately to bad news is what turned a problem at Salomon from one that could have easily been disposed of into one that almost caused the demise of a firm with 8,000 employees.[19]

Chapter 13

Management Principles and Practices

Every day, in countless ways, the competitive position of each of our businesses grows either weaker or stronger. If we are delighting customers, eliminating unnecessary costs and improving our products and services, we gain strength. . . . On a daily basis the effects of our actions are imperceptible; cumulatively, though, their consequences are enormous.[1]

. . . Berkshire's ownership may make even the best of managers more effective. First, we eliminate all of the ritualistic and non productive activities that normally go with the job of CEO. Our managers are totally in charge of their personal schedules. Second, we give each a simple mission: Just run your business as if: 1) you own 100% of it; 2) it is the only asset that you and your family have or will have; and 3) you can't sell or merge it for at least a century.[2]

We regard product quality as sacred.[3]

—WARREN BUFFETT

Long-Term Economic Goals

In good years and bad, Charlie and I simply focus on four goals:

(1) Maintaining Berkshire's Gibraltar-like financial position, which features huge amounts excess liquidity, near-term obligations that are modest, and dozens of sources of earnings and cash;

99

(2) Widening the "moats" around our operating businesses that give them durable competitive advantages;

(3) Acquiring and developing new and varied streams of earnings;

(4) Expanding and nurturing the cadre of outstanding operating managers who, over the years, have delivered Berkshire exceptional results.[4]

Measuring Managerial Economic Performance

The primary test of managerial economic performance is the achievement of a high earnings rate on equity capital employed (without undue leverage, accounting gimmickry, etc.) and not the achievement of consistent gains in earnings per share. In our view, many businesses would be better understood by their shareholder owners, as well as the general public, if managements and financial analysts modified the primary emphasis they place upon earnings per share, and upon yearly changes in that figure.[5]

■ ■ ■

When returns on capital are ordinary, an earn-more-by-putting-up-more record is no great managerial achievement. You can get the same result personally while operating from your rocking chair. Just quadruple the capital you commit to a savings account and you will quadruple your earnings. You would hardly expect hosannas for that particular accomplishment. Yet, retirement announcements regularly sing the praises of CEOs who have, say, quadrupled earnings of their widget company during their reign—with no one examining whether this gain was attributable simply to many years of retained earnings and the workings of compound interest.

If the widget company consistently earned a superior return on capital throughout the period, or if capital employed only doubled during the CEO's reign, the praise for him may be well deserved. But if return on capital was lackluster and capital employed increased in pace with earnings, applause should be withheld. A savings account in which interest was reinvested would achieve the same year-by-year increase in earnings—and, at only 8% interest, would quadruple its annual earnings in 18 years.

The power of this simple math is often ignored by companies to the detriment of their shareholders. Many corporate compensation plans reward managers handsomely for earnings increases produced solely, or in large part, by retained earnings—i.e., earnings withheld from owners. For example, ten-year, fixed-price stock options are granted routinely, often by companies whose dividends are only a small percentage of earnings.[6]

Businesses—the Great, the Good, and the Gruesome

Let's take a look at what kind of businesses turn us on. And while we're at it, let's also discuss what we wish to avoid.

Charlie and I look for companies that have a) a business we understand; b) favorable long-term economics; c) able and trustworthy management; and d) a sensible price tag. We like to buy the whole business or, if management is our partner, at least 80%. When control-type purchases of quality aren't available, though, we are also happy to simply buy small portions of great businesses by way of stock market purchases. It's better to have a part interest in the Hope Diamond than to own all of a rhinestone.

A truly great business must have an enduring "moat" that protects excellent returns on invested capital. The dynamics of capitalism guarantee that competitors will repeatedly assault any business "castle" that is earning high returns. Therefore a formidable barrier such as a company's being the low-cost producer (GEICO, Costco) or possessing a powerful world-wide brand (Coca-Cola, Gillette, American Express) is essential for sustained success. Business history is filled with "Roman Candles," companies whose moats proved illusory and were soon crossed.

But if a business *requires* a superstar to produce great results, the business itself cannot be deemed great. A medical partnership led by your area's premier brain surgeon may enjoy outsized and growing earnings, but that tells little about its future. The partnership's moat will go when the surgeon goes. You can count, though, on the moat of the Mayo Clinic to endure, even though you can't name its CEO.

Now let's move to the gruesome. The worst sort of business is one that grows rapidly, requires significant capital to engender the growth, and then earns little or no money. Think airlines. Here a *durable* competitive advantage has proven elusive ever since the days of the Wright Brothers. Indeed, if a farsighted capitalist had been present at Kitty Hawk, he would have done his successors a huge favor by shooting Orville down.

To sum up, think of three types of "savings accounts." The great one pays an extraordinarily high interest rate that will rise as the years pass. The good one pays an attractive rate of interest that will be earned also on deposits that are added. Finally, the gruesome account both pays an inadequate interest rate and requires you to keep adding money at those disappointing returns.[7]

Cost of Capital

What you find in practice, of course—the test used by most CEO's—is that the cost of capital is about ¼ of 1% below the return promised by any deal that the CEO wants to do. It's very simple.

When we have capital around, we have three questions—leaving aside whether we want to borrow money, which we generally don't want to do. First, "Does it make more sense to pay it out to the shareholders than to keep it within the company?" The sub-question on that is, "If we pay it out, is it better off to do it via repurchases or via dividend? The test of whether we pay it out in dividends is, "Can we create more than a dollar by retaining it rather than paying it out?"

And you never know the answer to that. But, so far, the answer, as judged by our results, is, "Yes we can." And we think that prospectively we can. But that's a hope on our part. It's justified to some extent by past history, but it's not a certainty.

Once we've crossed *that* threshold, then we ask ourselves, "Should we repurchase stock?" Well obviously. If you can buy your stock at significant discount from conservatively calculated intrinsic value and you can buy a reasonable quantity, that's a sensible use of capital.

So once we cross the threshold of deciding that we can deploy capital so as to create more than a dollar of present value for every dollar retained, then it's just a question of doing the most intelligent thing you can find. And the cost of every deal that we do is measured by the second best deal that's around at a given time—including doing more of some of the things we're already in.

And I've listened to cost of capital discussions of all kinds of corporate board meetings and everything else. And I've never found anything that made very much sense in it—except for the fact that it's what they learned in business school and what the consultants talked about. And most of the board members would nod their heads without knowing what the hell was going on. So that's been my history with the cost of capital.[8]

Capital Allocation

Once they become CEOs, they face new responsibilities. They now must make capital allocation decisions, a critical job that they may have never tackled and that is not easily mastered. To stretch the point, it's as if the final step for a highly-talented musician was not to perform at Carnegie Hall but, instead, to be named Chairman of the Federal Reserve.

The lack of skill that many CEOs have at capital allocation is no small matter: After ten years on the job, a CEO whose company annually retains earnings equal to 10% of net worth will have been responsible for the deployment of more than 60% of all the capital at work in the business.

CEOs who recognize their lack of capital-allocation skills (which not all do) will often try to compensate by turning to their staffs, management consultants, or investment bankers. Charlie and I have frequently observed the consequences of such "help." On balance, we feel it is more likely to accentuate the capital-allocation problem than to solve it.

In the end, plenty of unintelligent capital allocation takes place in corporate America. (That's why you hear so much about "restructuring.") Berkshire, however, has been fortunate. At the companies that are our major non-controlled holdings, capital has generally been well-deployed and, in some cases, brilliantly so.[9]

■ ■ ■

Over time, the skill with which a company's managers allocate capital has an enormous impact on the enterprise's value. Almost by definition, a really good business generates far more money (at least after its early years) than it can use internally. The company could, of course, distribute the money to shareholders by way of dividends or share repurchases. But often the CEO asks a strategic planning staff, consultants or investment bankers whether an acquisition or two might make sense. That's like asking your interior decorator whether you need a $50,000 rug.

Understanding intrinsic value is as important for managers as it is for investors. When managers are making capital allocation decisions— including decisions to repurchase shares—it's vital that they act in ways that increase per-share intrinsic value and avoid moves that decrease it. This principle may seem obvious but we constantly see it violated. And, when misallocations occur, shareholders are hurt.[10]

Dividend Policy

Dividend policy is often reported to shareholders, but seldom explained. A company will say something like, "Our goal is to pay out 40% to 50% of earnings and to increase dividends at a rate at least equal to the rise in the CPI." And that's it—no analysis will be supplied as to why that particular policy is best for the owners of the business. Yet, allocation of capital is crucial to business and investment management. Because it is, we believe managers and owners should think hard about the circumstances under which earnings should be retained and under which they should be distributed.

The first point to understand is that all earnings are not created equal. In many businesses—particularly those that have high asset/profit ratios—inflation causes some or all of the reported earnings to become ersatz. The ersatz portion—let's call these earnings "restricted"—cannot, if the business is to retain its economic position, be distributed as dividends. Were these earnings to be paid out, the business would lose ground in one or more of the following areas: its ability to maintain its unit volume of sales, its long-term competitive position, its financial strength. No matter how conservative its payout ratio, a company that consistently distributes restricted earnings is destined for oblivion unless equity capital is otherwise infused.

Restricted earnings are seldom valueless to owners, but they often must be discounted heavily. In effect, they are conscripted by the business, no matter how poor its economic potential. (This retention-no-matter-how-unattractive-the-return situation was communicated unwittingly in a marvelously ironic way by Consolidated Edison a decade ago. At the time, a punitive regulatory policy was a major factor causing the company's stock to sell as low as one-fourth of book value; i.e., every time a dollar of earnings was retained for reinvestment in the business, that dollar was transformed into only 25 cents of market value. But, despite this gold-into-lead process, most earnings were reinvested in the business rather than paid to owners. Meanwhile, at construction and maintenance sites throughout New York, signs proudly proclaimed the corporate slogan, "Dig We Must.")

Restricted earnings need not concern us further in this dividend discussion. Let's turn to the much-more-valued unrestricted variety. These earnings may, with equal feasibility be retained or distributed. In our opinion, management should choose whichever course makes greater sense for the owners of the business.

This principle is not universally accepted. For a number of reasons managers like to withhold unrestricted, readily distributable earnings from shareholders—to expand the corporate empire over which the managers rule, to operate from a position of exceptional financial comfort, etc. But we believe there is only one valid reason for retention. Unrestricted earnings should be retained only when there is a reasonable prospect—backed preferably by historical evidence or, when appropriate, by a thoughtful analysis of the future—that *for every dollar retained by the corporation, at least one dollar of market value will be created for owners.* This will happen only if the capital retained produces incremental earnings equal to, or above, those generally available to investors.

In judging whether managers should retain earnings, shareholders should not simply compare total incremental earnings in recent years to total incremental capital because that relationship may be distorted by what is going on in a core business. During an inflationary period, companies with a core business characterized by extraordinary economics can use small amounts of incremental capital in that business at very high rates of return (as was discussed in last year's section on Goodwill). But, unless they are experiencing tremendous unit growth, outstanding businesses by definition generate large amounts of excess cash. If a company sinks most of this money in other businesses that earn low returns, the company's overall return on retained capital may nevertheless appear excellent because of the extraordinary returns being earned by the portion of earnings incrementally invested in the core business. The situation is analogous to a Pro-Am golf event: even if all of the amateurs are hopeless duffers, the team's best-ball score will be respectable because of the dominating skills of the professional.

Many corporations that consistently show good returns both on equity and on overall incremental capital have, indeed, employed a large portion of their retained earnings on an economically unattractive, even disastrous, basis. Their marvelous core businesses, however, whose earnings grow year after year, camouflaged repeated failures in capital allocation elsewhere (usually involving high-priced acquisitions of businesses that have inherently mediocre economics). The managers at fault periodically report on the lessons they have learned from the latest disappointment. They then usually seek out future lessons. (Failure seems to go to their heads.)

In such cases, shareholders would be far better off if earnings were retained only to expand the high-return business, with the balance paid in dividends or used to repurchase stock (an action that increases the owners' interest in the exceptional business while sparing them participation in subpar businesses). Managers of high-return businesses who consistently employ much of the cash thrown off by those businesses in other ventures with low returns should be held to account for those allocation decisions, regardless of how profitable the overall enterprise is.[11]

Franchises, Businesses, and Moats

An economic franchise arises from a product or service that: (1) is needed or desired; (2) is thought by its customers to have no close substitute and; (3) is not subject to price regulation. The existence of all three conditions will be demonstrated by a company's ability to regularly price its product or service aggressively and thereby to earn high rates of return on capital. Moreover, franchises can tolerate mis-management. Inept managers may diminish a franchise's profitability, but they cannot inflict mortal damage.

In contrast, "a business" earns exceptional profits only if it is the low-cost operator or if supply of its product or service is tight. Tightness in supply usually does not last long. With superior management, a company may maintain its status as a low-cost operator for a much longer time, but even then unceasingly faces the possibility of competitive attack. And a business, unlike a franchise, can be killed by poor management.[12]

■■■

Experience, however, indicates that the best business returns are usually achieved by companies that are doing something quite similar today to what they were doing five or ten years ago. That is no argument for managerial complacency. Businesses always have opportunities to improve service, product lines, manufacturing techniques, and the like, and obviously these opportunities should be seized. But a business that constantly encounters major change also encounters many chances for major error. Furthermore, economic terrain that is forever shifting violently is ground on which it is difficult to build a fortress-like business franchise. Such a franchise is usually the key to sustained high returns.[13]

Every day, in countless ways, the competitive position of each of our businesses grows either weaker or stronger. If we are delighting customers, eliminating unnecessary costs and improving our products and services, we gain strength. But if we treat customers with indifference or tolerate bloat, our businesses will wither. On a daily basis, the effects of our actions are imperceptible; cumulatively, though, their consequences are enormous.

When our long-term competitive position improves as a result of these almost unnoticeable actions, we describe the phenomenon as "widening the moat." And doing that is essential if we are to have the kind of business we want a decade or two from now. We always, of course, hope to earn more money in the short-term. But when short-term and long-term conflict, widening the moat *must* take precedence. If a management makes bad decisions in order to hit short-term earnings targets, and consequently gets behind the eight-ball in terms of costs, customer satisfaction or brand strength, no amount of subsequent brilliance will overcome the damage that has been inflicted. Take a look at the dilemmas of managers in the auto and airline industries today as they struggle with the huge problems handed them by their predecessors. Charlie is fond of quoting Ben Franklin's "An ounce of prevention is worth a pound of cure." But sometimes no amount of cure will overcome the mistakes of the past.

Our managers focus on moat-widening—and are brilliant at it. Quite simply, they are passionate about their businesses. Usually, they were running those long before we came along; our only function since has been to stay out of the way. If you see these heroes—and our four heroines as well—at the annual meeting, thank them for the job they do for you. [14]

Acquisition Policies

In the past, I've observed that many acquisition-hungry managers were apparently mesmerized by their childhood reading of the story about the frog-kissing princess. Remembering her success, they pay dearly for the right to kiss corporate toads, expecting wondrous transfigurations. Initially, disappointing results only deepen their desire to round up new toads. ("Fanaticism," said Santyana, "consists of redoubling your effort when you've forgotten your aim.") Ultimately, even the most optimistic manager must face reality. Standing knee-deep in unresponsive toads, he then announces an enormous "restructuring" charge. In this corporate equivalent of a Head Start program, the CEO receives the education but the stockholders pay the tuition.

In my early days as a manager I, too, dated a few toads. They were cheap dates—I've never been much of a sport—but my results matched those of acquirers who courted higher-priced toads. I kissed and they croaked.

After several failures of this type, I finally remembered some useful advice I once got from a golf pro (who, like all pros who have had anything to do with my game, wishes to remain anonymous). Said the pro: "Practice doesn't make perfect; practice makes permanent." And thereafter I revised my strategy and tried to buy good businesses at fair prices rather than fair businesses at good prices.[15]

■ ■ ■

On the other hand, we frequently get approached about acquisitions that don't come close to meeting our tests: new ventures, turnarounds, auction-like sales, and the ever-popular (among brokers) "I'm-sure-something-will-work-out-if-you-people-get-to-know-each-other." None of these attracts us in the least.[16]

■ ■ ■

Charlie and I frequently get approached about acquisitions that don't come close to meeting our tests: We've found that if you advertise an interest in buying collies, a lot of people will call hoping to sell you their cocker spaniels. A line from a country song expresses our feeling about new ventures, turnarounds, or auction-like sales: "When the phone don't ring, you'll know it's me."[17]

■ ■ ■

Talking to *Time Magazine* a few years back, Peter Drucker got to the heart of things: "I will tell you a secret: Deal making beats working. Deal making is exciting and fun, and working is grubby. Running anything is primarily an enormous amount of grubby detail work . . . deal making is romantic, sexy. That's why you have deals that make no sense."[18]

■ ■ ■

Furthermore, we completed two significant acquisitions that we negotiated in 1999 and initiated six more. All told, these purchases have cost us about $8 billion, with 97% of that amount paid in cash and 3% in stock. The eight businesses we've acquired have aggregate sales of about $13 billion and employ 58,000 people. Still, we incurred no debt in making these purchases, and our shares outstanding have increased only 1/3 of 1%. Better yet, we remain awash in liquid assets and are both eager and ready for even larger acquisitions.

I will detail our purchases in the next section of the report. But I will tell you now that we have embraced the 21st century by entering such cutting-edge industries as brick, carpet, insulation and paint. Try to control your excitement.[19]

■ ■ ■

My conclusion from my own experiences and from much observation of other businesses is that a good managerial record (measured by economic returns) is far more a function of what business boat you get into than it is of how effectively you row (though intelligence and effort help considerably, of course, in any business, good or bad). Some years ago I wrote: "When a management with a reputation for brilliance tackles a business with a reputation for poor fundamental economics, it is the reputation of the business that remains intact." Nothing has since changed my point of view on that matter. Should you find yourself in a chronically-leaking boat, energy devoted to changing vessels is likely to be more productive than energy devoted to patching leaks.[20]

■ ■ ■

On November 12, 2005, an article ran in the *Wall Street Journal* dealing with Berkshire's unusual acquisition and managerial practices. In it Pete declared, "It was easier to sell my business than to renew my driver's license."

In New York, Cathy Baron Tamraz read the article, and it struck a chord. On November 21, she sent me a letter that began, "As president of Business Wire, I'd like to introduce you to my company, as I believe it fits the profile of Berkshire Hathaway subsidiary companies as detailed in a recent *Wall Street Journal* article."

By the time I finished Cathy's two-page letter, I felt Business Wire and Berkshire were a fit. I particularly liked her penultimate paragraph: "We run a tight ship and keep unnecessary spending under wraps. No secretaries or management layers here. Yet we'll invest big dollars to gain a technological advantage and move the business forward."[21]

■ ■ ■

On that occasion, we had a significant investment in a bank whose management was hell-bent on expansion. (Aren't they all?) When our bank wooed a smaller bank, its owner demanded a stock swap on a basis that valued the acquiree's net worth and earning power at over twice that of the acquirer's. Our management—visibly in heat—quickly capitulated. The owner of the acquiree then insisted on one other condition: "You must promise me," he said in effect, "that once our merger is done and I have become a major shareholder, you'll never again make a deal this dumb."[22]

■ ■ ■

In making acquisitions, we have a further advantage: As payment, we can offer sellers a stock backed by an extraordinary collection of outstanding businesses. An individual or a family wishing to dispose of a single fine business, but also wishing to defer personal taxes indefinitely, is apt to find Berkshire stock a particularly comfortable holding. I believe, in fact, that this calculus played an important part in the two acquisitions for which we paid shares in 1995.

Beyond that, sellers sometimes care about placing their companies in a corporate home that will both endure and provide pleasant, productive working conditions for their managers. Here again, Berkshire offers something special. Our managers operate with extraordinary autonomy. Additionally, our ownership structure enables sellers to know that when I say we are buying to keep, the promise means something. For our part, we like dealing with owners who care what happens to their companies and people. A buyer is likely to find fewer unpleasant surprises dealing with that type of seller than with one simply auctioning off his business.

In addition to the foregoing being an explanation of our acquisition style, it is, of course, a not-so-subtle sales pitch. If you own or represent a business earning $25 million or more before tax, and it fits the criteria listed on page 23, just give me a call. Our discussion will be confidential. And if you aren't interested now, file our proposition in the back of your mind: We are never going to lose our appetite for buying companies with good economics and excellent management.

Concluding this little dissertation on acquisitions, I can't resist repeating a tale told me last year by a corporate executive. The business he grew up in was a fine one, with a long-time record of leadership in its industry. Its main product, however, was distressingly glamorless. So several decades ago, the company hired a management consultant who—naturally—advised diversification, the then-current fad. ("Focus" was not yet in style.) Before long, the company acquired a number of businesses, each after the consulting firm had gone through a long—and expensive—acquisition study. And the outcome? Said the executive sadly, "When we started, we were getting 100% of our earnings from the original business. After ten years, we were getting 150%."[23]

■ ■ ■

Our acquisitions usually develop in the same way. At other companies, executives may devote themselves to pursuing acquisition possibilities with investment bankers, utilizing an auction process that has become standardized. In this exercise the bankers prepare a "book" that makes me think of the Superman comics of my youth. In the Wall Street version, a formerly mild-mannered company emerges from the investment banker's phone booth able to leap over competitors in a single bound and with earnings moving faster than a speeding bullet. Titillated by the book's description of the acquiree's powers, acquisition-hungry CEOs—Lois Lanes all, beneath their cool exteriors—promptly swoon.

What's particularly entertaining in these books is the precision with which earnings are projected for many years ahead. If you ask the author-banker, however, what his own firm will earn *next month*, he will go into a protective crouch and tell you that business and markets are far too uncertain for him to venture a forecast.

Here's one story I can't resist relating: In 1985, a major investment banking house undertook to sell Scott Fetzer, offering it widely—but with no success. Upon reading of this strikeout, I wrote Ralph Schey, then and now Scott Fetzer's CEO, expressing an interest in buying the business. I had never met Ralph, but within a week we had a deal. Unfortunately, Scott Fetzer's letter of engagement with the banking firm provided it a $2.5 million fee upon sale, even if it had nothing to do with finding the buyer. I guess the lead banker felt he should do something for his payment, so he graciously offered us a copy of the book on Scott Fetzer that his firm had prepared. With his customary tact, Charlie responded: "I'll pay $2.5 million *not* to read it."

At Berkshire, our carefully-crafted acquisition strategy is simply to wait for the phone to ring. Happily, it sometimes does so, usually because a manager who sold to us earlier has recommended to a friend that he think about following suit.[24]

■ ■ ■

It may seem strange that we exult over a year in which we made three acquisitions, given that we have regularly used these pages to question the acquisition activities of most managers. Rest assured, Charlie and I haven't lost our skepticism: We believe most deals do damage to the shareholders of the acquiring company. Too often, the words from *HMS Pinafore* apply: "Things are seldom what they seem, skim milk masquerades as cream." Specifically, sellers and their representatives invariably present financial projections having more entertainment value than educational value. In the production of rosy scenarios, Wall Street can hold its own against Washington.

In any case, why potential buyers even look at projections prepared by sellers baffles me. Charlie and I never give them a glance, but instead keep in mind the story of the man with an ailing horse. Visiting the vet, he said: "Can you help me? Sometimes my horse walks just fine and sometimes he limps." The vet's reply was pointed: "No problem—when he's walking fine, sell him." In the world of mergers and acquisitions, that horse would be peddled as Secretariat.

At Berkshire, we have all the difficulties in perceiving the future that other acquisition-minded companies do. Like they also, we face the inherent problem that the seller of a business practically always knows far more about it than the buyer and also picks the time of sale—a time when the business is likely to be walking "just fine."

Even so, we do have a few advantages, perhaps the greatest being that we *don't* have a strategic plan. Thus we feel no need to proceed in an ordained direction (a course leading almost invariably to silly purchase prices) but can instead simply decide what makes sense for our owners. In doing that, we always mentally compare any move we are contemplating with dozens of other opportunities open to us, including the purchase of small pieces of the best businesses in the world via the stock market. Our practice of making this comparison—acquisitions against passive investments—is a discipline that managers focused simply on expansion seldom use.[25]

■ ■ ■

From the economic standpoint of the acquiring company, the worst deal of all is a stock-for-stock acquisition. Here, a huge price is often paid without there being any step-up in the tax basis of either the stock of the acquiree or its assets. If the acquired entity is subsequently sold, its owner may owe a large capital gains tax (at a 35% or greater rate), even though the sale may truly be producing a major economic loss.[26]

■ ■ ■

For example, in contemplating business mergers and acquisitions, many managers tend to focus on whether the transaction is immediately dilutive or anti-dilutive to earnings per share (or, at financial institutions, to per-share book value). An emphasis of this sort carries great dangers. Going back to our college-education example, imagine that a 25-year-old first-year MBA student is considering merging his future economic interests with those of a 25-year-old day laborer. The MBA student, a non-earner, would find that a "share-for-share" merger of his equity interest in himself with that of the day laborer would enhance his near-term earnings (in a big way!). But what could be sillier for the student than a deal of this kind?

In corporate transactions, it's equally silly for the would-be purchaser to focus on current earnings when the prospective acquiree has either different prospects, different amounts of non-operating assets, or a different capital structure. At Berkshire, we have rejected many merger and purchase opportunities that would have boosted current and near-term earnings but that would have reduced per-share intrinsic value. Our approach, rather, has been to follow Wayne Gretzky's advice: "Go to where the puck is going to be, not to where it is." As a result, our shareholders are now many billions of dollars richer than they would have been if we had used the standard catechism.

The sad fact is that most major acquisitions display an egregious imbalance: They are a bonanza for the shareholders of the acquiree; they increase the income and status of the acquirer's management; and they are a honey pot for the investment bankers and other professionals on both sides. But, alas, they usually reduce the wealth of the acquirer's shareholders, often to a substantial extent. That happens because the acquirer typically gives up more intrinsic value than it receives. Do that enough, says John Medlin, the retired head of Wachovia Corp., and "you are running a chain letter in reverse."[27]

■■■

Over the years, our current businesses, in aggregate, should deliver modest growth in operating earnings. But they will not in themselves produce truly satisfactory gains. We will need major acquisitions to get that job done.

In this quest, 2005 was encouraging. We agreed to five purchases: two that were completed last year, one that closed after yearend and two others that we expect to close soon. None of the deals involve the issuance of Berkshire shares. That's a crucial, but often ignored, point: When a management proudly acquires another company for stock, the shareholders of the acquirer are concurrently selling part of their interest in everything they own. I've made this kind of deal a few times myself—and, on balance, my actions have cost you money.[28]

■ ■ ■

Unlike many business buyers, Berkshire has no "exit strategy." We buy to keep. We do, though, have an entrance strategy, looking for businesses in this country or abroad that meet our six criteria and are available at a price that will produce a reasonable return. If you have a business that fits, give me a call. Like a hopeful teenage girl, I'll be waiting by the phone.[29]

Planning and Administrative Practices

Your company is run on the principle of centralization of financial decisions at the top (the very top, it might be added), and rather extreme delegation of operating authority to a number of key managers at the individual company or business unit level. We could just field a basketball team with our corporate headquarters group (which utilizes only about 1500 square feet of space).

This approach produces an occasional major mistake that might have been eliminated or minimized through closer operating controls. But it also eliminates large layers of costs and dramatically speeds decision-making. Because everyone has a great deal to do, a very great deal gets done. Most important of all, it enables us to attract and retain some extraordinarily talented individuals—people who simply can't be hired in the normal course of events—who find working for Berkshire to be almost identical to running their own show.[30]

■ ■ ■

Berkshire's collection of managers is unusual in several important ways. As one example, a very high percentage of these men and women are independently wealthy, having made fortunes in the businesses that they run. They work neither because they need the money nor because they are contractually obligated to—we have no contracts at Berkshire. Rather, they work long and hard because they love their businesses. And I use the word "their" advisedly, since these managers are truly in charge—there are no show-and-tell presentations in Omaha, no budgets to be approved by headquarters, no dictums issued about capital expenditures. We simply ask our managers to run their companies as if these are the sole asset of their families and will remain so for the next century.

With managers like ours, my partner, Charlie Munger, and I have little to do with operations. In fact, it is probably fair to say that if we did more, less would be accomplished. We have no corporate meetings, no corporate budgets, and no performance reviews (though our managers, of course, oftentimes find such procedures useful at their operating units).[31]

■ ■ ■

Fault me for dithering. (Charlie calls it thumb-sucking.) When a problem exists, whether in personnel or in business operations, the time to act is *now*.[32]

■ ■ ■

Charlie and I do not believe in flexible operating budgets, as in "Nondirect expenses can be X if revenues are Y, but must be reduced if revenues are Y—5%." Should we really cut our news hole at the Buffalo

News, or the quality of product and service at See's, simply because profits are down during a given year or quarter? Or, conversely, should we add a staff economist, a corporate strategist, an institutional advertising campaign or something else that does Berkshire no good simply because the money currently is rolling in?

That makes no sense to us. We neither understand the adding of unneeded people or activities because profits are booming, nor the cutting of essential people or activities because profitability is shrinking. That kind of yo-yo approach is neither business-like nor humane. Our goal is to do what makes sense for Berkshire's customers and employees at all times, and never to add the unneeded. ("But what about the corporate jet?" you rudely ask. Well, occasionally a man must rise above principle.)[33]

■ ■ ■

At Berkshire, we believe in Charlie's dictum—"Just tell me the bad news; the good news will take care of itself"—and that is the behavior we expect of our managers when they are reporting to us. Consequently, I also owe you—Berkshire's owners—a report on three operations that, though they continued to earn decent (or better) returns on invested capital, experienced a decline in earnings last year. Each encountered a different type of problem.[34]

■ ■ ■

The most important thing to do when you find yourself in a hole is to stop digging.[35]

Hiring Policies

An observer might conclude from our hiring practices that Charlie and I were traumatized early in life by an EEOC bulletin on age discrimination. The real explanation, however, is self-interest: It's difficult to teach a new dog old tricks. The many Berkshire managers who are past

70 hit home runs today at the same pace that long ago gave them reputations as young slugging sensations. Therefore, to get a job with us, just employ the tactic of the 76-year-old who persuaded a dazzling beauty of 25 to marry him. "How did you ever get her to accept?" asked his envious contemporaries. The comeback: "I told her I was 86."[36]

■ ■ ■

I recall that one woman, upon being asked to describe the perfect spouse, specified an archeologist: "The older I get," she said, "the more he'll be interested in me." She would have liked my tastes: I treasure those extraordinary Berkshire managers who are working well past normal retirement age and who concomitantly are achieving results much superior to those of their younger competitors. While I understand and empathize with the decision of Verne and Gladys to retire when the calendar says it's time, theirs is not a step I wish to encourage. It's hard to teach a new dog old tricks.[37]

■ ■ ■

Naturally, a business that follows a no-layoff policy must be especially careful to avoid overstaffing when times are good. Thirty years ago Tom Murphy, then CEO of Cap Cities, drove this point home to me with a hypothetical tale about an employee who asked his boss for permission to hire an assistant. The employee assumed that adding $20,000 to the annual payroll would be inconsequential. But his boss told him the proposal should be evaluated as a $3 million decision, given that an additional person would probably cost at least that amount over his lifetime, factoring in raises, benefits and other expenses (more people, more toilet paper). And unless the company fell on very hard times, the employee added would be unlikely to be dismissed, however marginal his contribution to the business.[38]

He is also experienced. Though I don't know Ralph's age, I do know that, like many of our managers, he is over 65. At Berkshire, we look to performance, not to the calendar. Charlie and I, at 71 and 64 respectively, now keep George Foreman's picture on our desks. You can make book that our scorn for a mandatory retirement age will grow stronger every year.[39]

■ ■ ■

Susan came to Borsheims 25 years ago as a $4-an-hour saleswoman. Though she lacked a managerial background, I did not hesitate to make her CEO in 1994. She's smart, she loves the business, and she loves her associates. That beats having an MBA degree any time.

(An aside: Charlie and I are not big fans of resumes. Instead, we focus on brains, passion and integrity. Another of our great managers is Cathy Baron Tamraz, who has significantly increased Business Wire's earnings since we purchased it early in 2006. She is an owner's dream. It is positively *dangerous* to stand between Cathy and a business prospect. Cathy, it should be noted, began her career as a cab driver.)[40]

■ ■ ■

At Berkshire, associations like these last a long time. We do not remove superstars from our lineup merely because they have attained a specified age—whether the traditional 65, or the 95 reached by Mrs. B on the eve of Hanukkah in 1988. Superb managers are too scarce a resource to be discarded simply because a cake gets crowded with candles. Moreover, our experience with newly-minted MBAs has not been that great. Their academic records always look terrific and the candidates always know just what to say; but too often they are short on personal commitment to the company and general business savvy. It's difficult to teach a new dog old tricks.[41]

■ ■ ■

Under this plan, I intend to hire a younger man or woman with the potential to manage a very large portfolio, who we hope will succeed me as Berkshire's chief investment officer when the need for someone to do that arises. As part of the selection process, we may in fact take on several candidates.

Picking the right person(s) will not be an easy task. It's not hard, of course, to find smart people, among them individuals who have impressive investment records. But there is far more to successful long-term investing than brains and performance that has recently been good.

Over time, markets will do extraordinary, even bizarre, things. A single, big mistake could wipe out a long string of successes. We therefore need someone genetically programmed to recognize and avoid serious risks, *including those never before encountered*. Certain perils that lurk in investment strategies cannot be spotted by use of the models commonly employed today by financial institutions.

Temperament is also important. Independent thinking, emotional stability, and a keen understanding of both human and institutional behavior is vital to long-term investment success. I've seen a lot of very smart people who have lacked these virtues.

Finally, we have a special problem to consider: our ability to keep the person we hire. Being able to list Berkshire on a resume would materially enhance the marketability of an investment manager. We will need, therefore, to be sure we can retain our choice, even though he or she could leave and make much more money elsewhere.[42]

Debt and Costs

Except for token amounts. . . . We are not interested in incurring any significant debt at Berkshire for acquisitions or operating purposes. Conventional business wisdom, of course, would argue that we are being too conservative and that there are added profits that could be safely earned if we injected moderate leverage into our balance sheet.[43]

■ ■ ■

We use debt sparingly and, when we do borrow, we attempt to structure our loans on a long-term fixed-rate basis. We will reject interesting opportunities rather than over-leverage our balance sheet. This conservatism has penalized our results but it is the only behavior that leaves us comfortable, considering our fiduciary obligations to policyholders, lenders and the many equity holders who have committed unusually large portions of their net worth to our care. As one of the Indianapolis "500" winners said: "To finish first, you must first finish."[44]

■ ■ ■

You may wonder why we borrow money while sitting on a mountain of cash. It's because of our "every tub on its own bottom" philosophy. We believe that any subsidiary lending money should pay an appropriate rate for the funds needed to carry its receivables and should not be subsidized by its parent. Otherwise, having a rich daddy can lead to sloppy decisions. Meanwhile, the cash we accumulate at Berkshire is destined for business acquisitions or for the purchase of securities that offer opportunities for significant profit.[45]

■ ■ ■

In general, we continue to have an aversion to debt, particularly the short-term kind. But we are willing to incur modest amounts of debt when it is both properly structured and of significant benefit to shareholders.[46]

■ ■ ■

Unlike many in the business world, we prefer to finance in anticipation of need rather than in reaction to it. A business obtains the best financial results possible by managing both sides of its balance sheet well. This means obtaining the highest-possible return on assets and the lowest-possible cost on liabilities. It would be convenient if opportunities for intelligent action on both fronts coincided. However, reason tells us that just the opposite is likely to be the case: Tight money conditions, which translate into high costs for liabilities, will create the best opportunities for acquisitions, and cheap money will cause assets to be bid to the sky. Our conclusion: Action on the liability side should sometimes be taken independent of any action on the asset side.[47]

■ ■ ■

Unlike most businesses, Berkshire did not finance because of any specific immediate needs. Rather, we borrowed because we think that, over a period far shorter than the life of the loan, we will have many opportunities to put the money to good use. The most attractive opportunities may present themselves at a time when credit is extremely expensive—or even unavailable. At such a time we want to have plenty of financial firepower.[48]

■ ■ ■

We cherish cost-consciousness at Berkshire. Our model is the widow who went to the local newspaper to place an obituary notice. Told there was a 25-cents-a-word charge, she requested "Fred Brown died." She was then informed there was a seven-word minimum. "Okay" the bereaved woman replied, "make it 'Fred Brown died, golf clubs for sale.'"[49]

■ ■ ■

I can't resist one more Candler quote: "Beginning this year about March 1st . . . we employed ten traveling salesmen by means of which, with systematic correspondence from the office, we covered almost the territory of the Union." That's my kind of sales force.[50]

■ ■ ■

Our experience has been that the manager of an already high-cost operation frequently is uncommonly resourceful in finding new ways to add to overhead, while the manager of a tightly-run operation usually continues to find additional methods to curtail costs, even when his costs are already well below those of his competitors. No one has demonstrated this latter ability better than Gene Abegg.[51]

■ ■ ■

Our failure here illustrates the importance of a guideline—*stay with simple propositions*—that we usually apply in investments as well as operations. If only one variable is key to a decision, and the variable has a 90% chance of going your way, the chance for a successful outcome is obviously 90%. But if ten independent variables need to break favorably for a successful result, and each has a 90% probability of success, the likelihood of having a winner is only 35%. In our zinc venture, we solved most of the problems. But one proved intractable, and that was one too many. Since a chain is no stronger than its weakest link, it makes sense to look for—if you'll excuse an oxymoron—mono-linked chains.[52]

■ ■ ■

Our after-tax overhead costs are under 1% of our reported operating earnings and less than 1/2 of 1% of our look-through earnings. We have no legal, personnel, public relations, investor relations, or strategic planning departments. In turn this means we don't need support personnel such as guards, drivers, messengers, etc. Finally, except for Verne, we employ no consultants. Professor Parkinson would like our operation—though Charlie, I must say, still finds it outrageously fat.

At some companies, corporate expense runs 10% or more of operating earnings. The tithing that operations thus makes to headquarters not only hurts earnings, but more importantly slashes capital values. If the business that spends 10% on headquarters' costs achieves earnings at its operating levels identical to those achieved by the business that incurs costs of only 1%, shareholders of the first enterprise suffer a 9% loss in the value of their holdings simply because of corporate overhead. Charlie and I have observed no correlation between high corporate costs and good corporate performance. In fact, we see the simpler, low-cost operation as more likely to operate effectively than its bureaucratic brethren. We're admirers of the Wal-Mart, Nucor, Dover, GEICO, Golden West Financial and Price Co. models.[53]

■ ■ ■

This crew occupies 9,708 square feet of space, and Charlie—at World Headquarters West in Los Angeles—uses another 655 square feet. Our home-office payroll, including benefits and counting both locations, totaled $3,531,978 last year. We're careful when spending your money.

Corporate bigwigs often complain about government spending, criticizing bureaucrats who they say spend taxpayers' money differently from how they would if it were their own. But sometimes the financial behavior of executives will also vary based on whose wallet is getting depleted. Here's an illustrative tale from my days at Salomon. In the 1980s the company had a barber, Jimmy by name, who came in weekly to give free haircuts to the top brass. A manicurist was also on tap. Then, because of a cost-cutting drive, patrons were told to pay their own way. One top executive (not the CEO) who had previously visited Jimmy weekly went immediately to a once-every-three-weeks schedule.[54]

■ ■ ■

The other group to which I owe enormous thanks is the home-office staff. After the eight acquisitions more than doubled our worldwide workforce to about 112,000, Charlie and I went soft last year and added one more person at headquarters. (Charlie, bless him, never lets me forget Ben Franklin's advice: "A small leak can sink a great ship.") Now we have 13.8 people.

This tiny band works miracles. In 2000 it handled all of the details connected with our eight acquisitions, processed extensive regulatory and tax filings (our tax return covers 4,896 pages), smoothly produced an annual meeting to which 25,000 tickets were issued, and accurately dispensed checks to 3,660 charities designated by our shareholders. In addition, the group dealt with all the routine tasks served up by a company with a revenue runrate of $40 billion and more than 300,000 owners. And, to add to all of this, the other 12.8 are a delight to be around.[55]

Stock Ownership and Stock Activity

We often are asked why Berkshire does not split its stock. The assumption behind this question usually appears to be that a split would be a pro-shareholder action. We disagree. Let me tell you why.

One of our goals is to have Berkshire Hathaway stock sell at a price rationally related to its intrinsic business value. (But note "rationally related," not "identical": if well-regarded companies are generally selling in the market at large discounts from value, Berkshire might well be priced similarly.) The key to a rational stock price is rational shareholders, both current and prospective.

If the holders of a company's stock and/or the prospective buyers attracted to it are prone to make irrational or emotion-based decisions, some pretty silly stock prices are going to appear periodically. Manic-depressive personalities produce manic-depressive valuations. Such aberrations may help us in buying and selling the stocks of other companies. But we think it is in both your interest and ours to minimize their occurrence in the market for Berkshire.

To obtain only high quality shareholders is no cinch. Mrs. Astor could select her 400, but anyone can buy any stock. Entering members of a shareholder "club" cannot be screened for intellectual capacity, emotional stability, moral sensitivity or acceptable dress. Shareholder eugenics, therefore, might appear to be a hopeless undertaking.

In large part, however, we feel that high quality ownership can be attracted and maintained if we consistently communicate our business and ownership philosophy—*along with no other conflicting messages*—and then let self selection follow its course. For example, self selection will draw a far different crowd to a musical event advertised as an opera than one advertised as a rock concert even though anyone can buy a ticket to either.

Through our policies and communications—our "advertisements"—we try to attract investors who will understand our operations, attitudes and expectations. (And, fully as important, we try to dissuade those who won't.) We want those who think of themselves as business owners and invest in companies with the intention of staying a long time. And, we want those who keep their eyes focused on business results, not market prices.[56]

■ ■ ■

Additionally, we enjoy a rare sort of managerial freedom. Most companies are saddled with institutional constraints. A company's history, for example, may commit it to an industry that now offers limited opportunity. A more common problem is a shareholder constituency that pressures its manager to dance to Wall Street's tune. Many CEOs resist, but others give in and adopt operating and capital allocation policies far different from those they would choose if left to themselves.

At Berkshire, neither history nor the demands of owners impede intelligent decision-making. When Charlie and I make mistakes, they are—in tennis parlance—unforced errors.[57]

■ ■ ■

Investors possessing those characteristics are in a small minority, but we have an exceptional collection of them. I believe well over 90%—probably over 95%—of our shares are held by those who were shareholders of Berkshire or Blue Chip five years ago. And I would guess that over 95% of our shares are held by investors for whom the holding is at least double the size of their next largest. Among companies with at least several thousand public shareholders and more than $1 billion of market value, we are almost certainly the leader in the degree to which our shareholders think and act like owners. Upgrading a shareholder group that possesses these characteristics is not easy.

Were we to split the stock or take other actions focusing on stock price rather than business value, we would attract an entering class of buyers inferior to the exiting class of sellers. At $1300, there are very few investors who can't afford a Berkshire share. Would a potential one-share purchaser be better off if we split 100 for 1 so he could buy 100 shares? Those who think so and who would buy the stock because of the split or in anticipation of one would definitely downgrade the quality of our present shareholder group. (Could we really improve our shareholder group by trading some of our present clear-thinking members for impressionable new ones who, preferring paper to value, feel wealthier with nine $10 bills than with one $100 bill?) People who buy for non-value reasons are likely to sell for non-value reasons. Their presence in the picture will accentuate erratic price swings unrelated to underlying business developments.

We will try to avoid policies that attract buyers with a short-term focus on our stock price and try to follow policies that attract informed long-term investors focusing on business values. Just as you purchased your Berkshire shares in a market populated by rational informed investors, you deserve a chance to sell—should you ever want to—in the same kind of market. We will work to keep it in existence.[58]

■ ■ ■

We much prefer owners who like our service and menu and who return year after year. It would be hard to find a better group to sit in the Berkshire Hathaway shareholder "seats" than those already occupying them. So we hope to continue to have a very low turnover among our owners, reflecting a constituency that understands our operation, approves of our policies, and shares our expectations. And we hope to deliver on those expectations.[59]

■ ■ ■

There is only one combination of facts that makes it advisable for a company to repurchase its shares: First, the company has available funds—cash plus sensible borrowing capacity—beyond the near-term needs of the business and, second, finds its stock selling in the market below its intrinsic value, conservatively-calculated. To this we add a caveat: Shareholders should have been supplied all the information they need for estimating that value. Otherwise, insiders could take advantage of their uninformed partners and buy out their interests at a function of true worth. We have, on rare occasions, seen that happen. Usually, of course, chicanery is employed to drive stock prices up, not down.[60]

■ ■ ■

In two respects our goals probably differ somewhat from those of most listed companies. First, we do not want to maximize the price at which Berkshire shares trade. We wish instead for them to trade in a narrow range centered at intrinsic business value (which we hope increases at a reasonable—or, better yet, unreasonable—rate). Charlie and I are bothered as much by significant overvaluation as significant undervaluation. Both extremes will inevitably produce results for many shareholders that will differ sharply from Berkshire's business results. If our stock price instead consistently mirrors business value, each of our shareholders will receive an investment result that roughly parallels the business results of Berkshire during his holding period.

Second, we wish for very little trading activity. If we ran a private business with a few passive partners, we would be disappointed if those partners, and their replacements, frequently wanted to leave the partnership. Running a public company, we feel the same way.

Our goal is to attract long-term owners who, at the time of purchase, have no timetable or price target for sale but plan instead to stay with us indefinitely. We don't understand the CEO who wants lots of stock activity, for that can be achieved only if many of his owners are constantly exiting. At what other organization—school, club, church, etc.—do leaders cheer when members leave? (However, if there were a broker whose livelihood depended upon the membership turnover in such organizations, you could be sure that there would be at least one proponent of activity, as in: "There hasn't been much going on in Christianity for a while; maybe we should switch to Buddhism next week.")[61]

■■■

We will not repurchase shares unless we believe Berkshire stock is selling well below intrinsic value, conservatively calculated. Nor will we attempt to talk the stock up or down. (Neither publicly or privately have I ever told anyone to buy or sell Berkshire shares.) Instead we will give all shareholders—and potential shareholders—the same value-related information we would wish to have if our positions were reversed.

Please be clear about one point: We will *never* make purchases with the intention of stemming a decline in Berkshire's price. Rather we will make them if and when we believe that they represent an attractive use of the Company's money. At best, repurchases are likely to have only a very minor effect on the future rate of gain in our stock's intrinsic value.[62]

Chapter 14

Executive Behavior

The job of CEO's is now to regain America's trust—and for the country's sake it's important that they do so. They will not succeed in this endeavor, however, by way of fatuous ads, meaningless policy statements, structural changes of boards and committees. Instead, CEO's must embrace stewardship as a way of life and treat owners as partners, not patsies. It's time for CEO's to walk the walk.[1]

—WARREN BUFFETT

I will keep well over 99% of my net worth in Berkshire. My wife and I have never sold a share nor do we intend to. Charlie and I are disgusted by the situation, so common in the last few years, in which disasters have walked with extraordinary wealth. Indeed, many of these people were urging investors to buy shares while concurrently dumping their own, sometimes using methods that hid their actions. To their shame, these business leaders view shareholders as patsies not partners.

Though Enron has been the symbol for shareholder abuse, there is no shortage of egregious conduct elsewhere in corporate America.[2]

■■■

Our equation is different. With 47% of Berkshire's stock, Charlie and I don't worry about being fired, and we receive our rewards as owners, not managers. Thus we behave with Berkshire's money as we would with our own. That frequently leads us to unconventional behavior both in investments and general business management.[3]

■ ■ ■

Our acquisitions usually develop in the same way. At other companies, executives may devote themselves to pursuing acquisition possibilities with investment bankers, utilizing an auction process that has become standardized. In this exercise the bankers prepare a "book" that makes me think of the Superman comics of my youth. In the Wall Street version, a formerly mild-mannered company emerges from the investment banker's phone booth able to leap over competitors in a single bound and with earnings moving faster than a speeding bullet. Titillated by the book's description of the acquiree's powers, acquisition-hungry CEOs—Lois Lanes all, beneath their cool exteriors—promptly swoon.[4]

■ ■ ■

Corporate bigwigs often complain about government spending, criticizing bureaucrats who they say spend taxpayers' money differently from how they would if it were their own. But sometimes the financial behavior of executives will also vary based on whose wallet is getting depleted. Here's an illustrative tale from my days at Salomon. In the 1980s the company had a barber, Jimmy by name, who came in weekly to give free haircuts to the top brass. A manicurist was also on tap. Then, because of a cost-cutting drive, patrons were told to pay their own way. One top executive (not the CEO) who had previously visited Jimmy weekly went immediately to a once-every-three-weeks schedule.[5]

■ ■ ■

The supreme irony of business management is that it is far easier for an inadequate CEO to keep his job than it is for an inadequate subordinate.

If a secretary, say, is hired for a job that requires typing ability of at least 80 words a minute and turns out to be capable of only 50 words a minute, she will lose her job in no time. There is a logical standard for this job; performance is easily measured; and if you can't make the grade, you're out. Similarly, if new salespeople fail to generate sufficient business quickly enough, they will be let go. Excuses will not be accepted as a substitute for orders.

However, a CEO who doesn't perform is frequently carried indefinitely. One reason is that performance standards for his job seldom exist. When they do, they are often fuzzy or they may be waived or explained away, even when the performance shortfalls are major and repeated. At too many companies, the boss shoots the arrow of managerial performance and then hastily paints the bullseye around the spot where it lands.

Another important, but seldom recognized, distinction between the boss and the foot soldier is that the CEO has no immediate superior whose performance is itself getting measured. The sales manager who retains a bunch of lemons in his sales force will soon be in hot water himself. It is in his immediate self-interest to promptly weed out his hiring mistakes. Otherwise, he himself may be weeded out. An office manager who has hired inept secretaries faces the same imperative.

But the CEO's boss is a Board of Directors that seldom measures itself and is infrequently held to account for substandard corporate performance. If the Board makes a mistake in hiring, and perpetuates that mistake, so what? Even if the company is taken over because of the mistake, the deal will probably bestow substantial benefits on the outgoing Board members. (The bigger they are, the softer they fall.)

Finally, relations between the Board and the CEO are expected to be congenial. At board meetings, criticism of the CEO's performance is often viewed as the social equivalent of belching. No such inhibitions restrain the office manager from critically evaluating the substandard typist.

These points should not be interpreted as a blanket condemnation of CEOs or Boards of Directors: Most are able and hard-working, and a number are truly outstanding. But the management failings that Charlie and I have seen make us thankful that we are linked with the managers of our three permanent holdings. They love their businesses, they think like owners, and they exude integrity and ability.[6]

■■■

Still, I believe that the behavior of managements has been even worse when it comes to restructurings and merger accounting. Here, many managements purposefully work at manipulating numbers and deceiving investors. And, as Michael Kinsley has said about Washington: "The scandal isn't in what's done that's *illegal* but rather in what's *legal*."

It was once relatively easy to tell the good guys in accounting from the bad: The late 1960's, for example, brought on an orgy of what one charlatan dubbed "bold, imaginative accounting" (the practice of which, incidentally, made him loved for a time by Wall Street because he never missed expectations). But most investors of that period knew who was playing games. And, to their credit, virtually all of America's most-admired companies then shunned deception.

In recent years, probity has eroded. Many major corporations still play things straight, but a significant and growing number of otherwise high-grade managers—CEOs you would be happy to have as spouses for your children or as trustees under your will—have come to the view that it's okay to manipulate earnings to satisfy what they believe are Wall Street's desires. Indeed, many CEOs think this kind of manipulation is not only okay, but actually their *duty*.

These managers start with the assumption, all too common, that their job at all times is to encourage the highest stock price possible (a premise with which we adamantly disagree). To pump the price, they strive, admirably, for operational excellence. But when operations don't produce the result hoped for, these CEOs resort to unadmirable accounting stratagems. These either manufacture the desired "earnings" or set the stage for them in the future.

Rationalizing this behavior, these managers often say that their shareholders will be hurt if their currency for doing deals—that is, their stock—is not fully-priced, and they also argue that in using accounting shenanigans to get the figures they want, they are only doing what everybody else does. Once such an everybody's-doing-it attitude takes hold, ethical misgivings vanish. Call this behavior Son of Gresham: Bad accounting drives out good.

The distortion *du jour* is the "restructuring charge," an accounting entry that can, of course, be legitimate but that too often is a device for manipulating earnings. In this bit of legerdemain, a large chunk of costs that should properly be attributed to a number of years is dumped into a single quarter, typically one already fated to disappoint investors. In some cases, the purpose of the charge is to clean up earnings misrepresentations of the past, and in others it is to prepare the ground for future misrepresentations. In either case, the size and timing of these charges is dictated by the cynical proposition that Wall Street will not mind if earnings fall short by $5 per share in a given quarter, just as long as this deficiency ensures that quarterly earnings in the future will consistently exceed expectations by five cents per share.

This dump-everything-into-one-quarter behavior suggests a corresponding "bold, imaginative" approach to—golf scores. In his first round of the season, a golfer should ignore his actual performance and simply fill his card with atrocious numbers—double, triple, quadruple bogeys—and then turn in a score of, say, 140. Having established this "reserve," he should go to the golf shop and tell his pro that he wishes to "restructure" his imperfect swing. Next, as he takes his new swing onto the course, he should count his good holes, but not the bad ones. These remnants from his old swing should be charged instead to the reserve established earlier. At the end of five rounds, then, his record will be 140, 80, 80, 80, 80 rather than 91, 94, 89, 94, 92. On Wall Street, they will ignore the 140—which, after all, came from a "discontinued" swing—and will classify our hero as an 80 shooter (and one who *never* disappoints).

For those who prefer to cheat up front, there would be a variant of this strategy. The golfer, playing alone with a cooperative caddy-auditor, should defer the recording of bad holes, take four 80s, accept the plaudits he gets for such athleticism and consistency, and then turn in a fifth card carrying a 140 score. After rectifying his earlier score-keeping sins with this "big bath," he may mumble a few apologies but will refrain from returning the sums he has previously collected from comparing scorecards in the clubhouse. (The caddy, need we add, will have acquired a loyal patron.)

Berkshire has kept entirely clear of these practices: If we are to disappoint you, we would rather it be with our earnings than with our accounting. In all of our acquisitions, we have left the loss reserve figures exactly as we found them. After all, we have consistently joined with insurance managers knowledgeable about their business and honest in their financial reporting. When deals occur in which liabilities are increased immediately and substantially, simple logic says that at least one of those virtues must have been lacking—or, alternatively, that the acquirer is laying the groundwork for future infusions of "earnings."

Here's a true story that illustrates an all-too-common view in corporate America. The CEOs of two large banks, one of them a man who'd made many acquisitions, were involved not long ago in a friendly merger discussion (which in the end didn't produce a deal). The veteran acquirer was expounding on the merits of the possible combination, only to be skeptically interrupted by the other CEO: "But won't that mean a huge charge," he asked, "perhaps as much as $1 billion?" The "sophisticate" wasted no words: "We'll make it bigger than that—that's why we're doing the deal."

A preliminary tally by R. G. Associates, of Baltimore, of special charges taken or announced during 1998—that is, charges for restructuring, in-process R&D, merger-related items, and write-downs—identified no less than 1,369 of these, totaling $72.1 billion. That is a staggering amount as evidenced by this bit of perspective: The 1997 earnings of the 500 companies in Fortune's famous list totaled $324 billion.

Clearly the attitude of disrespect that many executives have today for accurate reporting is a business disgrace. And auditors, as we have already suggested, have done little on the positive side. Though auditors *should* regard the investing public as their client, they tend to kowtow instead to the managers who choose them and dole out their pay. ("Whose bread I eat, his song I sing.")[7]

■ ■ ■

A far more serious problem occurs when the management of a great company gets sidetracked and neglects its wonderful base business while purchasing other businesses that are so-so or worse. When that happens, the suffering of investors is often prolonged. Unfortunately, that is precisely what transpired years ago at both Coke and Gillette. (Would you believe that a few decades back they were growing shrimp at Coke and exploring for oil at Gillette?) Loss of focus is what most worries Charlie and me when we contemplate investing in businesses that in general look outstanding. All too often, we've seen value stagnate in the presence of hubris or of boredom that caused the attention of managers to wander. That's not going to happen again at Coke and Gillette, however—not given their current and prospective managements.[8]

■ ■ ■

I mean it's just the scope of human beings to do crazy things, self-destructive things, things as a mob they do. You saw it on October 19, 1987. . . . You saw Long-Term Capital Management. You've seen all kinds of things. There will be other things in the future. They will have similar factors. The human factor will be at the bottom of them. They won't be exactly the same. But it's like Mark Twain said, "You know history doesn't repeat itself, but it rhymes." We will see some things that rhyme with 1929 or whatever it may be.

Well I've seen all kinds of people with 160 IQ's with intense interest in the subject, lots of experience in the investment world. I've seen them self destruct. And you have to have a certain amount of natural flow of juices just to be excited about the game and down there participating. And the trick of course is to keep control of those juices. And most people, even smart people, have trouble not getting caught up in the game and thinking I'll just dance one more dance like Cinderella at five minutes till twelve or something like that because they think they are smarter than the rest of the public. . . . Or they don't protect themselves against something that will come totally from right field. Long-Term Capital Management is a good example of that.[9]

■ ■ ■

Some years back, a CEO friend of mine—in jest, it must be said—unintentionally described the pathology of many big deals. This friend, who ran a property-casualty insurer, was explaining to his directors why he wanted to acquire a certain life insurance company. After droning rather unpersuasively through the economics and strategic rationale for the acquisition, he abruptly abandoned the script. With an impish look, he simply said: "Aw, fellas, all the other kids have one."[10]

■ ■ ■

Most managers have very little incentive to make the intelligent-but-with-some-chance-of-looking-like-an-idiot decision. Their personal gain/loss ratio is all too obvious: if an unconventional decision works out well, they get a pat on the back and, if it works out poorly, they get a pink slip. (Failing conventionally is the route to go; as a group, lemmings may have a rotten image, but no individual lemming has ever received bad press.)[11]

■ ■ ■

One further thought while I'm on my soapbox: Charlie and I think it is both deceptive and dangerous for CEOs to predict growth rates for their companies. They are, of course, frequently egged on to do so by both analysts and their own investor relations departments. They should resist, however, because too often these predictions lead to trouble.

It's fine for a CEO to have his own internal goals and, in our view, it's even appropriate for the CEO to publicly express some hopes about the future, if these expectations are accompanied by sensible caveats. But for a major corporation to predict that its per-share earnings will grow over the long term at, say, 15% annually is to court trouble.

That's true because a growth rate of that magnitude can only be maintained by a very small percentage of large businesses. Here's a test: Examine the record of, say, the 200 highest earning companies from 1970 or 1980 and tabulate how many have increased per-share earnings by 15% annually since those dates. You will find that only a handful have. I would wager you a very significant sum that fewer than 10 of the 200 most profitable companies in 2000 will attain 15% annual growth in earnings-per-share over the next 20 years.

The problem arising from lofty predictions is not just that they spread unwarranted optimism. Even more troublesome is the fact that they corrode CEO behavior. Over the years, Charlie and I have observed many instances in which CEOs engaged in uneconomic operating maneuvers so that they could meet earnings targets they had announced. Worse still, after exhausting all that operating acrobatics would do, they sometimes played a wide variety of accounting games to "make the numbers." These accounting shenanigans have a way of snowballing: Once a company moves earnings from one period to another, operating shortfalls that occur thereafter require it to engage in further accounting maneuvers that must be even more "heroic." These can turn fudging into fraud. (More money, it has been noted, has been stolen with the point of a pen than at the point of a gun.)

Charlie and I tend to be leery of companies run by CEOs who woo investors with fancy predictions. A few of these managers will prove prophetic—but others will turn out to be congenital optimists, or even charlatans. Unfortunately, it's not easy for investors to know in advance which species they are dealing with.[12]

■ ■ ■

The blue ribbon for mischief-making should go to the zero-coupon issuer unable to make its interest payments on a current basis. Our advice: Whenever an investment banker starts talking about EBDIT— or whenever someone creates a capital structure that does not allow all interest, both payable and accrued, to be comfortably met out of current cash flow net of *ample capital expenditures*—zip up your wallet. Turn the tables by suggesting that the promoter and his high-priced entourage accept zero-coupon fees, deferring their take until the zero-coupon bonds have been paid in full. See then how much enthusiasm for the deal endures.

Our comments about investment bankers may seem harsh. But Charlie and I—in our hopelessly old-fashioned way—believe that they should perform a gatekeeping role, guarding investors against the promoter's propensity to indulge in excess. Promoters, after all, have throughout time exercised the same judgment and restraint in accepting money that alcoholics have exercised in accepting liquor. At a minimum, therefore, the banker's conduct should rise to that of a responsible bartender who, when necessary, refuses the profit from the next drink to avoid sending a drunk out on the highway. In recent years, unfortunately, many leading investment firms have found bartender morality to be an intolerably restrictive standard. Lately, those who have traveled the high road in Wall Street have not encountered heavy traffic.[13]

Chapter 15

Mistakes I've Made

Agonizing over errors is a mistake. But acknowledging and analyzing them can be useful, although that practice is rare in corporate boardrooms. . . . Dumb decisions either get no follow-up or are rationalized.[1]

—Warren Buffett

Mistakes of the First Twenty-Five Years
(A Condensed Version)

To quote Robert Benchley, "Having a dog teaches a boy fidelity, perseverance, and to turn around three times before lying down." Such are the shortcomings of experience. Nevertheless, it's a good idea to review past mistakes before committing new ones. So let's take a quick look at the last 25 years.

- My first mistake, of course, was in buying control of Berkshire. Though I knew its business—textile manufacturing—to be unpromising, I was enticed to buy because the price looked cheap. Stock purchases of that kind had proved reasonably rewarding in my early years, though by the time Berkshire came along in 1965, I was becoming aware that the strategy was not ideal.

    If you buy a stock at a sufficiently low price, there will usually be some hiccup in the fortunes of the business that gives you a chance to unload at a decent profit, even though the long-term performance of the business may be terrible. I call this the "cigar butt" approach to investing. A cigar butt found on the street that has only one puff left in it may not offer much of a smoke, but the "bargain purchase" will make that puff all profit.

Unless you are a liquidator, that kind of approach to buying businesses is foolish. First, the original "bargain" price probably will not turn out to be such a steal after all. In a difficult business, no sooner is one problem solved than another surfaces—never is there just one cockroach in the kitchen. Second, any initial advantage you secure will be quickly eroded by the low return that the business earns. For example, if you buy a business for $8 million that can be sold or liquidated for $10 million and promptly take either course, you can realize a high return. But the investment will disappoint if the business is sold for $10 million in ten years and in the interim has annually earned and distributed only a few percent on cost. Time is the friend of the wonderful business, the enemy of the mediocre.

You might think this principle is obvious, but I had to learn it the hard way—in fact, I had to learn it several times over. Shortly after purchasing Berkshire, I acquired a Baltimore department store, Hochschild Kohn, buying through a company called Diversified Retailing that later merged with Berkshire. I bought at a substantial discount from book value, the people were first-class, and the deal included some extras—unrecorded real estate values and a significant LIFO inventory cushion. How could I miss? So-o-o—three years later I was lucky to sell the business for about what I had paid. After ending our corporate marriage to Hochschild Kohn, I had memories like those of the husband in the country song, "My Wife Ran Away With My Best Friend and I Still Miss Him a Lot."

I could give you other personal examples of "bargain-purchase" folly but I'm sure you get the picture: It's far better to buy a wonderful company at a fair price than a fair company at a wonderful price. Charlie understood this early; I was a slow learner. But now, when buying companies or common stocks, we look for first-class businesses accompanied by first-class managements.

- That leads right into a related lesson: Good jockeys will do well on good horses, but not on broken-down nags. Both Berkshire's textile business and Hochschild, Kohn had able and honest people running them. The same managers employed in a business with good economic characteristics would have achieved fine records. But they were never going to make any progress while running in quicksand.

  I've said many times that when a management with a reputation for brilliance tackles a business with a reputation for bad economics, it is the reputation of the business that remains intact. I just wish I hadn't been so energetic in creating examples. My behavior has matched that admitted by Mae West: "I was Snow White, but I drifted."

- A further related lesson: Easy does it. After 25 years of buying and supervising a great variety of businesses, Charlie and I have *not* learned how to solve difficult business problems. What we have learned is to avoid them. To the extent we have been successful, it is because we concentrated on identifying one-foot hurdles that we could step over rather than because we acquired any ability to clear seven-footers.

  The finding may seem unfair, but in both business and investments it is usually far more profitable to simply stick with the easy and obvious than it is to resolve the difficult. On occasion, tough problems *must* be tackled as was the case when we started our Sunday paper in Buffalo. In other instances, a great investment opportunity occurs when a marvelous business encounters a one-time huge, but solvable, problem as was the case many years back at both American Express and GEICO. Overall, however, we've done better by avoiding dragons than by slaying them.

- My most surprising discovery: the overwhelming importance in business of an unseen force that we might call "the institutional imperative." In business school, I was given no hint of the imperative's existence and I did not intuitively understand it when I entered the business world. I thought then that decent, intelligent, and experienced managers would automatically make rational business decisions. But I learned over time that isn't so. Instead, rationality frequently wilts when the institutional imperative comes into play.

For example: (1) As if governed by Newton's First Law of Motion, an institution will resist any change in its current direction; (2) Just as work expands to fill available time, corporate projects or acquisitions will materialize to soak up available funds; (3) Any business craving of the leader, however foolish, will be quickly supported by detailed rate-of-return and strategic studies prepared by his troops; and (4) The behavior of peer companies, whether they are expanding, acquiring, setting executive compensation or whatever, will be mindlessly imitated.

Institutional dynamics, not venality or stupidity, set businesses on these courses, which are too often misguided. After making some expensive mistakes because I ignored the power of the imperative, I have tried to organize and manage Berkshire in ways that minimize its influence. Furthermore, Charlie and I have attempted to concentrate our investments in companies that appear alert to the problem.

- After some other mistakes, I learned to go into business only with people whom I like, trust, and admire. As I noted before, this policy of itself will not ensure success: A second-class textile or department-store company won't prosper simply because its managers are men that you would be pleased to see your daughter marry. However, an owner—or investor—can accomplish wonders if he manages to associate himself with such people in businesses that possess decent economic characteristics. Conversely, we do not wish to join with managers who lack admirable qualities, no matter how attractive the prospects of their business. We've never succeeded in making a good deal with a bad person.

- Some of my worst mistakes were not publicly visible. These were stock and business purchases whose virtues I understood and yet didn't make. It's no sin to miss a great opportunity outside one's area of competence. But I have passed on a couple of really big purchases that were served up to me on a platter and that I was fully capable of understanding. For Berkshire's shareholders, myself included, the cost of this thumb-sucking has been huge.

Our consistently-conservative financial policies may appear to have been a mistake, but in my view were not. In retrospect, it is clear

that significantly higher, though still conventional, leverage ratios at
Berkshire would have produced considerably better returns on equity
than the 23.8% we have actually averaged. Even in 1965, perhaps we
could have judged there to be a 99% probability that higher leverage
would lead to nothing but good. Correspondingly, we might have seen
only a 1% chance that some shock factor, external or internal, would
cause a conventional debt ratio to produce a result falling somewhere
between temporary anguish and default.

We wouldn't have liked those 99:1 odds—and never will. A small
chance of distress or disgrace cannot, in our view, be offset by a
large chance of extra returns. If your actions are sensible, you are certain to get good results; in most such cases, leverage just moves things
along faster. Charlie and I have never been in a big hurry: We enjoy
the process far more than the proceeds—though we have learned to
live with those also.[2]

■■■

Charlie and I have almost never witnessed a candid post-mortem of a
failed decision, *particularly one involving an acquisition*. A notable exception to this never-look-back approach is that of The Washington Post
Company, which unfailingly and objectively reviews its acquisitions
three years after they are made. Elsewhere, triumphs are trumpeted, but
dumb decisions either get no follow-up or are rationalized.[3]

■■■

I've made three decisions relating to Dexter that have hurt you in a
major way: (1) buying it in the first place; (2) paying for it with stock;
and (3) procrastinating when the need for changes in its operations was
obvious. I would like to lay these mistakes on Charlie (or anyone else,
for that matter) but they were mine. Dexter, prior to our purchase—
and indeed for a few years after—prospered despite low-cost foreign
competition that was brutal. I concluded that Dexter could continue to
cope with that problem, and I was wrong.[4]

■■■

And now it's confession time: I'm sure I could have saved you $100 million or so, pre-tax, if I had acted more promptly to shut down Gen Re Securities. Both Charlie and I knew at the time of the General Reinsurance merger that its derivatives business was unattractive. Reported profits struck us as illusory, and we felt that the business carried sizable risks that could not effectively be measured or limited. Moreover, we knew that any major problems the operation might experience would likely correlate with troubles in the financial or insurance world that would affect Berkshire elsewhere. In other words, if the derivatives business were ever to need shoring up, it would commandeer the capital and credit of Berkshire at just the time we could otherwise deploy those resources to huge advantage. (A historical note: We had just such an experience in 1974 when we were the victim of a major insurance fraud. We could not determine for some time how much the fraud would ultimately cost us and therefore kept more funds in cash-equivalents than we normally would have.)[5]

Mistake Du Jour

In the 1989 annual report I wrote about "Mistakes of the First 25 Years" and promised you an update in 2015. My experiences in the first few years of this second "semester" indicate that my backlog of matters to be discussed will become unmanageable if I stick to my original plan. Therefore, I will occasionally unburden myself in these pages in the hope that public confession may deter further bumblings. (Postmortems prove useful for hospitals and football teams; why not for businesses and investors?)

Typically, our most egregious mistakes fall in the omission, rather than the commission, category. That may spare Charlie and me some embarrassment, since you don't see these errors; but their invisibility does not reduce their cost. In this mea culpa, I am not talking about missing out on some company that depends upon an esoteric invention (such as Xerox), high-technology (Apple), or even brilliant merchandising (Wal-Mart). We will never develop the competence to spot such businesses early. Instead I refer to business situations that Charlie and I can understand and that seem clearly attractive—but in which we nevertheless end up sucking our thumbs rather than buying.

Every writer knows it helps to use striking examples, but I wish the one I now present wasn't quite so dramatic: In early 1988, we decided to buy 30 million shares (adjusted for a subsequent split) of Federal National Mortgage Association (Fannie Mae), which would have been a $350–$400 million investment. We had owned the stock some years earlier and understood the company's business. Furthermore, it was clear to us that David Maxwell, Fannie Mae's CEO, had dealt superbly with some problems that he had inherited and had established the company as a financial powerhouse—with the best yet to come. I visited David in Washington and confirmed that he would not be uncomfortable if we were to take a large position.

After we bought about 7 million shares, the price began to climb. In frustration, I stopped buying (a mistake that, thankfully, I did not repeat when Coca-Cola stock rose similarly during our purchase program). In an even sillier move, I surrendered to my distaste for holding small positions and sold the 7 million shares we owned.

I wish I could give you a halfway rational explanation for my amateurish behavior vis-a-vis Fannie Mae. But there isn't one. What I *can* give you is an estimate as of year-end 1991 of the approximate gain that Berkshire *didn't* make because of your Chairman's mistake: about $1.4 billion.[6]

■ ■ ■

And now it's confession time. It should be noted that no consultant, board of directors or investment banker pushed me into the mistakes I will describe. In tennis parlance, they were all unforced errors.

To begin with, I almost blew the See's purchase. The seller was asking $30 million, and I was adamant about not going above $25 million. Fortunately, he caved. Otherwise I would have balked, and that $1.35 billion would have gone to somebody else.

About the time of the See's purchase, Tom Murphy, then running Capital Cities Broadcasting, called and offered me the Dallas-Fort Worth NBC station for $35 million. The station came with the Fort Worth paper that Capital Cities was buying, and under the "cross-ownership" rules Murph had to divest it. I knew that TV stations were See's-like businesses that required virtually no capital investment and had excellent prospects for growth. They were simple to run and showered cash on their owners. Moreover, Murph, then as now, was a close friend, a man I admired as an extraordinary manager and outstanding human being. He knew the television business forward and backward and would not have called me unless he felt a purchase was certain to work. In effect Murph whispered "buy" into my ear. But I didn't listen.

In 2006, the station earned $73 million pre-tax, bringing its total earnings since I turned down the deal to at least $1 billion—almost all available to its owner for other purposes. Moreover, the property now has a capital value of about $800 million. Why did I say "no"? The only explanation is that my brain had gone on vacation and forgot to notify me. (My behavior resembled that of a politician Molly Ivins once described: "If his IQ (style) was any lower, you would have to water him twice a day.")

Finally, I made an even worse mistake when I said "yes" to Dexter, a shoe business I bought in 1993 for $433 million in Berkshire stock (25,203 shares of A). What I had assessed as durable competitive advantage vanished within a few years. But that's just the beginning: By using Berkshire stock, I compounded this error hugely. That move made the cost to Berkshire shareholders not $400 million, but rather $3.5 billion. In essence, I gave away 1.6% of a wonderful business— one now valued at $220 billion to buy a worthless business.

To date, Dexter is the worst deal that I've made. But I'll make more mistakes in the future—you can bet on that. A line from Bobby Bare's country song explains what too often happens with acquisitions: "I've never gone to bed with an ugly woman, but I've sure woke up with a few."[7]

■ ■ ■

I've mentioned that we strongly prefer to use cash rather than Berkshire stock in acquisitions. A study of the record will tell you why: If you aggregate all of our stock-only mergers (excluding those we did with two affiliated companies, Diversified Retailing and Blue Chip Stamps), you will find that our shareholders are slightly worse off than they would have been had I not done the transactions. Though it hurts me to say it, when I've issued stock, I've cost you money.

Be clear about one thing: This cost has *not* occurred because we were misled in any way by sellers or because they thereafter failed to manage with diligence and skill. On the contrary, the sellers were completely candid when we were negotiating our deals and have been energetic and effective ever since.

Instead, our problem has been that we own a truly marvelous collection of businesses, which means that trading away a portion of them for something new almost never makes sense. When we issue shares in a merger, we reduce your ownership in all of our businesses—partly-owned companies such as Coca-Cola, Gillette and American Express, and all of our terrific operating companies as well. An example from sports will illustrate the difficulty we face: For a baseball team, acquiring a player who can be expected to bat .350 is almost always a wonderful event—*except* when the team must trade a .380 hitter to make the deal.[8]

■ ■ ■

When Richard Branson, the wealthy owner of Virgin Atlantic Airways, was asked how to become a millionaire, he had a quick answer: "There's really nothing to it. Start as a billionaire and then buy an airline."[9]

■ ■ ■

The resuscitation of US Airways borders on the miraculous. Those who have watched my moves in this investment know that I have compiled a record that is unblemished by success. I was wrong in originally purchasing the stock, and I was wrong later, in repeatedly trying to unload our holdings at 50 cents on the dollar.

Two changes at the company coincided with its remarkable rebound: 1) Charlie and I left the board of directors and 2) Stephen Wolf became CEO. Fortunately for our egos, the second event was the key: Stephen Wolf's accomplishments at the airline have been phenomenal.

There still is much to do at US Airways, but survival is no longer an issue. Consequently, the company made up the dividend arrearages on our preferred during 1997, adding extra payments to compensate us for the delay we suffered. The company's common stock, furthermore, has risen from a low of $4 to a recent high of $73.

Our preferred has been called for redemption on March 15. But the rise in the company's stock has given our conversion rights, which we thought worthless not long ago, great value. It is now almost certain that our US Airways shares will produce a decent profit—that is, if my cost for Maalox is excluded—and the gain could even prove indecent.

Next time I make a big, dumb decision, Berkshire shareholders will know what to do: *Phone Mr. Wolf.*[10]

■ ■ ■

Charlie Rose: Dumbest mistake you ever made?

Warren Buffett: The dumbest mistake I ever made was, probably, will be in the future. No, you make plenty of mistakes, plenty of mistakes, Charlie. I can look back on every year in terms of mistakes I've made.[11]

Chapter 16

Personal Investing

Our equity-investing strategy remains little changed from what it was fifteen years ago, when we said in the 1977 annual report: We select our marketable equity securities in much the way we would evaluate a business for acquisition in its entirety. We want the business to be one (a) that we can understand; (b) with favorable long-term prospects; (c) operated by honest and competent people; and (d) available at a very attractive price.[1]

—WARREN BUFFETT

The Only Investment Advice You Will Ever Need

Let me add a few thoughts about your own investments. Most investors, both institutional and individual, will find that the best way to own common stocks is through an index fund that charges minimal fees. Those following this path are sure to beat the net results (after fees and expenses) delivered by the great majority of investment professionals.

Should you choose, however, to construct your own portfolio, there are a few thoughts worth remembering. Intelligent investing is not complex, though that is far from saying that it is easy. What an investor needs is the ability to correctly evaluate selected businesses. Note that word "selected": You don't have to be an expert on every company, or even many. You only have to be able to evaluate companies within your circle of competence. The size of that circle is not very important; knowing its boundaries, however, is vital.

To invest successfully, you need not understand beta, efficient markets, modern portfolio theory, option pricing or emerging markets. You may, in fact, be better off knowing nothing of these. That, of course, is not the prevailing view at most business schools, whose finance curriculum tends to be dominated by such subjects. In our view, though, investment students need only two well-taught courses—How to Value a Business, and How to Think About Market Prices.

Your goal as an investor should simply be to purchase, at a rational price, a part interest in an easily-understandable business whose earnings are virtually certain to be materially higher five, ten and twenty years from now. Over time, you will find only a few companies that meet these standards—so when you see one that qualifies, you should buy a meaningful amount of stock. You must also resist the temptation to stray from your guidelines: If you aren't willing to own a stock for ten years, don't even think about owning it for ten minutes. Put together a portfolio of companies whose aggregate earnings march upward over the years, and so also will the portfolio's market value.

Though it's seldom recognized, this is the exact approach that has produced gains for Berkshire shareholders: Our look-through earnings have grown at a good clip over the years, and our stock price has risen correspondingly. Had those gains in earnings not materialized, there would have been little increase in Berkshire's value.[2]

■ ■ ■

Charlie and I decided long ago that in an investment lifetime it's just too hard to make hundreds of smart decisions. That judgment became ever more compelling as Berkshire's capital mushroomed and the universe of investments that could significantly affect our results shrank dramatically. Therefore, we adopted a strategy that required our being smart—and not too smart at that—only a very few times. Indeed, we'll now settle for one good idea a year. (Charlie says it's my turn.)

The strategy we've adopted precludes our following standard diversification dogma. Many pundits would therefore say the strategy must be riskier than that employed by more conventional investors. We disagree. We believe that a policy of portfolio concentration may well *decrease* risk if it raises, as it should, both the intensity with which an investor thinks about a business and the comfort-level he must feel with its economic characteristics before buying into it. In stating this opinion, we define risk, using dictionary terms, as "the possibility of loss or injury."

Academics, however, like to define investment "risk" differently, averring that it is the relative volatility of a stock or portfolio of stocks—that is, their volatility as compared to that of a large universe of stocks. Employing data bases and statistical skills, these academics compute with precision the "beta" of a stock—its relative volatility in the past—and then build arcane investment and capital-allocation theories around this calculation. In their hunger for a single statistic to measure risk, however, they forget a fundamental principle: It is better to be approximately right than precisely wrong.

For owners of a business—and that's the way we think of shareholders—the academics' definition of risk is far off the mark, so much so that it produces absurdities. For example, under beta-based theory, a stock that has dropped very sharply compared to the market—as had Washington Post when we bought it in 1973—becomes "riskier" at the lower price than it was at the higher price. Would that description have then made any sense to someone who was offered the entire company at a vastly-reduced price?

In fact, the true investor *welcomes* volatility. Ben Graham explained why in Chapter 8 of *The Intelligent Investor.* There he introduced "Mr. Market," an obliging fellow who shows up every day to either buy from you or sell to you, whichever you wish. The more manic-depressive this chap is, the greater the opportunities available to the investor. That's true because a wildly fluctuating market means that irrationally low prices will periodically be attached to solid businesses. It is impossible to see how the availability of such prices can be thought of as increasing the hazards for an investor who is totally free to either ignore the market or exploit its folly.

In assessing risk, a beta purist will disdain examining what a company produces, what its competitors are doing, or how much borrowed money the business employs. He may even prefer not to know the company's name. What he treasures is the price history of its stock. In contrast, we'll happily forgo knowing the price history and instead will seek whatever information will further our understanding of the company's business. After we buy a stock, consequently, we would not be disturbed if markets closed for a year or two. We don't need a daily quote on our 100% position in See's or H. H. Brown to validate our well-being. Why, then, should we need a quote on our 7% interest in Coke?[3]

Aesop's Investment Axiom

Leaving aside tax factors, the formula we use for evaluating stocks and businesses is identical. Indeed, the formula for valuing *all* assets that are purchased for financial gain has been unchanged since it was first laid out by a very smart man in about 600 B.C. (though he wasn't smart enough to know it was 600 B.C.).

The oracle was Aesop and his enduring, though somewhat incomplete, investment insight was "a bird in the hand is worth two in the bush." To flesh out this principle, you must answer only three questions. How certain are you that there are indeed birds in the bush? When will they emerge and how many will there be? What is the risk-free interest rate (which we consider to be the yield on long-term U.S. bonds)? If you can answer these three questions, you will know the maximum value of the bush—and the maximum number of the birds you now possess that should be offered for it. And, of course, don't literally think birds. Think dollars.

Aesop's investment axiom, thus expanded and converted into dollars, is immutable. It applies to outlays for farms, oil royalties, bonds, stocks, lottery tickets, and manufacturing plants. And neither the advent of the steam engine, the harnessing of electricity nor the creation of the automobile changed the formula one iota—nor will the Internet. Just insert the correct numbers, and you can rank the attractiveness of all possible uses of capital throughout the universe.

Common yardsticks such as dividend yield, the ratio of price to earnings or to book value, and even growth rates have *nothing* to do with valuation except to the extent they provide clues to the amount and timing of cash flows into and from the business. Indeed, growth can destroy value if it requires cash inputs in the early years of a project or enterprise that exceed the discounted value of the cash that those assets will generate in later years. Market commentators and investment managers who glibly refer to "growth" and "value" styles as contrasting approaches to investment are displaying their ignorance, not their sophistication. Growth is simply a component—usually a plus, sometimes a minus—in the value equation.

Alas, though Aesop's proposition and the third variable—that is, interest rates—are simple, plugging in numbers for the other two variables is a difficult task. Using precise numbers is, in fact, foolish; working with a range of possibilities is the better approach. Usually, the range must be so wide that no useful conclusion can be reached. Occasionally, though, even very conservative estimates about the future emergence of birds reveal that the price quoted is startlingly low in relation to value. (Let's call this phenomenon the IBT—Inefficient Bush Theory.) To be sure, an investor needs some general understanding of business economics as well as the ability to think independently to reach a well-founded positive conclusion. But the investor does not need brilliance nor blinding insights.

At the other extreme, there are many times when the *most* brilliant of investors can't muster a conviction about the birds to emerge, not even when a very broad range of estimates is employed. This kind of uncertainty frequently occurs when new businesses and rapidly changing industries are under examination. In cases of this sort, *any* capital commitment must be labeled speculative.[4]

■ ■ ■

Now, speculation—in which the focus is not on what an asset will produce but rather on what the next fellow will pay for it—is neither illegal, immoral nor un-American. But it is not a game in which Charlie and I wish to play. We bring nothing to the party, so why should we expect to take anything home?

The line separating investment and speculation, which is never bright and clear, becomes blurred still further when most market participants have recently enjoyed triumphs. Nothing sedates rationality like large doses of effortless money. After a heady experience of that kind, normally sensible people drift into behavior akin to that of Cinderella at the ball. They know that overstaying the festivities—that is, continuing to speculate in companies that have gigantic valuations relative to the cash they are likely to generate in the future—will eventually bring on pumpkins and mice. But they nevertheless hate to miss a single minute of what is one helluva party. Therefore, the giddy participants all plan to leave just seconds before midnight. There's a problem, though: They are dancing in a room in which the clocks have no hands. Last year, we commented on the exuberance—and, yes, it was irrational—that prevailed, noting that investor expectations had grown to be several multiples of probable returns. One piece of evidence came from a Paine Webber–Gallup survey of investors conducted in December 1999, in which the participants were asked their opinion about the annual returns investors could expect to realize over the decade ahead. Their answers averaged 19%. That, for sure, was an irrational expectation: For American business as a whole, there couldn't possibly be enough birds in the 2009 bush to deliver such a return.

Far more irrational still were the huge valuations that market participants were then putting on businesses almost certain to end up being of modest or no value. Yet investors, mesmerized by soaring stock prices and ignoring all else, piled into these enterprises. It was as if some virus, racing wildly among investment professionals as well as amateurs, induced hallucinations in which the values of stocks in certain sectors became decoupled from the values of the businesses that underlay them.

This surreal scene was accompanied by much loose talk about "value creation." We readily acknowledge that there has been a huge amount of true value created in the past decade by new or young businesses, and that there is much more to come. But value is destroyed, not created, by any business that loses money over its lifetime, no matter how high its interim valuation may get.

What actually occurs in these cases is wealth *transfer*, often on a massive scale. By shamelessly merchandising birdless bushes, promoters have in recent years moved billions of dollars from the pockets of the public to their own purses (and to those of their friends and associates). The fact is that a bubble market has allowed the creation of bubble companies, entities designed more with an eye to making money *off* investors rather than *for* them. Too often, an IPO, not profits, was the primary goal of a company's promoters. At bottom, the "business model" for these companies has been the old-fashioned chain letter, for which many fee-hungry investment bankers acted as eager postmen.

But a pin lies in wait for every bubble. And when the two eventually meet, a new wave of investors learns some very old lessons: First, many in Wall Street—a community in which quality control is not prized—will sell investors anything they will buy. Second, speculation is most dangerous when it looks easiest.

At Berkshire, we make *no* attempt to pick the few winners that will emerge from an ocean of unproven enterprises. We're not smart enough to do that, and we know it. Instead, we try to apply Aesop's 2,600-year-old equation to opportunities in which we have reasonable confidence as to how many birds are in the bush and when they will emerge (a formulation that my grandsons would probably update to "A girl in a convertible is worth five in the phonebook."). Obviously, we can never precisely predict the timing of cash flows in and out of a business or their exact amount. We try, therefore, to keep our estimates conservative and to focus on industries where business surprises are unlikely to wreak havoc on owners. Even so, we make many mistakes: I'm the fellow, remember, who thought he understood the future economics of trading stamps, textiles, shoes and second-tier department stores.[5]

■ ■ ■

We've long felt that the only value of stock forecasters is to make fortune tellers look good. Even now, Charlie and I continue to believe that short-term market forecasts are poison and should be kept locked up in a safe place, away from children and also from grown-ups who behave in the market like children.[6]

■ ■ ■

Ben Graham told a story 40 years ago that illustrates why investment professionals behave as they do: An oil prospector, moving to
his heavenly reward, was met by St. Peter with bad news. "You're
qualified for residence," said St. Peter, "but, as you can see, the compound reserved for oil men is packed. There's no way to squeeze you
in." After thinking a moment, the prospector asked if he might say
just four words to the present occupants. That seemed harmless to
St. Peter, so the prospector cupped his hands and yelled, "Oil discovered in hell." Immediately the gate to the compound opened
and all of the oil men marched out to head for the nether regions.
Impressed, St. Peter invited the prospector to move in and make
himself comfortable. The prospector paused. "No," he said, "I think
I'll go along with the rest of the boys. There might be some truth to
that rumor after all."[7]

■ ■ ■

Common stocks, of course, are the most fun. When conditions are
right that is, when companies with good economics and good management sell well below intrinsic business value—stocks sometimes
provide grand-slam home runs. But we currently find no equities
that come close to meeting our tests. This statement in no way translates into a stock market prediction: we have no idea—and never have
had—whether the market is going to go up, down, or sideways in the
near- or intermediate-term future.

What we do know, however, is that occasional outbreaks of
those two super-contagious diseases, fear and greed, will forever
occur in the investment community. The timing of these epidem-
ics will be unpredictable. And the market aberrations produced by
them will be equally unpredictable, both as to duration and degree.
Therefore, we never try to anticipate the arrival or departure of
either disease. Our goal is more modest: we simply attempt to be
fearful when others are greedy and to be greedy only when others
are fearful.[8]

How We Think About Market Fluctuations

A short quiz: If you plan to eat hamburgers throughout your life and are not a cattle producer, should you wish for higher or lower prices for beef? Likewise, if you are going to buy a car from time to time but are not an auto manufacturer, should you prefer higher or lower car prices? These questions, of course, answer themselves.

But now for the final exam: If you expect to be a net saver during the next five years, should you hope for a higher or lower stock market during that period? Many investors get this one wrong. Even though they are going to be net buyers of stocks for many years to come, they are elated when stock prices rise and depressed when they fall. In effect, they rejoice because prices have risen for the "hamburgers" they will soon be buying. This reaction makes no sense. Only those who will be sellers of equities in the near future should be happy at seeing stocks rise. Prospective purchasers should much prefer sinking prices.[9]

■ ■ ■

"*Dis*investors lose as market falls—but investors gain." Though writers often forget this truism, there is a buyer for every seller and what hurts one necessarily helps the other. (As they say in golf matches: "Every putt makes *someone* happy.")

We gained enormously from the low prices placed on many equities and businesses in the 1970s and 1980s. Markets that then were hostile to investment transients were friendly to those taking up permanent residence. In recent years, the actions we took in those decades have been validated, but we have found few new opportunities. In its role as a corporate "saver," Berkshire continually looks for ways to sensibly deploy capital, but it may be some time before we find opportunities that get us truly excited.[10]

■ ■ ■

Ted Williams wrote a book called "The Science of Hitting." In that book he had a grid of 77 little zones in the strike zone. Se said if he only swung at the balls in this one area, "the sweet spot," he would bat over 400; if he swung at the balls on the outside corner and low but still a strike, he would bat at about 225. So he said everything in life is about waiting for the right pitch. In baseball if you have 2 strikes already and you get one of those 225 balls you still have to swing at it because there aren't any more balls. In investing, you never have to swing. Now, if you swing and miss, it's a strike, but if you wait and the pitcher gets tired and he keeps throwing balls at you and finally you see one right in your sweet spot and you understand and you swing at it and you only have to do that a few times in a lifetime. You only have to get a few hits, you don't have to get up everyday and take five at bats and swing at every ball.[11]

Excerpt from the Warren Buffett Article, "The Superinvestors of Graham-And-Doddsville"

Before we begin this examination, I would like you to imagine a national coin-flipping contest. Let's assume we get 225 million Americans up tomorrow morning and we ask them all to wager a dollar. They go out in the morning at sunrise, and they all call the flip of a coin. If they call correctly, they win a dollar from those who called wrong. Each day the losers drop out, and on the subsequent day the stakes build as all previous winnings are put on the line. After ten flips on ten mornings, there will be approximately 220,000 people in the United States who have correctly called ten flips in a row. They each will have won a little over $1,000.

Now this group will probably start getting a little puffed up about this, human nature being what it is. They may try to be modest, but at cocktail parties they will occasionally admit to attractive members of the opposite sex what their technique is, and what marvelous insights they bring to the field of flipping.

Assuming that the winners are getting the appropriate rewards from the losers, in another ten days we will have 215 people who have successfully called their coin flips 20 times in a row and who, by this exercise, each have turned one dollar into a little over $1 million. $225 million would have been lost, $225 million would have been won.

By then, this group will really lose their heads. They will probably write books on "How I Turned a Dollar into a Million in Twenty Days Working Thirty Seconds a Morning." Worse yet, they'll probably start jetting around the country attending seminars on efficient coin-flipping and tackling skeptical professors with, "If it can't be done, why are there 215 of us?"

By then some business school professor will probably be rude enough to bring up the fact that if 225 million orangutans had engaged in a similar exercise, the results would be much the same—215 egotistical orangutans with 20 straight winning flips.

I would argue, however, that there are some important differences in the examples I am going to present. For one thing, if (a) you had taken 225 million orangutans distributed roughly as the U.S. population is; if (b) 215 winners were left after 20 days; and if (c) you found that 40 came from a particular zoo in Omaha, you would be pretty sure you were on to something. So you would probably go out and ask the zookeeper about what he's feeding them, whether they had special exercises, what books they read, and who knows what else. That is, if you found any really extraordinary concentrations of success, you might want to see if you could identify concentrations of unusual characteristics that might be causal factors.

Scientific inquiry naturally follows such a pattern. If you were trying to analyze possible causes of a rare type of cancer—with, say, 1,500 cases a year in the United States—and you found that 400 of them occurred in some little mining town in Montana, you would get very interested in the water there, or the occupation of those afflicted, or other variables. You know it's not random chance that 400 come from a small area. You would not necessarily know the causal factors, but you would know where to search.

I submit to you that there are ways of defining an origin other than geography. In addition to geographical origins, there can be what I call an *intellectual* origin. I think you will find that a disproportionate number of successful coin-flippers in the investment world came from a very small intellectual village that could be called Graham-and-Doddsville. A concentration of winners that simply cannot be explained by chance can be traced to this particular intellectual village.

Conditions could exist that would make even that concentration unimportant. Perhaps 100 people were simply imitating the coin-flipping call of some terribly persuasive personality. When he called heads, 100 followers automatically called that coin the same way. If the leader was part of the 215 left at the end, the fact that 100 came from the same intellectual origin would mean nothing. You would simply be identifying one case as a hundred cases. Similarly, let's assume that you lived in a strongly patriarchal society and every family in the United States conveniently consisted of ten members. Further assume that the patriarchal culture was so strong that, when the 225 million people went out the first day, every member of the family identified with the father's call. Now, at the end of the 20-day period, you would have 215 winners, and you would find that they came from only 21.5 families. Some naive types might say that this indicates an enormous hereditary factor as an explanation of successful coin-flipping. But, of course, it would have no significance at all because it would simply mean that you didn't have 215 individual winners, but rather 21.5 randomly distributed families who were winners.

In this group of successful investors that I want to consider, there has been a common intellectual patriarch, Ben Graham. But the children who left the house of this intellectual patriarch have called their "flips" in very different ways. They have gone to different places and bought and sold different stocks and companies, yet they have had a combined record that simply cannot be explained by the fact that they are all calling flips identically because a leader is signaling the calls for them to make. The patriarch has merely set forth the intellectual theory for making coin-calling decisions, but each student has decided on his own manner of applying the theory.

The common intellectual theme of the investors from Graham-and-Doddsville is this: they search for discrepancies between the *value* of a business and the *price* of small pieces of that business in the market. Essentially, they exploit those discrepancies without the efficient market theorist's concern as to whether the stocks are bought on Monday or Thursday, or whether it is January or July, etc. Incidentally, when businessmen buy businesses, which is just what our Graham & Dodd investors are doing through the purchase of marketable stocks—I doubt that many are cranking into their purchase decision the day of the week or the month in which the transaction is going to occur. If it doesn't make any difference whether all of a business is being bought on a Monday or a Friday, I am baffled why academicians invest extensive time and effort to see whether it makes a difference when buying small pieces of those same businesses. Our Graham & Dodd investors, needless to say, do not discuss beta, the capital asset pricing model, or covariance in returns among securities. These are not subjects of any interest to them. In fact, most of them would have difficulty defining those terms. The investors simply focus on two variables: price and value.

I always find it extraordinary that so many studies are made of price and volume behavior, the stuff of chartists. Can you imagine buying an entire business simply because the price of the business had been marked *up* substantially last week and the week before? Of course, the reason a lot of studies are made of these price and volume variables is that now, in the age of computers, there are almost endless data available about them. It isn't necessarily because such studies have any utility; it's simply that the data are there and academicians have [worked] hard to learn the mathematical skills needed to manipulate them. Once these skills are acquired, it seems sinful not to use them, even if the usage has no utility or negative utility. As a friend said, to a man with a hammer, everything looks like a nail.[13]

Chapter 17

Buffett, the Teacher

I believe in going to work for businesses you admire and people you admire. Anytime you are around somebody that you're getting something out of and you feel good about the organization, you just have to have a good result. I advise you never to do anything because you think its miserable now but it's going to be great 10 years from now, or because you think I've got x dollars now, but I'll have 10x. If you are not enjoying it today, you're probably not going to enjoy it 10 years from now.[1]

—WARREN BUFFETT

Charlie Rose: You've always, always taken the position that you don't have to make speeches except to students and kids. What's the idea?

Warren Buffett: The idea is that they listen and you may change some lives. I mean the things I heard when I was 20 from somebody I wanted to listen to changed my behavior. The people I listened to at age 74, I wanted to be entertained, but it's not going to change anything. If I talk to 50–60 year olds, basically they want to be entertained by my predictions and if I talk to 20 year olds or even 25 year olds, they ask me the questions on their minds. They really get what's on their minds and what's on their faces. Then they write me afterwards and it changes some lives. Thinking they would go into this line because it looks good on their resume or they get a little more assurance. I tell them why wait till their 80 to do something you like. It's like saving up sex for your old age. While you want to have patience for what you do, why go through life waiting for the big moment.

Warren Buffett: Yeah, I tell students if you make a million dollars one way or another or a 100 billion dollars, let's call it a billion to make it easy, I say if you make a billion doing things that you are fine doing and if you do a bunch of things and associate with people you don't like and everything else and when you died your obituary says he died with a billion, one hundred million, so what. I mean it just doesn't make any difference. The real question is how you live.[2]

■ ■ ■

WB: A University of Chicago graduate student asked me once, what are we being taught that is wrong? In business school the amount of time spent teaching option pricing is total nonsense. You only need two courses: (1) how to value a business, and (2) how to think about stock market fluctuations. The thing is that instructors know the formulas and you don't, so they have something to fill the time. It has nothing to do with investment success—what matters is buying businesses at the right price. If you were teaching Biblical studies and you could read the Bible forward, backward, and in four different languages, you would find it hard to tell everyone that it comes down to the Ten Commandments. The priests want to spend a lot of time preaching. You must have an attitude where you aren't influenced by the market. You need a mindset, and you need to have the attitude to divorce yourself from letting the market influence you.

CM: Students learn corporate finance at business schools. They are taught that the whole secret is diversification. But the exact rule is the opposite. The "know-nothing" investor should practice diversification, but it is crazy if you are an expert. The goal of investment is to find situations where it is safe *not* to diversify. If you only put 20% into the opportunity of a lifetime, you are not being rational. Very seldom do we get to buy as much of any good idea as we would like to.

Q13: (*from a teacher trying to help introverts*) **What advice would you give to the quieter, introverted population, in order to raise their visibility and gain the recognition they deserve?**

WB: I avoided all classes that had public speaking; I got physically ill if I had to speak. I signed up for a Dale Carnegie course. I gave them a check for $100, and then I went home and stopped payment on the check. I was in Omaha, and finally took $100 cash to Wally Kean. I took that Carnegie course, and then I went to the University of Omaha to start teaching—knowing I had to get in front of people. Ability to communicate in writing and speaking—it is undertaught—and enormously important. If you can communicate well, you have an enormous advantage. Force yourself into situations where you have to develop those abilities. It helps to do it in front of similar people to start. At Dale Carnegie—they made us stand on tables. I may have gone too far. You are doing something very worthwhile if you are helping introverted people get outside of themselves.

Q12: Germany (high school student). What should I do with my life?

WB: We prefer questions that are harder. [*laughter*]

Q12 CONT: What would you do if you started over?

WB: You have to find your passion in life. I would choose the same job. I enjoy it. It is a terrible mistake to sleepwalk through your life. Unless Shirley MacLaine is right, you won't have another one. My dad had a business with [investment] books on his shelves, and they turned me on. This was before *Playboy*. If he was a minister, I'm not sure I would have been as enthused. If you have obligations, you have to deal with realities. I tell students to go work for an organization you admire or an individual you admire, which usually means that most MBAs I meet become self-employed. [*laughter*] I went to work for Ben Graham. I never asked my salary. Get the right spouse. Charlie talks about the man who spent twenty years looking for the perfect woman and found her. Unfortunately, she was looking for the perfect man. If you are lucky, you will be happy and as a result, you will behave better. It makes it easier.

CM: You'll do better if you have passion for something in which you have aptitude. If Warren had gone into ballet, no one would have heard of him.

Q46: Florida. I teach at a community college in Florida, teaching students to invest in themselves. Financial independence and freedom. Slow and steady wins the race. Law of reciprocity. Etc., etc., etc. What else should I be doing?

WB: [*Laughing*] I'm ready to hire your entire class right now. The most important investment is in themselves. Potential horsepower is rarely achieved. Just imagine you are 16 and your parents are going to give you the car of your choice. But the catch is that it is the only car you would get for the rest of your life. How would you choose to proceed? Of course, you will read the manual 5 times. How would you treat it? You'll keep it garaged, change the oil twice as frequently as you're supposed to, and keep rust to a minimum because you know it needs to last a lifetime. I tell students that you get only one body and one mind. You'd better treat them the same way. It's hard to change habits at age 50 or 60. Anything students do to invest in body and mind is good, particularly in the mind. We didn't work too hard on bodies around here. It pays off in an extraordinary way. The best asset is your own self. You can become, to an enormous degree, the person you want to be. When I talk to university classes, I ask them to buy one classmate to own [his or her earnings] for the rest of their life. They would pick the person not with the highest IQ, but the ones who are the most effective; the ones you want to be around. These people are easy to work with, generous, on time, don't claim credit, help others. Those are good habits to develop. Leaders are effective because people want to be around them.[3]

Cynthia Milligan Interview

Warren: The best ethical leadership people receive is from their parents. Every kid wants heroes, and they may pick the wrong ones. The natural heroes are the parents. Kids usually emulate their parents, and if the parents behave well, the kids are very, very likely to behave well.

I think that what you do at school by emphasizing ethical values is that you will keep those kids on track and pull in a few that aren't.

Cynthia: What about the value of good leadership skills and ethics in business?

Warren: I have seen plenty of people succeed that don't have either one. And I have also seen an awful lot of people succeed that do; and those are the ones I admire and they are the ones I want to associate with. Honesty is a terrific policy. What do you look back on in terms of whether you have been a success? You have certain things you want to achieve, but if you don't have the love and respect of people, you are always a failure. That is the one thing you must earn, it can never be bought. No one that has the love and respect of others is ever a failure.

Cynthia: A donor gave us $1 million to develop an ethics program, and every year he asks us if we really think this makes a difference. I agree with you, often the students come with high ethical standards, but what we are doing is exposing them to some ethical issues that might trip them up at some point in their career. We want them to understand the issues and understand they can influence those around them with their own standards. Do you agree with that approach?

Warren: The simple test of good ethics, is how would you feel about any act, if a reasonably intelligent, but unfriendly reporter were to write it up and put it in tomorrow's paper for everyone to see. If it passes that test, it's okay, and if you have to think about it, it probably isn't the right thing to do.

Cynthia: Our philosophy is that technology is a part of every element in our curriculum. We do not have an e-commerce or an e-business major. It should be infused into everything; it has changed accounting, it has changed all aspects of business.

Warren: It's a tool. For a student to leave business school and not know how technology affects business and a mind to keep up with the progress of technology would be insupportable. Technology is the future of business. It is transforming society. If I were starting out in business today, I would be very focused on technology.

Cynthia: Do you think an MBA is an important degree for students to have today?

Warren: If you are interested in business, or likely to be in business, an MBA is very useful. But, what is really important is what you bring to a class in terms of being interested in the subject. If you view a course like accounting as a drudge and a requirement, you are missing the whole game. Any course can be exciting. Mastering accounting is like mastering a new language, it can be so much fun. The attitude should be one of discovery, that you are coming there and discovering. Accounting is the Rosetta Stone of business.

Economics is fascinating, the first page of economics describes how mankind deals with insatiable wants and creates the systems to fulfill these wants. It's great stuff. Really how the world works. Business is a subsection, a fairly understandable subsection, not like black holes, which are fairly hard to visualize, but business is every day stuff and you are learning how the world works. You are 18–19 years old and learning about the world, understanding how this great world works. The GDP per capita in the 20th century increased 6 to 1. Think of that, six times. Why does that work here in the U.S., why doesn't it work other places? The U.S. is a small part of the universe, but a very important part and understanding that and seeing everything else against that backdrop for the rest of your life is fabulous.

Cynthia: We have 3,200 students in the Business College, just beginning their paths to a career. What advice would you give students who are preparing for a business career?

Warren: My advice generally is to sop up everything you can. You're not going to run out of storage room in your brain, so take advantage of everything that is of interest. You will never have another opportunity like this in your lifetime.

Cynthia: Our students are always interested in knowing what you look for when you hire someone? What specific qualities do you seek?

Warren: You look for three things: you look for intelligence, you look for energy and you look for integrity. You don't need to be brilliant, just reasonably intelligent. Ray Kroc, for example, has good intelligence, which he combined with good business principles and passion for business and a passion for his particular business. Every business student you have has the requisite intelligence and requisite energy. Integrity is not hard wired into your DNA. A student at that age can pretty much decide what kind [of] a person they are going to be at sixty. If they don't have integrity, they never will. The chains of habit are sometimes too heavy to be broken. Students can forge their own chains. Just pick a person to admire and ask why you admire them, usually it is because they are generous, decent, kind people, and those are the kind of people to emulate.[4]

Speech before University of Florida MBA Students—September 4, 2006

I would like to talk for just one minute to the students about your future when you leave here. Because you will learn a tremendous amount about investments, you all have the ability to do well; you all have the IQ to do well. You all have the energy and initiative to do well or you wouldn't be here. Most of you will succeed in meeting your aspirations. But in determining whether you succeed there is more to it than intellect and energy. I would like to talk just a second about that. In fact, there was a guy, Pete Kiewit in Omaha, who used to say, he looked for three things in hiring people: integrity, intelligence and energy. And he said if the person did not have the first two, the later two would kill him, because if they don't have integrity, you want them dumb and lazy.

We want to talk about the first two because we know you have the last two. You are all second-year MBA students, so you have gotten to know your classmates. Think for a moment that I granted you the right—you can buy 10% of one of your classmate's earnings for the rest of their lifetime. You can't pick someone with a rich father; you have to pick someone who is going to do it on his or her own merit. And I gave you an hour to think about it.

Will you give them an IQ test and pick the one with the highest IQ? I doubt it. Will you pick the one with the best grades? The most energetic? You will start looking for qualitative factors, in addition to (the quantitative) because everyone has enough brains and energy. You would probably pick the one you responded the best to, the one who has the leadership qualities, the one who is able to get other people to carry out their interests. That would be the person who is generous, honest and who gave credit to other people for their own ideas. All types of qualities. Whomever you admire the most in the class. Then I would throw in a hooker. In addition to this person you had to go short one of your classmates.

That is more fun. Who do I want to go short? You wouldn't pick the person with the lowest IQ, you would think about the person who turned you off, the person who is egotistical, who is greedy, who cuts corners, who is slightly dishonest.

As you look at those qualities on the left and right hand side, there is one interesting thing about them; it is not the ability to throw a football 60 yards, it is not the ability to run the 100 yard dash in 9.3 seconds, it is not being the best looking person in the class—they are all qualities that if you really want to have the ones on the left hand side, you can have them.

They are qualities of behavior, temperament, character that are achievable; they are not forbidden to anybody in this group. And if you look at the qualities on the right hand side, the ones that turn you off in other people, there is not a quality there that you have to have. You can get rid of it. You can get rid of it a lot easier at your age than at my age, because most behaviors are habitual. The chains of habit are too light to be felt until they are too heavy to be broken. There is no question about it. I see people with these self destructive behavior patterns at my age or even twenty years younger and they really are entrapped by them.

They go around and do things that turn off other people right and left. They don't need to be that way but by a certain point they get so they can hardly change it. But at your age you can have any habits, any patterns of behavior that you wish. It is simply a question of which you decide.

If you did this. . . . Ben Graham looked around at the people he admired and Ben Franklin did this before him. Ben Graham did this in his low teens and he looked around at the people he admired and he said, "I want to be admired, so why don't I behave like them?" And he found out that there was nothing impossible about behaving like them. Similarly he did the same thing on the reverse side in terms of getting rid of those qualities. I would suggest that if you write those qualities down and think about them a while and make them habitual, you will be the one you want to buy 10% of when you are all through. And the beauty of it is that you already own 100% of yourself and you are stuck with it. So you might as well be that person, that somebody else. Well that is a short little sermon.[5]

■ ■ ■

That does not take away from the fact that State Farm is one of America's greatest business stories. I've urged that the company be studied at business schools because it has achieved fabulous success while following a path that in many ways defies the dogma of those institutions. Studying counter-evidence is a highly useful activity, though not one always greeted with enthusiasm at citadels of learning.

State Farm was launched in 1922, by a 45-year-old, semi-retired Illinois farmer, to compete with long established insurers—haughty institutions in New York, Philadelphia and Hartford—that possessed overwhelming advantages in capital, reputation, and distribution. Because State Farm is a mutual company, its board members and managers could not be owners, and it had no access to capital markets during its years of fast growth. Similarly, the business never had the stock options or lavish salaries that many people think vital if an American enterprise is to attract able managers and thrive.

In the end, however, State Farm eclipsed all its competitors. In fact, by 1999 the company had amassed a tangible net worth exceeding that of all but four American businesses.If you want to read how this happened, get a copy of *The Farmer from Merna*.[6]

■ ■ ■

Other colleges and universities have now come calling. This school year we will have visiting classes, ranging in size from 30 to 100 students, from Chicago, Dartmouth (Tuck), Delaware State, Florida State, Indiana, Iowa, Iowa State, Maryland, Nebraska, Northwest Nazarene, Pennsylvania (Wharton), Stanford, Tennessee, Texas, Texas A&M, Toronto (Rotman), Union and Utah. Most of the students are MBA candidates, and I've been impressed by their quality. They are keenly interested in business and investments, but their questions indicate that they also have more on their minds than simply making money. I always feel good after meeting them.[7]

Chapter 18

Humor and Stories

A gorgeous woman slinks up to a CEO at a party and through her moist lips purrs "I'll do anything—anything. Just tell me what you would like." With no hesitation, he replies, "reprice my options."[1]

—WARREN BUFFETT

S ome major financial institutions have, however, experienced staggering problems because they engaged in the "weakened lending practices" I described in last year's letter. John Stumpf, CEO of Wells Fargo, aptly dissected the recent behavior of many lenders: "It is interesting that the industry has invented new ways to lose money when the old ways seemed to work just fine."[2]

■ ■ ■

The attitude of our managers vividly contrasts with that of the young man who married a tycoon's only child, a decidedly homely and dull lass. Relieved, the father called in his new son-in-law after the wedding and began to discuss the future:

"Son, you're the boy I always wanted and never had. Here's a stock certificate for 50% of the company. You're my equal partner from now on."

"Thanks, dad."

"Now, what would you like to run? How about sales?"

"I'm afraid I couldn't sell water to a man crawling in the Sahara."

"Well then, how about heading human relations?"

175

"I really don't care for people."

"No problem, we have lots of other spots in the business. What would you like to do?"

"Actually, nothing appeals to me. Why don't you just buy me out?"[3]

■ ■ ■

My own role in operations may best be illustrated by a small tale concerning my granddaughter, Emily, and her fourth birthday party last fall. Attending were other children, adoring relatives, and Beemer the Clown, a local entertainer who includes magic tricks in his act.

Beginning these, Beemer asked Emily to help him by waving a "magic wand" over "the box of wonders." Green handkerchiefs went into the box, Emily waved the wand, and Beemer removed blue ones. Loose handkerchiefs went in and, upon a magisterial wave by Emily, emerged knotted. After four such transformations, each more amazing than its predecessor, Emily was unable to contain herself. Her face aglow, she exulted: "Gee, I'm really good at this."[4]

■ ■ ■

What we do know is that our ignorance means we must follow the course prescribed by Pascal in his famous wager about the existence of God. As you may recall, he concluded that since he didn't know the answer, his personal gain/loss ratio dictated an affirmative conclusion.[5]

■ ■ ■

Gypsy Rose Lee announced on one of her later birthdays: "I have everything I had last year; it's just that it's all two inches lower." As the table shows, during 1987 almost all of our businesses aged in a more upbeat way.[6]

■ ■ ■

Our exemplar is the older man who crashed his grocery cart into that of a much younger fellow while both were shopping. The elderly man explained apologetically that he had lost track of his wife and was pre-occupied searching for her. His new acquaintance said that by coinci-dence his wife had also wandered off and suggested that it might be more efficient if they jointly looked for the two women. Agreeing, the older man asked his new companion what his wife looked like. "She's a gorgeous blonde," the fellow answered, "with a body that would cause a bishop to go through a stained glass window, and she's wearing tight white shorts. How about yours?" The senior citizen wasted no words: "Forget her, we'll look for yours."[7]

∎∎∎

In this ambition, we hope—metaphorically—to avoid the fate of the elderly couple who had been romantically challenged for some time. As they finished dinner on their 50th anniversary, however, the wife—stimulated by soft music, wine and candlelight—felt a long-absent tickle and demurely suggested to her husband that they go upstairs and make love. He agonized for a moment and then replied, "I can do one or the other, but not both."[8]

∎∎∎

At our sessions, I tell the newcomers the story of the Tennessee group and its spotting of Clayton Homes. I do this in the spirit of the farmer who enters his hen house with an ostrich egg and admonishes the flock: "I don't like to complain, girls, but this is just a small sample of what the competition is doing." To date, our new scouts have not brought us deals. But their mission in life has been made clear to them.[9]

∎∎∎

Soooo . . . "except for" a couple of favorable breaks, our pre-tax earn-ings last year would have been about $500 million less than we actually reported. We're happy, nevertheless, to bank the excess. As Jack Benny once said upon receiving an award: "I don't deserve this honor—but, then, I have arthritis, and I don't deserve that either."[10]

■ ■ ■

A story I told you some years back illustrates our problem in accurately estimating our loss liability: A fellow was on an important business trip in Europe when his sister called to tell him that their dad had died. Her brother explained that he couldn't get back but said to spare nothing on the funeral, whose cost he would cover. When he returned, his sister told him that the service had been beautiful and presented him with bills totaling $8,000. He paid up but a month later received a bill from the mortuary for $10. He paid that, too—and still another $10 charge he received a month later. When a third $10 invoice was sent to him the following month, the perplexed man called his sister to ask what was going on. "Oh," she replied, "I forgot to tell you. We buried Dad in a rented suit."[11]

■ ■ ■

The change brings to mind a *New Yorker* cartoon in which the grateful borrower rises to shake the hand of the bank's lending officer and gushes: "I don't know how I'll ever repay you."[12]

■ ■ ■

There's a story behind my unwillingness to throw the curve ball. As some of you may know, Candy Cummings invented the curve in 1867 and used it to great effect in the National Association, where he never won less than 28 games in a season. The pitch, however, drew immediate criticism from the very highest of authorities, namely Charles Elliott, then president of Harvard University, who declared, "I have heard that this year we at Harvard won the baseball championship because we have a pitcher who has a fine curve ball. I am further instructed that the purpose of the curve ball is to deliberately deceive the batter. Harvard is not in the business of teaching deception." (I'm not making this up.)

Ever since I learned of President Elliott's moral teachings on this subject, I have scrupulously refrained from using my curve, however devastating its effect might have been on hapless batters. Now, however, it is time for my karma to run over Elliott's dogma and for me to quit holding back. Visit the park on Saturday night and marvel at the majestic arc of my breaking ball.[13]

■■■

Woody Allen once explained why eclecticism works: "The real advantage of being bisexual is that it doubles your chances for a date on Saturday night."[14]

■■■

Our exposures are large: We have one policy that calls for us to pay $100 million to the policyholder if a specified catastrophe occurs. (Now you know why I suffer eyestrain: from watching The Weather Channel.)[15]

■■■

Charlie doesn't like it when I equate the jet with bacteria; he feels it's degrading to the bacteria. His idea of traveling in style is an air-conditioned bus, a luxury he steps up to only when bargain fares are in effect. My own attitude toward the jet can be summarized by the prayer attributed, apocryphally I'm sure, to St. Augustine as he contemplated leaving a life of secular pleasures to become a priest. Battling the conflict between intellect and glands, he pled: "Help me, Oh Lord, to become chaste—but not yet." Naming the plane has not been easy. I initially suggested "The Charles T. Munger." Charlie countered with "The Aberration." We finally settled on "The Indefensible."[16]

■■■

"My ideas about food and diet were irrevocably formed quite early. The product of a widely successful party that celebrated my fifth birthday. On that occasion we had hot dogs, hamburgers, soft drinks, popcorn and ice cream."[17]

■ ■ ■

Managers thinking about accounting issues should never forget one of Abraham Lincoln's favorite riddles: "How many legs does a dog have if you call his tail a leg?" The answer: "Four, because calling a tail a leg does not make it a leg." It behooves managers to remember that Abe's right even if an auditor is willing to certify that the tail is a leg.[18]

■ ■ ■

"Last night Warren Buffett came to me in a dream
and whispered in my ear, but it was just sexual."

(Reprinted with permission from www.CartoonStock.com.)

Appendix A

Warren E. Buffett, A Chronological History

(A Condensed Version)

1930–1931

Warren E. Buffett was born August 30, 1930, in Omaha, Nebraska, to Howard and Leila Buffett. Warren adored his father, who called Warren "Fireball."

His father was a stockbroker and in 1931 founded Buffett-Falk & Company after he lost his job at a bank that had closed the year before. He also served as a U.S. Representative from 1942–1948 and from 1950–1952.

1936

Warren's first business was selling Cokes. He would buy six for 25 cents from Buffett & Son, the family grocery store, and sell them for 5 cents each.

1942

Warren and his sister purchase six shares of Cities Service preferred stock at a cost of $38 per share. The price declines to $27, rebounds to $40 and Buffett sells. A few years later, the price increased to over $200 per share.

1943

Buffett files his first income tax return, deducting his bicycle as a work expense.

1945–1947

Warren delivers (earning $175 a month) *Washington Post* newspapers. He and a high school friend purchased a 1928 Rolls-Royce for $350 and rented it out for $35 a day. They also ran a peanut vending machine and pinball machine business in local barber shops. They sold the business, Wilson Coin-Operated Machine Company, for $1,200.

Warren purchases 40 acres of farmland for $1,200.

Warren has earned $5,000 and enrolls as a freshman at the Wharton School of Finance and Commerce.

1949–1950

Warren, dissatisfied, leaves Wharton after his junior year and transfers to the University of Nebraska-Lincoln College of Business Administration and graduates with a B.S. degree. His savings are now $9,800.

In 1950, Warren applies for admission to Harvard Business School but is turned down. He enrolls at Columbia Business School after learning that Benjamin Graham and David Dodd are professors there. In his senior year at Nebraska, he had read Graham's book, *The Intelligent Investor.*

He invests three-fourths of his net worth in GEICO.

1951

Buffett receives a master's degree in economics from Columbia, reportedly receiving the only A+ ever given out by Benjamin Graham.

After being turned down to work for Graham, Warren returns to Omaha to work as a stockbroker at Buffett-Falk. Buffett takes a Dale Carnegie public speaking course and teaches a night class, "Investor Principles," at the University of Nebraska.

Warren begins dating Susan Thompson. She was Warren's sister's roommate at Northwestern University.

1952

Warren and Susan marry and have their first child, Susie.

1954

Ben Graham offers Warren a position at his partnership for $12,000. He accepts and he and Susie move to New York.

His second child, Howard, is born.

1956

Ben Graham retires and Warren returns to Omaha. His savings have grown to over $140,000.

Warren opens his first partnership with seven partners, friends and family members, $105,000. Warren's investment is $100.

1957–1969

In 1957, Warren purchases his first and only residence on Farnam Street for $31,500.

Warren's third child, Peter, is born in 1958.

In 1959, Warren and Charlie Munger meet and become lifelong friends and partners.

Buffett sets up several investment partnerships, which are merged into one in 1961.

At the beginning of 1962, the partnership had 90 partners and $7.2 million in assets, with $1 million owned by Buffett.

In 1962, the Buffett Partnership began purchasing Berkshire Hathaway at $7.60 per share and shortly thereafter becomes the largest shareholder.

At the end of 1965, the partnership has $44 million of assets, with $6.8 million owned by Buffett. Two years later, the partnership has $65 million of assets, with $10 million owned by Buffett.

In 1967, Berkshire acquires National Indemnity.

One investment alone, American Express, returns a gain of $20 million after being purchased at very depressed levels resulting from a salad oil scandal.

In 1969, Warren closes the partnership, now worth $100 million, with his share being $25 million.

The Buffett partnership liquidates. Among the assets distributed are Berkshire Hathaway shares.

For the period of 1957–1968, the Buffett Partnership, LTD had an average annual return of 31.6%.

1970

The Buffett Partnership is now completely liquidated. Warren owns 29% of the outstanding stock of Berkshire Hathaway.

Berkshire begins buying the Washington Post.

1971

Berkshire purchases See's Candies, its biggest investment to date.

1973

By October, Berkshire is the Washington Post's largest outside shareholder.

1974

In a declining stock market, Buffett's personal wealth declines by over 50%.

1976

In April, Berkshire invests an additional $40 million in GEICO.

1977–1987

In 1977, Susie Buffett moved to San Francisco. She and Warren never divorced and remained close friends until her death in 2004. A year later, Astrid Menks and Warren began living together.

Three days before Black Monday, Berkshire traded at $3,890 only to decline to $3,170.

In 1983, Berkshire purchases 90% of the Nebraska Furniture Mart for $55 million.

1988–1989

By early 1989, Berkshire has acquired approximately 7% of Coca-Cola.

1990

Berkshire purchases additional Wells Fargo stock, increasing its percentage ownership to just under 10%.

1991–1992

Buffett serves as interim CEO and Chairman of Salomon Brothers after the firm's illegal bond trading scandal.

1993–2001

Berkshire acquisitions include:
- Helzberg's Diamond Shops
- R.C. Willey Home Furnishings
- Star Furniture

- Dairy Queen
- General Reinsurance
- NetJets

In 1995, Berkshire acquires remaining 50% of GEICO for $2.3 billion.

In 1995, Berkshire's net worth gained $5.3 billion, or 45.0%. Over the past 31 years, per-share book value has grown from $19 to $14,426, or at a rate of 23.6% compounded annually.

In 1996, Berkshire issued B shares (at one-thirtieth the price of the A shares) to discourage the formation of mutual funds for investors who could not afford the purchase of A shares.

In 2001, Berkshire incurred a $2.2 billion underwriting loss from the 9/11 attack on the World Trade Center.

2002–2007

Berkshire acquisitions include:

- Garan
- CTB International
- The Pampered Chef
- McLane Company
- Clayton Homes
- Burlington Industries
- Forest River, Inc.
- Business Wire
- Russell Corporation
- TTI, Inc.
- Boat America Corporation
- Jordan's Furniture
- Part interest in Mid American Energy Holdings Company
- Ben Bridge Jeweler
- Justin Brands
- Benjamin Moore
- John Manville
- MiTek Inc.

- XTRA
- Fruit of the Loom

2004

Susan Buffett dies of a stroke in Wyoming.

Bill Gates is elected a Director of Berkshire Hathaway.

2005

Berkshire's net worth increased by $5.6 billion, which increased the per-share book value of Berkshire stock by 6.4%. Insurance business did well despite estimated hurricane losses from Katrina of $2.5 billion and Rita and Wilma of an additional $9 billion.

2006

Warren announces donation (approximately $37 billion) of most of his wealth to the Bill and Melinda Gates Foundation and four other family foundations. It's the largest donation in U.S. history.

In his will, it is stipulated that the proceeds from all Berkshire shares owned at his death are to be used for philanthropic purposes within 10 years after his estate is enclosed.

On August 30, Warren's birthday, he marries Astrid Menks, his long-time companion.

2007

Buffett announces that a management succession plan has been approved by the Berkshire Board.

Berkshire acquires 60% of Marmon Holdings, Inc., formally owned by the Jay Pritzker family.

2008

Berkshire's net worth declined by $11.5 billion, which reduced the book value of Berkshire shares by 9.6%. Over the last 44 years, book value has grown from $19 to $70,530, a rate of 20.3% compounded annually.

Appendix B

Berkshire Hathaway Inc., An Owner's Manual, Owner-Related Business Principles, January 1999

In June 1996, Berkshire's Chairman, Warren E. Buffett, issued a booklet entitled "**An Owner's Manual**" to Berkshire's Class A and Class B shareholders. The purpose of the manual was to explain Berkshire's broad economic principles of operation. An updated version is reproduced on this and the following pages.

Owner-Related Business Principles

At the time of the Blue Chip merger in 1983, I set down 13 owner-related business principles that I thought would help new shareholders understand our managerial approach. As is appropriate for "principles," all 13 remain alive and well today, and they are stated here.

1. Although our form is corporate, our attitude is partnership. Charlie Munger and I think of our shareholders as owner-partners, and of ourselves as managing partners. (Because of the size of our shareholdings we are also, for better or worse, controlling partners.) We do not view the company itself as the ultimate owner of our business assets but instead view the company as a conduit through which our shareholders own the assets.

   Charlie and I hope that you do not think of yourself as merely owning a piece of paper whose price wiggles around daily and that is a candidate for sale when some economic or political event makes you nervous. We hope you instead visualize yourself as a part owner of a business that you expect to stay with indefinitely, much as you might if you owned a farm or apartment house in partnership with members of your family. For our part, we do not view Berkshire shareholders as faceless members of an ever-shifting crowd, but rather as co-venturers who have entrusted their funds to us for what may well turn out to be the remainder of their lives.

   The evidence suggests that most Berkshire shareholders have indeed embraced this long-term partnership concept. The annual percentage turnover in Berkshire's shares is a small fraction of that occurring in the stocks of other major American corporations, even when the shares I own are excluded from the calculation.

   In effect, our shareholders behave in respect to their Berkshire stock much as Berkshire itself behaves in respect to companies in which it has an investment. As owners of, say, Coca-Cola or American Express shares, we think of Berkshire as being a non-managing partner in two extraordinary businesses, in which we measure our success by the long-term progress of the companies rather than by the month-to-month movements of their stocks. In fact, we would not care in the least if several years went by in which there was no trading, or quotation of prices, in the stocks of those companies. If we have good long-term expectations, short-term price changes are meaningless for us except to the extent they offer us an opportunity to increase our ownership at an attractive price.

2. In line with Berkshire's owner-orientation, most of our directors have a major portion of their net worth invested in the company. We eat our own cooking.

Charlie's family has 90% or more of its net worth in Berkshire shares; I have about 99%. In addition, many of my relatives—my sisters and cousins, for example—keep a huge portion of their net worth in Berkshire stock.

Charlie and I feel totally comfortable with this eggs-in-one-basket situation because Berkshire itself owns a wide variety of truly extraordinary businesses. Indeed, we believe that Berkshire is close to being unique in the quality and diversity of the businesses in which it owns either a controlling interest or a minority interest of significance.

Charlie and I cannot promise you results. But we can guarantee that your financial fortunes will move in lockstep with ours for whatever period of time you elect to be our partner. We have no interest in large salaries or options or other means of gaining an "edge" over you. We want to make money only when our partners do and in exactly the same proportion. Moreover, when I do something dumb, I want you to be able to derive some solace from the fact that my financial suffering is proportional to yours.

3. Our long-term economic goal (subject to some qualifications mentioned later) is to maximize Berkshire's average annual rate of gain in intrinsic business value on a per-share basis. We do not measure the economic significance or performance of Berkshire by its size; we measure by per-share progress. We are certain that the rate of per-share progress will diminish in the future—a greatly enlarged capital base will see to that. But we will be disappointed if our rate does not exceed that of the average large American corporation.

4. Our preference would be to reach our goal by directly owning a diversified group of businesses that generate cash and consistently earn above-average returns on capital. Our second choice is to own parts of similar businesses, attained primarily through purchases of marketable common stocks by our insurance subsidiaries. The price and availability of businesses and the need for insurance capital determine any given year's capital allocation.

In recent years we have made a number of acquisitions. Though there will be dry years, we expect to make many more in the decades to come, and our hope is that they will be large. If these purchases approach the quality of those we have made in the past, Berkshire will be well served.

The challenge for us is to generate ideas as rapidly as we generate cash. In this respect, a depressed stock market is likely to present us with significant advantages. For one thing, it tends to reduce the prices at which entire companies become available for purchase. Second, a depressed market makes it easier for our insurance companies to buy small pieces of wonderful businesses—including additional pieces of businesses we already own—at attractive prices. And third, some of those same wonderful businesses, such as Coca-Cola, are consistent buyers of their own shares, which means that they, and we, gain from the cheaper prices at which they can buy.

Overall, Berkshire and its long-term shareholders benefit from a sinking stock market much as a regular purchaser of food benefits from declining food prices. So when the market plummets—as it will from time to time—neither panic nor mourn. It's good news for Berkshire.

5. Because of our two-pronged approach to business ownership and because of the limitations of conventional accounting, consolidated reported earnings may reveal relatively little about our true economic performance. Charlie and I, both as owners and managers, virtually ignore such consolidated numbers. However, we will also report to you the earnings of each major business we control, numbers we consider of great importance. These figures, along with other information we will supply about the individual businesses, should generally aid you in making judgments about them.

To state things simply, we try to give you in the annual report the numbers and other information that really matter. Charlie and I pay a great deal of attention to how well our businesses are doing, and we also work to understand the environment in which each business is operating. For example, is one of our businesses enjoying an industry tailwind or is it facing a headwind? Charlie and I need to know exactly which situation prevails and to adjust our expectations accordingly. We will also pass along our conclusions to you.

Over time, the large majority of our businesses have exceeded our expectations. But sometimes we have disappointments, and we will try to be as candid in informing you about those as we are in describing the happier experiences. When we use unconventional measures to chart our progress—for instance, you will be reading in our annual reports about insurance "float"—we will try to explain these concepts and why we regard them as important. In other words, we believe in telling you how we think so that you can evaluate not only Berkshire's businesses but also assess our approach to management and capital allocation.

6. Accounting consequences do not influence our operating or capital-allocation decisions. When acquisition costs are similar, we much prefer to purchase $2 of earnings that is not reportable by us under standard accounting principles than to purchase $1 of earnings that is reportable. This is precisely the choice that often faces us since entire businesses (whose earnings will be fully reportable) frequently sell for double the pro-rata price of small portions (whose earnings will be largely unreportable). In aggregate and over time, we expect the unreported earnings to be fully reflected in our intrinsic business value through capital gains.

We have found over time that the undistributed earnings of our investees, in aggregate, have been fully as beneficial to Berkshire as if they had been distributed to us (and therefore had been included in the earnings we officially report). This pleasant result has occurred because most of our investees are engaged in truly outstanding businesses that can often employ incremental capital to great advantage, either by putting it to work in their businesses or by repurchasing their shares. Obviously, every capital decision that our investees have made has not benefitted us as shareholders, but overall we have garnered far more than a dollar of value for each dollar they have retained. We consequently regard look-through earnings as realistically portraying our yearly gain from operations.

7. We use debt sparingly and, when we do borrow, we attempt to structure our loans on a long-term fixed-rate basis. We will reject

interesting opportunities rather than over-leverage our balance sheet. This conservatism has penalized our results but it is the only behavior that leaves us comfortable, considering our fiduciary obligations to policyholders, lenders and the many equity holders who have committed unusually large portions of their net worth to our care. (As one of the Indianapolis "500" winners said: "To finish first, you must first finish.")

The financial calculus that Charlie and I employ would never permit our trading a good night's sleep for a shot at a few extra percentage points of return. I've never believed in risking what my family and friends have and need in order to pursue what they don't have and don't need.

Besides, Berkshire has access to two low-cost, non-perilous sources of leverage that allow us to safely own far more assets than our equity capital alone would permit: deferred taxes and "float," the funds of others that our insurance business holds because it receives premiums before needing to pay out losses. Both of these funding sources have grown rapidly and now total about $68 billion.

Better yet, this funding to date has often been cost-free. Deferred tax liabilities bear no interest. And as long as we can break even in our insurance underwriting the cost of the float developed from that operation is zero. Neither item, of course, is equity; these are real liabilities. But they are liabilities without covenants or due dates attached to them. In effect, they give us the benefit of debt—an ability to have more assets working for us—but saddle us with none of its drawbacks.

Of course, there is no guarantee that we can obtain our float in the future at no cost. But we feel our chances of attaining that goal are as good as those of anyone in the insurance business. Not only have we reached the goal in the past (despite a number of important mistakes by your Chairman), our 1996 acquisition of GEICO materially improved our prospects for getting there in the future.

8. A managerial "wish list" will not be filled at shareholder expense. We will not diversify by purchasing entire businesses at control prices that ignore long-term economic consequences to our shareholders. We will only do with your money what we would do with our own,

weighing fully the values you can obtain by diversifying your own portfolios through direct purchases in the stock market.

Charlie and I are interested only in acquisitions that we believe will raise the per-share intrinsic value of Berkshire's stock. The size of our paychecks or our offices will never be related to the size of Berkshire's balance sheet.

9. We feel noble intentions should be checked periodically against results. We test the wisdom of retaining earnings by assessing whether retention, over time, delivers shareholders at least $1 of market value for each $1 retained. To date, this test has been met. We will continue to apply it on a five-year rolling basis. As our net worth grows, it is more difficult to use retained earnings wisely.

We continue to pass the test, but the challenges of doing so have grown more difficult. If we reach the point that we can't create extra value by retaining earnings, we will pay them out and let our shareholders deploy the funds.

10. We will issue common stock only when we receive as much in business value as we give. This rule applies to all forms of issuance—not only mergers or public stock offerings, but stock-for-debt swaps, stock options, and convertible securities as well. We will not sell small portions of your company—and that is what the issuance of shares amounts to—on a basis inconsistent with the value of the entire enterprise.

When we sold the Class B shares in 1996, we stated that Berkshire stock was not undervalued—and some people found that shocking. That reaction was not well-founded. Shock should have registered instead had we issued shares when our stock was undervalued. Managements that say or imply during a public offering that their stock is undervalued are usually being economical with the truth or uneconomical with their existing shareholders' money: Owners unfairly lose if their managers deliberately sell assets for 80¢ that in fact are worth $1. We didn't commit that kind of crime in our offering of Class B shares and we never will. (We did not, however, say at the time of the sale that our stock was overvalued, though many media have reported that we did.)

11. You should be fully aware of one attitude Charlie and I share that hurts our financial performance: Regardless of price, we have no interest at all in selling any good businesses that Berkshire owns. We are also very reluctant to sell sub-par businesses as long as we expect them to generate at least some cash and as long as we feel good about their managers and labor relations. We hope not to repeat the capital-allocation mistakes that led us into such sub-par businesses. And we react with great caution to suggestions that our poor businesses can be restored to satisfactory profitability by major capital expenditures. (The projections will be dazzling and the advocates sincere, but, in the end, major additional investment in a terrible industry usually is about as rewarding as struggling in quicksand.) Nevertheless, gin rummy managerial behavior (discard your least promising business at each turn) is not our style. We would rather have our overall results penalized a bit than engage in that kind of behavior.

   We continue to avoid gin rummy behavior. True, we closed our textile business in the mid–1980s after 20 years of struggling with it, but only because we felt it was doomed to run never-ending operating losses. We have not, however, given thought to selling operations that would command very fancy prices nor have we dumped our laggards, though we focus hard on curing the problems that cause them to lag.

12. We will be candid in our reporting to you, emphasizing the pluses and minuses important in appraising business value. Our guideline is to tell you the business facts that we would want to know if our positions were reversed. We owe you no less. Moreover, as a company with a major communications business, it would be inexcusable for us to apply lesser standards of accuracy, balance and incisiveness when reporting on ourselves than we would expect our news people to apply when reporting on others. We also believe candor benefits us as managers: The CEO who misleads others in public may eventually mislead himself in private.

   At Berkshire you will find no "big bath" accounting maneuvers or restructurings nor any "smoothing" of quarterly or annual results. We will always tell you how many strokes we have taken on each hole and never play around with the scorecard. When the numbers are a very rough "guesstimate," as they necessarily must be in insurance reserving, we will try to be both consistent and conservative in our approach.

We will be communicating with you in several ways. Through the annual report, I try to give all shareholders as much value-defining information as can be conveyed in a document kept to reasonable length. We also try to convey a liberal quantity of condensed but important information in the quarterly reports we post on the internet, though I don't write those (one recital a year is enough). Still another important occasion for communication is our Annual Meeting, at which Charlie and I are delighted to spend five hours or more answering questions about Berkshire. But there is one way we can't communicate: on a one-on-one basis. That isn't feasible given Berkshire's many thousands of owners.

In all of our communications, we try to make sure that no single shareholder gets an edge: We do not follow the usual practice of giving earnings "guidance" or other information of value to analysts or large shareholders. Our goal is to have all of our owners updated at the same time.

13. Despite our policy of candor, we will discuss our activities in marketable securities only to the extent legally required. Good investment ideas are rare, valuable and subject to competitive appropriation just as good product or business acquisition ideas are. Therefore we normally will not talk about our investment ideas. This ban extends even to securities we have sold (because we may purchase them again) and to stocks we are incorrectly rumored to be buying. If we deny those reports but say "no comment" on other occasions, the no-comments become confirmation.

Though we continue to be unwilling to talk about specific stocks, we freely discuss our business and investment philosophy. I benefitted enormously from the intellectual generosity of Ben Graham, the greatest teacher in the history of finance, and I believe it appropriate to pass along what I learned from him, even if that creates new and able investment competitors for Berkshire just as Ben's teachings did for him.

Two Added Principles

14. To the extent possible, we would like each Berkshire shareholder to record a gain or loss in market value during his period of ownership that is proportional to the gain or loss in per-share intrinsic value recorded by the company during that holding period. For this to come about, the relationship between the intrinsic value and the market price of a Berkshire share would need to remain constant, and by our preferences at 1-to-1. As that implies, we would rather see Berkshire's stock price at a fair level than a high level. Obviously, Charlie and I can't control Berkshire's price. But by our policies and communications, we can encourage informed, rational behavior by owners that, in turn, will tend to produce a stock price that is also rational. Our it's-as-bad-to-be-overvalued-as-to-be-undervalued approach may disappoint some shareholders. We believe, however, that it affords Berkshire the best prospect of attracting long-term investors who seek to profit from the progress of the company rather than from the investment mistakes of their partners.

15. We regularly compare the gain in Berkshire's per-share book value to the performance of the S&P 500. Over time, we hope to outpace this yardstick. Otherwise, why do our investors need us? The measurement, however, has certain shortcomings that are described in the next section. Moreover, it now is less meaningful on a year-to-year basis than was formerly the case. That is because our equity holdings, whose value tends to move with the S&P 500, are a far smaller portion of our net worth than they were in earlier years. Additionally, gains in the S&P stocks are counted in full in calculating that index, whereas gains in Berkshire's equity holdings are counted at 65% because of the federal tax we incur. We, therefore, expect to outperform the S&P in lackluster years for the stock market and underperform when the market has a strong year.

The Managing of Berkshire

I think it's appropriate that I conclude with a discussion of Berkshire's management, today and in the future. As our first owner-related principle tells you, Charlie and I are the managing partners of Berkshire. But we subcontract all of the heavy lifting in this business to the managers of our subsidiaries. In fact, we delegate almost to the point of abdication: Though Berkshire has about 246,000 employees, only 19 of these are at headquarters.

Charlie and I mainly attend to capital allocation and the care and feeding of our key managers. Most of these managers are happiest when they are left alone to run their businesses, and that is customarily just how we leave them. That puts them in charge of all operating decisions and of dispatching the excess cash they generate to headquarters. By sending it to us, they don't get diverted by the various enticements that would come their way were they responsible for deploying the cash their businesses throw off. Furthermore, Charlie and I are exposed to a much wider range of possibilities for investing these funds than any of our managers could find in his or her own industry.

Most of our managers are independently wealthy, and it's therefore up to us to create a climate that encourages them to choose working with Berkshire over golfing or fishing. This leaves us needing to treat them fairly and in the manner that we would wish to be treated if our positions were reversed.

As for the allocation of capital, that's an activity both Charlie and I enjoy and in which we have acquired some useful experience. In a general sense, grey hair doesn't hurt on this playing field: You don't need good hand-eye coordination or well-toned muscles to push money around (thank heavens). As long as our minds continue to function effectively, Charlie and I can keep on doing our jobs pretty much as we have in the past.

On my death, Berkshire's ownership picture will change but not in a disruptive way: None of my stock will have to be sold to take care of the cash bequests I have made or for taxes. Other assets of mine will take care of these requirements. All Berkshire shares will be left to foundations that will likely receive the stock in roughly equal installments over a dozen or so years.

At my death, the Buffett family will not be involved in managing the business but, as very substantial shareholders, will help in picking and overseeing the managers who do. Just who those managers will be, of course, depends on the date of my death. But I can anticipate what the management structure will be: Essentially my job will be split into two parts. One executive will become CEO and responsible for operations. The responsibility for investments will be given to one or more executives. If the acquisition of new businesses is in prospect, these executives will cooperate in making the decisions needed, subject, of course, to board approval. We will continue to have an extraordinarily shareholder-minded board, one whose interests are solidly aligned with yours.

Were we to need the management structure I have just described on an immediate basis, our directors know my recommendations for both posts. All candidates currently work for or are available to Berkshire and are people in whom I have total confidence.

I will continue to keep the directors posted on the succession issue. Since Berkshire stock will make up virtually my entire estate and will account for a similar portion of the assets of various foundations for a considerable period after my death, you can be sure that the directors and I have thought through the succession question carefully and that we are well prepared. You can be equally sure that the principles we have employed to date in running Berkshire will continue to guide the managers who succeed me and that our unusually strong and well-defined culture will remain intact.

Lest we end on a morbid note, I also want to assure you that I have never felt better. I love running Berkshire, and if enjoying life promotes longevity, Methuselah's record is in jeopardy.

Warren E. Buffett
Chairman

Appendix C

Berkshire Hathaway Inc., Code of Business Conduct and Ethics

A. Scope

This Code of Business Conduct and Ethics applies to all Berkshire Hathaway directors, officers and employees, as well as to directors, officers and employees of each subsidiary of Berkshire Hathaway. Such directors, officers and employees are referred to herein collectively as the "Covered Parties." Berkshire Hathaway and its subsidiaries are referred to herein collectively as the "Company."

B. Purpose

The Company is proud of the values with which it conducts business. It has and will continue to uphold the highest levels of business ethics and personal integrity in all types of transactions and interactions. To this end, this Code of Business Conduct and Ethics serves to (1) emphasize the Company's commitment to ethics and compliance with the law; (2) set forth basic standards of ethical and legal behavior; (3) provide reporting mechanisms for known or suspected ethical or legal violations; and (4) help prevent and detect wrongdoing.

Given the variety and complexity of ethical questions that may arise in the Company's course of business, this Code of Business Conduct and Ethics serves only as a rough guide. Confronted with ethically ambiguous situations, the Covered Parties should remember the Company's commitment to the highest ethical standards and seek advice from supervisors, managers or other appropriate personnel to ensure that all actions they take on behalf of the Company honor this commitment. When in doubt, remember Warren Buffett's rule of thumb:

> ". . . I want employees to ask themselves whether they are willing to have any contemplated act appear the next day on the front page of their local paper—to be read by their spouses, children and friends—with the reporting done by an informed and critical reporter."

C. Ethical Standards

1. Conflicts of Interest

A conflict of interest exists when a person's private interest interferes in any way with the interests of the Company. A conflict can arise when a Covered Party takes actions or has interests that may make it difficult to perform his or her work for the Company objectively and effectively. Conflicts of interest may also arise when a Covered Party, or members of his or her family, receives improper personal benefits as a result of his or her position at the Company. Loans to, or guarantees of obligations of, Covered Parties and their family members may create conflicts of interest. It is almost always a conflict of interest for a Covered Party to work simultaneously for a competitor, customer or supplier.

Conflicts of interest may not always be clear-cut, so if you have a question, you should consult with your supervisor or manager or, if circumstances warrant, the chief financial officer or chief legal officer of the Company. Any Covered Party who becomes aware of a conflict or potential conflict should bring it to the attention of a supervisor, manager or other appropriate personnel or consult the procedures described in Section E of this Code.

All directors and executive officers of the Company, and the chief executive officers and chief financial officers of Berkshire Hathaway's subsidiaries, shall disclose any material transaction or relationship that reasonably could be expected to give rise to such a conflict to the Chairman of the Company's Audit Committee. No action may be taken with respect to such transaction or party unless and until such action has been approved by the Audit Committee.

2. Corporate Opportunities

Covered Parties are prohibited from taking for themselves opportunities that are discovered through the use of corporate property, information or position without the consent of the Board of Directors of the Company. No Covered Party may use corporate property, information or position for improper personal gain and no employee may compete with the Company directly or indirectly. Covered Parties owe a duty to the Company to advance its legitimate interests whenever possible.

3. Fair Dealing

Covered Parties shall behave honestly and ethically at all times and with all people. They shall act in good faith, with due care, and shall engage only in fair and open competition, by treating ethically competitors, suppliers, customers, and colleagues. Stealing proprietary information, possessing trade secret information that was obtained without the owner's consent, or inducing such disclosures by past or present employees of other companies is prohibited. No Covered Party should take unfair advantage of anyone through manipulation, concealment, abuse of privileged information, misrepresentation of material facts, or any other unfair practice.

The purpose of business entertainment and gifts in a commercial setting is to create good will and sound working relationships, not to gain unfair advantage with customers. No gift or entertainment should ever be offered or accepted by a Covered Party or any family member of a Covered Party unless it (1) is consistent with customary business practices, (2) is not excessive in value, (3) cannot be construed as a bribe or payoff and (4) does not violate any laws or regulations. The offer or acceptance of cash gifts by any Covered Party is prohibited. Covered Parties should discuss with their supervisors, managers or other appropriate personnel any gifts or proposed gifts which they think may be inappropriate.

4. Insider Trading

Covered Parties who have access to confidential information are not permitted to use or share that information for stock trading purposes or for any other purpose except the conduct of the Company's business. All non-public information about the Company should be considered confidential information. It is always illegal to trade in Berkshire Hathaway securities while in possession of material, non-public information, and it is also illegal to communicate or "tip" such information to others.

5. Confidentiality

Covered Parties must maintain the confidentiality of confidential information entrusted to them, except when disclosure is authorized by an appropriate legal officer of the Company or required by laws or regulations. Confidential information includes all non-public information that might be of use to competitors or harmful to the Company or its customers if disclosed. It also includes information that suppliers and customers have entrusted to the Company. The obligation to preserve confidential information continues even after employment ends.

6. Protection and Proper Use of Company Assets

All Covered Parties should endeavor to protect the Company's assets and ensure their efficient use. Theft, carelessness, and waste have a direct impact on the Company's profitability. Any suspected incident of fraud or theft should be immediately reported for investigation. The Company's equipment should not be used for non-Company business, though incidental personal use is permitted.

The obligation of Covered Parties to protect the Company's assets includes its proprietary information. Proprietary information includes intellectual property such as trade secrets, patents, trademarks, and copyrights, as well as business, marketing and service plans, engineering and manufacturing ideas, designs, databases, records, salary information and any unpublished financial data and reports. Unauthorized use or distribution of this information would violate Company policy. It could also be illegal and result in civil or criminal penalties.

7. Compliance with Laws, Rules and Regulations

Obeying the law, both in letter and in spirit, is the foundation on which the Company's ethical standards are built. In conducting the business of the Company, the Covered Parties shall comply with applicable governmental laws, rules and regulations at all levels of government in the United States and in any non-U.S. jurisdiction in which the Company does business. Although not all Covered Parties are expected to know the details of these laws, it is important to know enough about the applicable local, state and national laws to determine when to seek advice from supervisors, managers or other appropriate personnel.

8. Timely and Truthful Public Disclosure

In reports and documents filed with or submitted to the Securities and Exchange Commission and other regulators by the Company, and in other public communications made by the Company, the Covered Parties involved in the preparation of such reports and documents (including those who are involved in the preparation of financial or other reports and the information included in such reports and documents) shall make disclosures that are full, fair, accurate, timely and understandable. Where applicable, these Covered Parties shall provide thorough and accurate financial and accounting data for inclusion in such disclosures. They shall not knowingly conceal or falsify information, misrepresent material facts or omit material facts necessary to avoid misleading the Company's independent public auditors or investors.

9. Significant Accounting Deficiencies

The CEO and each senior financial officer shall promptly bring to the attention of the Audit Committee any information he or she may have concerning (a) significant deficiencies in the design or operation of internal control over financial reporting which could adversely affect the Company's ability to record, process, summarize and report financial data or (b) any fraud, whether or not material, that involves management or other employees who have a significant role in the Company's financial reporting, disclosures or internal control over financial reporting.

D. Waivers

Any waiver of this Code for executive officers or directors may be made only by the Company's Board of Directors or its Audit Committee and will be promptly disclosed as required by law or stock exchange regulation.

E. Violations of Ethical Standards

1. Reporting Known or Suspected Violations

The Company's directors, CEO, senior financial officers and chief legal officer shall promptly report any known or suspected violations of this Code to the Chairman of the Company's Audit Committee. All other Covered Parties should talk to supervisors, managers or other appropriate personnel about known or suspected illegal or unethical behavior. These Covered Parties may also report questionable behavior in the same manner as they may report complaints regarding accounting, internal accounting controls or auditing matters by calling (anonymously, if desired) a third party organization called Global Compliance. No retaliatory action of any kind will be permitted against anyone making such a report in good faith, and the Company's Audit Committee will strictly enforce this prohibition.

2. Accountability for Violations

If the Company's Audit Committee or its designee determines that this Code has been violated, either directly, by failure to report a violation, or by withholding information related to a violation, the offending Covered Party may be disciplined for non-compliance with penalties up to and including removal from office or dismissal. Such penalties may include written notices to the individual involved that a violation has been determined, censure by the Audit Committee, demotion or re-assignment of the individual involved and suspension with or without pay or benefits. Violations of this Code may also constitute violations of law and may result in criminal penalties and civil liabilities for the offending Covered Party and the Company. All Covered Parties are expected to cooperate in internal investigations of misconduct.

F. Compliance Procedures

We must all work together to ensure prompt and consistent action against violations of this Code. In some situations, however, it is difficult to know if a violation has occurred. Because we cannot anticipate every situation that will arise, it is important that we have a way to approach a new question or problem. These are the steps to keep in mind:

- *Make sure you have all the facts.* In order to reach the right solutions, we must be as informed as possible.

- *Ask yourself: What specifically am I being asked to do? Does it seem unethical or improper?* Use your judgment and common sense. If something seems unethical or improper, it probably is.
- *Clarify your responsibility and role.* In most situations, there is shared responsibility. Are your colleagues informed? It may help to get others involved and discuss the problem.
- *Discuss the problem with your supervisor.* This is the basic guidance for all situations. In many cases, your supervisor will be more knowledgeable about the questions, and he or she will appreciate being consulted as part of the decision-making process.
- *Seek help from Company resources.* In rare cases where it would be inappropriate or uncomfortable to discuss an issue with your supervisor, or where you believe your supervisor has given you an inappropriate answer, discuss it locally with your office manager or your human resources manager.
- *You may report ethical violations in confidence without fear of retaliation.* If your situation requires that your identity be kept secret, your anonymity will be protected to the maximum extent consistent with the Company's legal obligations. The Company in all circumstances prohibits retaliation of any kind against those who report ethical violations in good faith.
- *Ask first, act later.* If you are unsure of what to do in any situation, seek guidance before you act.

Appendix D

July 23, 2008, Memo to Berkshire Hathaway Managers

BERKSHIRE HATHAWAY INC.
1440 KIEWIT PLAZA
OMAHA, NEBRASKA 68131
TELEPHONE (402) 346-1400
FAX (402) 346-0476

WARREN E. BUFFETT, CHAIRMAN

Memo

To: Berkshire Hathaway Managers ("The All-Stars")

cc: Berkshire Directors

From: Warren E. Buffett

Date: July 23, 2008

This is my biennial letter to reemphasize Berkshire's top priority and to get your help on succession planning.

The priority is that all of us continue to zealously guard Berkshire's reputation. We can't be perfect but we can try to be. As I've said in these memos for over 20 years: "We can afford to lose money – even a lot of money. But we can't afford to lose reputation – even a shred of reputation." We *must* continue to measure every act against not only what is legal but also what we would be happy to have written about on the front page of a national newspaper in an article written by an unfriendly but intelligent reporter.

Sometimes your associates will say "Everybody else is doing it." This rationale is almost always a bad one if it is the main justification for a business action. It is totally unacceptable when evaluating a moral decision. Whenever somebody offers that phrase as a rationale, in effect they are saying that they can't come up with a *good* reason. If anyone offers this explanation, tell them to try using it with a reporter or a judge and see how far it gets them.

If you see anything whose propriety or legality causes you to hesitate, be sure to give me a call. However, it's very likely that if a given course of action evokes hesitation *per se*, it's too close to the line and should be abandoned. There's plenty of money to be made in the center of the court. If it's questionable whether some action is close to the line, just assume it is outside and forget it.

As a corollary, let me know promptly if there's any significant bad news. I can handle bad news but I don't like to deal with it after it has festered for awhile. A reluctance to face up immediately to bad news is what turned a problem at Salomon from one that could have easily been disposed of into one that almost caused the demise of a firm with 8,000 employees.

In other respects, talk to me about what is going on as little or as much as you wish. Each of you does a first-class job of running your operation with your own individual style and you don't need me to help. The only items you need to clear with me are any changes in post-retirement benefits and any unusually large capital expenditures or acquisitions.

* * * * * * * * * * * *

I need your help in respect to the question of succession (*yours* not mine). I'm not looking for any of you to retire and I hope you all live to 100. (In Charlie's case, 110.) But just in case you don't, please send me a letter giving your recommendation as who should take over tomorrow if you should become incapacitated overnight. These letters will be seen by no one but me unless I'm no longer CEO, in which case my successor will need the information. Please summarize the strengths and weaknesses of your primary candidate as well as any possible alternates you may wish to include. Most of you have participated in this exercise in the past and others have offered your ideas verbally. However, it's important to me to get a periodic update, and now that we have added so many businesses, I need to have your thoughts in writing rather than trying to carry them around in my memory. Of course, there are a few operations that are run by two or more of you – such as the Blumkins, the Bridges, the pair at Applied Underwriters, etc. – and in these cases, just forget about this item. Your note can be short, informal, handwritten, etc. Just mark it "Personal for Warren."

Thanks for your help on all of this. And thanks for the way you run your businesses.

WEB/db

P.S. Another minor request: Please turn down all proposals for me to speak, make contributions, intercede with the Gates Foundation, etc. Sometimes these requests for you to act as intermediary will be accompanied by "It can't hurt to ask." It will be easier for both of us if you just say "no." As an added favor, don't suggest that they instead write or call me. Multiply 76 businesses by the periodic "I think he'll be interested in this one" and you can understand why it is better to say no firmly and immediately.

Appendix E

Berkshire Hathaway Inc., Corporate Governance Guidelines, as Amended on February 27, 2006

The Board of Directors has adopted the following guidelines to promote the effective governance of the Company. The Board will also review and amend these guidelines as it deems necessary or appropriate.

On behalf of the Company's shareholders, the Board is responsible for overseeing the management of the business and affairs of the Company. The Board acts as the ultimate decision-making body of the Company, except on those matters reserved to or shared with the shareholders of the Company under the laws of Delaware.

1. Director Qualifications

In choosing directors, the Company seeks individuals who have very substantial personal and family ownership stakes in the Company's stock. Such individuals must also have very high integrity, business savvy, shareholder orientation and a genuine interest in the Company. The Company is required to elect a majority of directors who are independent. All references to "independent directors" in these guidelines are to directors who are independent according to the criteria for independence established by Section 303A of the New York Stock Exchange Listed Company Manual. The Board does not have limits on the number of terms a director may serve. The Board does not have any retirement or tenure policies that would limit the ability of a director to be nominated for reelection. The Governance, Compensation and Nominating Committee is responsible for nominating directors for election or reelection.

2. Board Size and Committees

The Board presently has 11 members (2 management directors, 2 non-management but not independent directors and 7 independent directors). Under the By-Laws of the Company, the Board has the authority to change its size, and the Board will periodically review its size as appropriate. The Board has three committees: (i) Audit; (ii) Governance, Compensation and Nominating; and (iii) Executive. The Audit and Governance, Compensation and Nominating Committees each consist solely of independent directors. The Board may, from time to time, establish and maintain additional or different committees, as it deems necessary or appropriate.

3. Voting for Directors

Any nominee for director in an uncontested election (i.e., an election where the number of nominees is not greater than the number of directors to be elected) who receives a greater number of votes "withheld" from his or her election than votes "for" such election shall, promptly following certification of the shareholder vote, offer his or her resignation to the Board for consideration in accordance with the following procedures. All of these procedures shall be completed within 90 days following certification of the shareholder vote.

The Qualified Independent Directors (as defined below) shall evaluate the best interest of the Company and its shareholders and shall decide on behalf of the Board the action to be taken with respect to such offered resignation, which can include: (i) accepting the resignation, (ii) maintaining the director but addressing what the Qualified Independent Directors believe to be the underlying cause of the withhold votes, (iii) resolving that the director will not be re-nominated in the future for election, or (iv) rejecting the resignation.

In reaching their decision, the Qualified Independent Directors shall consider all factors they deem relevant, including: (i) any stated reasons why shareholders withheld votes from such director, (ii) any alternatives for curing the underlying cause of the withheld votes, (iii) the director's tenure, (iv) the director's qualifications, (v) the director's past and expected future contributions to the Company, and (vi) the overall composition of the Board, including whether accepting the resignation would cause the Company to fail to meet any applicable SEC or NYSE requirements.

Following the Board's determination, the Company shall promptly disclose publicly in a document furnished or filed with the SEC the Board's decision of whether or not to accept the resignation offer. The disclosure shall also include an explanation of how the decision was reached, including, if applicable, the reasons for rejecting the offered resignation.

A director who is required to offer his or her resignation in accordance with this Section 3 shall not be present during the deliberations or voting whether to accept his or her resignation or, except as otherwise provided below, a resignation offered by any other director in accordance with this Section 3. Prior to voting, the Qualified Independent Directors will afford the affected director an opportunity to provide any information or statement that he or she deems relevant.

For purposes of this Section 3, the term "Qualified Independent Directors" means:

(a) All directors who (1) are independent directors (as defined in accordance with the NYSE Corporate Governance Rules) and (2) are not required to offer their resignation in accordance with this Section 3.

(b) If there are fewer than three independent directors then serving on the Board who are not required to offer their resignations in accordance with this Section 3, then the Qualified Independent Directors shall mean all of the independent directors and each independent director who is required to offer his or her resignation in accordance with this Section 3 shall recuse himself or herself from the deliberations and voting only with respect to his or her individual offer to resign. The foregoing procedures will be summarized and disclosed each year in the proxy statement for the Company's annual meeting of shareholders.

4. Director Responsibilities

The basic responsibility of the directors is to exercise their business judgment to act in what they reasonably believe to be in the best interests of the Company and its shareholders, and to conduct themselves in accordance with their duties of care and loyalty. Directors are expected to attend Board meetings and meetings of the committees on which they serve, and to spend the time needed to carry out their responsibilities as directors, including meeting as frequently as necessary to properly discharge those responsibilities. Directors are also expected to review in advance all materials for the meetings of the Board and the Committee(s) on which they serve.

5. Director Access to Management and Advisors

Each director has full and free access to the officers and employees of the Company and its subsidiaries. The Board and each of its Committees has the authority to hire independent legal, financial or other advisors as it may deem to be necessary without consulting or obtaining the advance approval of any officer of the Company.

6. Board Meetings

The Chairman of the Board is responsible for establishing the agenda for each Board meeting. Each director is free to suggest items for inclusion on the agenda and to raise at any Board meeting subjects that are not on the agenda for that meeting. At least once a year, the Board reviews the Company's long-term plans and the principal issues that the Company will face in the future.

7. Executive Sessions

The non-management directors meet in regularly scheduled executive session (i.e., without directors who are members of management). The independent directors also meet in a separate executive session consisting solely of independent directors at least once a year. The presiding director at each executive session is chosen by the directors present at that meeting.

8. Director Compensation

Only directors who are neither an employee of the Company or a subsidiary nor a spouse of an employee receive compensation for serving on the Board. Director fees are nominal and are limited to immediate compensation. Changes in the form and amount of director compensation are determined by the full Board, taking into consideration the Company's policy that the fees should be of no consequence to any director serving the Company. The Board critically reviews any amounts that a director might receive directly or indirectly from the Company, as well as any charitable contributions the Company may make to organizations with which a director is affiliated, in determining whether a director is independent. The Company does not purchase directors and officers liability insurance for its directors or officers.

9. Orientation and Continuing Education

All new directors receive an orientation from the Chief Executive Officer and are expected to maintain the necessary level of expertise to perform his or her responsibilities as a director. The Company does not maintain any formal orientation or continuing education programs.

Appendix F

Intrinsic Value

Now let's focus on a term that I mentioned earlier and that you will encounter in future annual reports.

Intrinsic value is an all-important concept that offers the only logical approach to evaluating the relative attractiveness of investments and businesses. Intrinsic value can be defined simply: It is the discounted value of the cash that can be taken out of a business during its remaining life.

The calculation of intrinsic value, though, is not so simple. As our definition suggests, intrinsic value is an estimate rather than a precise figure, and it is additionally an estimate that must be changed if interest rates move or forecasts of future cash flows are revised. Two people looking at the same set of facts, moreover—and this would apply even to Charlie and me—will almost inevitably come up with at least slightly different intrinsic value figures. That is one reason we never give you our estimates of intrinsic value. What our annual reports do supply, though, are the facts that we ourselves use to calculate this value.

Meanwhile, we regularly report our per-share book value, an easily calculable number, though one of limited use. The limitations do not arise from our holdings of marketable securities, which are carried on our books at their current prices. Rather the inadequacies of book value have to do with the companies we control, whose values as stated on our books may be far different from their intrinsic values.

The disparity can go in either direction. For example, in 1964 we could state with certitude that Berkshire's per-share book value was $19.46. However, that figure considerably overstated the company's intrinsic value, since all of the company's resources were tied up in a sub-profitable textile business. Our textile assets had neither going-concern nor liquidation values equal to their carrying values. Today, however, Berkshire's situation is reversed: Now, our book value far understates Berkshire's intrinsic value, a point true because many of the businesses we control are worth much more than their carrying value.

Inadequate though they are in telling the story, we give you Berkshire's book-value figures because they today serve as a rough, albeit significantly understated, tracking measure for Berkshire's intrinsic value. In other words, the percentage change in book value in any given year is likely to be reasonably close to that year's change in intrinsic value.

You can gain some insight into the differences between book value and intrinsic value by looking at one form of investment, a college education. Think of the education's cost as its "book value." If this cost is to be accurate, it should include the earnings that were foregone by the student because he chose college rather than a job.

For this exercise, we will ignore the important non-economic benefits of an education and focus strictly on its economic value. First, we must estimate the earnings that the graduate will receive over his lifetime and subtract from that figure an estimate of what he would have earned had he lacked his education. That gives us an excess earnings figure, which must then be discounted, at an appropriate interest rate, back to graduation day. The dollar result equals the intrinsic economic value of the education.

Some graduates will find that the book value of their education exceeds its intrinsic value, which means that whoever paid for the education didn't get his money's worth. In other cases, the intrinsic value of an education will far exceed its book value, a result that proves capital was wisely deployed. In all cases, what is clear is that book value is meaningless as an indicator of intrinsic value.

■ ■ ■

What counts, however, is intrinsic value—the figure indicating what all of our constituent businesses are rationally worth. With perfect foresight, this number can be calculated by taking all future cash flows of a business—in and out—and discounting them at prevailing interest rates. So valued, all businesses, from manufacturers of buggy whips to operators of cellular phones, become economic equals.

Appendix G

The Superinvestors of Graham-and-Doddsville

by Warren E. Buffett

Editor's Note: This article is an edited transcript of a talk given at Columbia University in 1984 commemorating the fiftieth anniversary of *Security Analysis*, written by Benjamin Graham and David L. Dodd. This specialized volume first introduced the ideas later popularized in *The Intelligent Investor*. Buffett's essay offers a fascinating study of how Graham's disciples have used Graham's value investing approach to realize phenomenal success in the stock market.

If you have a high-speed Internet connection, you may prefer to read this version of the speech (a 1.6 MB .pdf file), which has all of the tables.

Note: The tables Buffett mentions are in *The Intelligent Investor*, but are not reproduced here. The Sequoia and Munger records are published here.

Is the Graham and Dodd "look for values with a significant margin of safety relative to prices" approach to security analysis out of date? Many of the professors who write textbooks today say yes. They argue that the stock market is efficient; that is, that stock prices reflect everything that is known about a company's prospects and about the state of the economy. There are no undervalued stocks, these theorists argue, because there are smart security analysts who utilize all available information to ensure unfailingly appropriate prices. Investors who seem to beat the market year after year are just lucky. "If prices fully reflect available information, this sort of investment adeptness is ruled out," writes one of today's textbook authors.

Well, maybe. But I want to present to you a group of investors who have, year in and year out, beaten the Standard & Poor's 500 stock index. The hypothesis that they do this by pure chance is at least worth examining. Crucial to this examination is the fact that these winners were all well known to me and pre-identified as superior investors, the most recent identification occurring over fifteen years ago. Absent this condition—that is, if I had just recently searched among thousands of records to select a few names for you this morning—I would advise you to stop reading right here. I should add that all of these records have been audited. And I should further add that I have known many of those who have invested with these managers, and the checks received by those participants over the years have matched the stated records.

Before we begin this examination, I would like you to imagine a national coin-flipping contest. Let's assume we get 225 million Americans up tomorrow morning and we ask them all to wager a dollar. They go out in the morning at sunrise, and they all call the flip of a coin. If they call correctly, they win a dollar from those who called wrong. Each day the losers drop out, and on the subsequent day the stakes build as all previous winnings are put on the line. After ten flips on ten mornings, there will be approximately 220,000 people in the United States who have correctly called ten flips in a row. They each will have won a little over $1,000.

Now this group will probably start getting a little puffed up about this, human nature being what it is. They may try to be modest, but at cocktail parties they will occasionally admit to attractive members of the opposite sex what their technique is, and what marvelous insights they bring to the field of flipping.

Assuming that the winners are getting the appropriate rewards from the losers, in another ten days we will have 215 people who have successfully called their coin flips 20 times in a row and who, by this exercise, each have turned one dollar into a little over $1 million. $225 million would have been lost, $225 million would have been won.

By then, this group will really lose their heads. They will probably write books on "How I Turned a Dollar into a Million in Twenty Days Working Thirty Seconds a Morning." Worse yet, they'll probably start jetting around the country attending seminars on efficient coin-flipping and tackling skeptical professors with, "If it can't be done, why are there 215 of us?"

By then some business school professor will probably be rude enough to bring up the fact that if 225 million orangutans had engaged in a similar exercise, the results would be much the same—215 egotistical orangutans with 20 straight winning flips.

I would argue, however, that there are some important differences in the examples I am going to present. For one thing, if (a) you had taken 225 million orangutans distributed roughly as the U.S. population is; if (b) 215 winners were left after 20 days; and if (c) you found that 40 came from a particular zoo in Omaha, you would be pretty sure you were on to something. So you would probably go out and ask the zookeeper about what he's feeding them, whether they had special exercises, what books they read, and who knows what else. That is, if you found any really extraordinary concentrations of success, you might want to see if you could identify concentrations of unusual characteristics that might be causal factors.

Scientific inquiry naturally follows such a pattern. If you were trying to analyze possible causes of a rare type of cancer—with, say, 1,500 cases a year in the United States—and you found that 400 of them occurred in some little mining town in Montana, you would get very interested in the water there, or the occupation of those afflicted, or other variables. You know it's not random chance that 400 come from a small area. You would not necessarily know the causal factors, but you would know where to search.

I submit to you that there are ways of defining an origin other than geography. In addition to geographical origins, there can be what I call an *intellectual* origin. I think you will find that a disproportionate number of successful coin-flippers in the investment world came from a very small intellectual village that could be called Graham-and-Doddsville. A concentration of winners that simply cannot be explained by chance can be traced to this particular intellectual village.

Conditions could exist that would make even that concentration unimportant. Perhaps 100 people were simply imitating the coin-flipping call of some terribly persuasive personality. When he called heads, 100 followers automatically called that coin the same way. If the leader was part of the 215 left at the end, the fact that 100 came from the same intellectual origin would mean nothing. You would simply be identifying one case as a hundred cases. Similarly, let's assume that you lived in a strongly patriarchal society and every family in the United States conveniently consisted of ten members. Further assume that the patriarchal culture was so strong that, when the 225 million people went out the first day, every member of the family identified with the father's call. Now, at the end of the 20-day period, you would have 215 winners, and you would find that they came from only 21.5 families. Some naive types might say that this indicates an enormous hereditary factor as an explanation of successful coin-flipping. But, of course, it would have no significance at all because it would simply mean that you didn't have 215 individual winners, but rather 21.5 randomly distributed families who were winners.

In this group of successful investors that I want to consider, there has been a common intellectual patriarch, Ben Graham. But the children who left the house of this intellectual patriarch have called their "flips" in very different ways. They have gone to different places and bought and sold different stocks and companies, yet they have had a combined record that simply cannot be explained by the fact that they are all calling flips identically because a leader is signaling the calls for them to make. The patriarch has merely set forth the intellectual theory for making coin-calling decisions, but each student has decided on his own manner of applying the theory.

The common intellectual theme of the investors from Graham-and-Doddsville is this: they search for discrepancies between the *value* of a business and the *price* of small pieces of that business in the market. Essentially, they exploit those discrepancies without the efficient market theorist's concern as to whether the stocks are bought on Monday or Thursday, or whether it is January or July, etc. Incidentally, when businessmen buy businesses, which is just what our Graham & Dodd investors are doing through the purchase of marketable stocks—I doubt that many are cranking into their purchase decision the day of the week or the month in which the transaction is going to occur. If it doesn't make any difference whether all of a business is being bought on a Monday or a Friday, I am baffled why academicians invest extensive time and effort to see whether it makes a difference when buying small pieces of those same businesses. Our Graham & Dodd investors, needless to say, do not discuss beta, the capital asset pricing model, or covariance in returns among securities. These are not subjects of any interest to them. In fact, most of them would have difficulty defining those terms. The investors simply focus on two variables: price and value.

I always find it extraordinary that so many studies are made of price and volume behavior, the stuff of chartists. Can you imagine buying an entire business simply because the price of the business had been marked *up* substantially last week and the week before? Of course, the reason a lot of studies are made of these price and volume variables is that now, in the age of computers, there are almost endless data available about them. It isn't necessarily because such studies have any utility; it's simply that the data are there and academicians have [worked] hard to learn the mathematical skills needed to manipulate them. Once these skills are acquired, it seems sinful not to use them, even if the usage has no utility or negative utility. As a friend said, to a man with a hammer, everything looks like a nail.

I think the group that we have identified by a common intellectual home is worthy of study. Incidentally, despite all the academic studies of the influence of such variables as price, volume, seasonality, capitalization size, etc., upon stock performance, no interest has been evidenced in studying the methods of this unusual concentration of value-oriented winners.

I begin this study of results by going back to a group of four of us who worked at Graham-Newman Corporation from 1954 through 1956. There were only four—I have not selected these names from among thousands. I offered to go to work at Graham-Newman for nothing after I took Ben Graham's class, but he turned me down as overvalued. He took this value stuff very seriously! After much pestering he finally hired me. There were three partners and four of us at the "peasant" level. All four left between 1955 and 1957 when the firm was wound up, and it's possible to trace the record of three.

The first example (see Table 1) is that of Walter Schloss. Walter never went to college, but took a course from Ben Graham at night at the New York Institute of Finance. Walter left Graham-Newman in 1955 and achieved the record shown here over 28 years. Here is what "Adam Smith"—after I told him about Walter—wrote about him in *Supermoney* (1972):

He has no connections or access to useful information. Practically no one in Wall Street knows him and he is not fed any ideas. He looks up the numbers in the manuals and sends for the annual reports, and that's about it.

In introducing me to (Schloss) Warren had also, to my mind, described himself. "He never forgets that he is handling other people's money, and this reinforces his normal strong aversion to loss." He has total integrity and a realistic picture of himself. Money is real to him and stocks are real—and from this flows an attraction to the "margin of safety" principle.

Walter has diversified enormously, owning well over 100 stocks currently. He knows how to identify securities that sell at considerably less than their value to a private owner. *And that's all he does.* He doesn't worry about whether it's January, he doesn't worry about whether it's Monday, he doesn't worry about whether it's an election year. He simply says, if a business is worth a dollar and I can buy it for 40 cents, something good may happen to me. And he does it over and over and over again. He owns many more stocks than I do—and is far less interested in the underlying nature of the business; I don't seem to have very much influence on Walter. That's one of his strengths; no one has much influence on him.

The second case is Tom Knapp, who also worked at Graham-Newman with me. Tom was a chemistry major at Princeton before the war; when he came back from the war, he was a beach bum. And then one day he read that Dave Dodd was giving a night course in investments at Columbia. Tom took it on a noncredit basis, and he got so interested in the subject from taking that course that he came up and enrolled at Columbia Business School, where he got the MBA degree. He took Dodd's course again, and took Ben Graham's course. Incidentally, 35 years later I called Tom to ascertain some of the facts involved here and I found him on the beach again. The only difference is that now he owns the beach!

In 1968, Tom Knapp and Ed Anderson, also a Graham disciple, along with one or two other fellows of similar persuasion, formed Tweedy, Browne Partners, and their investment results appear in Table 2. Tweedy, Browne built that record with very wide diversification. They occasionally bought control of businesses, but the record of the passive investments is equal to the record of the control investments.

Table 3 describes the third member of the group who formed Buffett Partnership in 1957. The best thing he did was to quit in 1969. Since then, in a sense, Berkshire Hathaway has been a continuation of the partnership in some respects. There is no single index I can give you that I would feel would be a fair test of investment management at Berkshire. But I think that any way you figure it, it has been satisfactory.

Table 4 shows the record of the Sequoia Fund, which is managed by a man whom I met in 1951 in Ben Graham's class, Bill Ruane. After getting out of Harvard Business School, he went to Wall Street. Then he realized that he needed to get a real business education so he came up to take Ben's course at Columbia, where we met in early 1951. Bill's record from 1951 to 1970, working with relatively small sums, was far better than average. When I wound up Buffett Partnership I asked Bill if he would set up a fund to handle all our partners, so he set up the Sequoia Fund. He set it up at a terrible time, just when I was quitting. He went right into the two-tier market and all the difficulties that made for comparative performance for value-oriented investors. I am happy to say that my partners, to an amazing degree, not only stayed with him but added money, with the happy result shown here.

There's no hindsight involved here. Bill was the only person I recommended to my partners, and I said at the time that if he achieved a four-point-per-annum advantage over the Standard & Poor's, that would be solid performance. Bill has achieved well over that, working with progressively larger sums of money. That makes things much more difficult. Size is the anchor of performance. There is no question about it. It doesn't mean you can't do better than average when you get larger, but the margin shrinks. And if you ever get so you're managing two trillion dollars, and that happens to be the amount of the total equity valuation in the economy, don't think that you'll do better than average!

I should add that in the records we've looked at so far, throughout this whole period there was practically no duplication in these portfolios. These are men who select securities based on discrepancies between price and value, but they make their selections very differently. Walter's largest holdings have been such stalwarts as Hudson Pulp & Paper and Jeddo Highland Coal and New York Trap Rock Company and all those other names that come instantly to mind to even a casual reader of the business pages. Tweedy Browne's selections have sunk even well below that level in terms of name recognition. On the other hand, Bill has worked with big companies. The overlap among these portfolios has been very, very low. These records do not reflect one guy calling the flip and fifty people yelling out the same thing after him.

Table 5 is the record of a friend of mine who is a Harvard Law graduate, who set up a major law firm. I ran into him in about 1960 and told him that law was fine as a hobby but he could do better. He set up a partnership quite the opposite of Walter's. His portfolio was concentrated in very few securities and therefore his record was much more volatile but it was based on the same discount-from-value approach. He was willing to accept greater peaks and valleys of performance, and he happens to be a fellow whose whole psyche goes toward concentration, with the results shown. Incidentally, this record belongs to Charlie Munger, my partner for a long time in the operation of Berkshire Hathaway. When he ran his partnership, however, his portfolio holdings were almost completely different from mine and the other fellows mentioned earlier.

Table 6 is the record of a fellow who was a pal of Charlie Munger's—another non-business school type—who was a math major at USC. He went to work for IBM after graduation and was an IBM salesman for a while. After I got to Charlie, Charlie got to him. This happens to be the record of Rick Guerin. Rick, from 1965 to 1983, against a compounded gain of 316 percent for the S&P, came off with 22,200 percent, which probably because he lacks a business school education, he regards as statistically significant.

One sidelight here: it is extraordinary to me that the idea of buying dollar bills for 40 cents takes immediately to people or it doesn't take at all. It's like an inoculation. If it doesn't grab a person right away, I find that you can talk to him for years and show him records, and it doesn't make any difference. They just don't seem able to grasp the concept, simple as it is. A fellow like Rick Guerin, who had no formal education in business, understands immediately the value approach to investing and he's applying it five minutes later. I've never seen anyone who became a gradual convert over a ten-year period to this approach. It doesn't seem to be a matter of IQ or academic training. It's instant recognition, or it is nothing.

Table 7 is the record of Stan Perlmeter. Stan was a liberal arts major at the University of Michigan who was a partner in the advertising agency of Bozell & Jacobs. We happened to be in the same building in Omaha. In 1965 he figured out I had a better business than he did, so he left advertising. Again, it took five minutes for Stan to embrace the value approach.

Perlmeter does not own what Walter Schloss owns. He does not own what Bill Ruane owns. These are records made *independently*. But every time Perlmeter buys a stock it's because he's getting more for his money than he's paying. That's the only thing he's thinking about. He's not looking at quarterly earnings projections, he's not looking at next year's earnings, he's not thinking about what day of the week it is, he doesn't care what investment research from any place says, he's not interested in price momentum, volume, or anything. He's simply asking: what is the business worth?

Table 8 and Table 9 are the records of two pension funds I've been involved in. They are not selected from dozens of pension funds with which I have had involvement; they are the only two I have influenced. In both cases I have steered them toward value-oriented managers. Very, very few pension funds are managed from a value standpoint. Table 8 is the Washington Post Company's Pension Fund. It was with a large bank some years ago, and I suggested that they would do well to select managers who had a value orientation.

As you can see, overall they have been in the top percentile ever since they made the change. The Post told the managers to keep at least 25 percent of these funds in bonds, which would not have been necessarily the choice of these managers. So I've included the bond performance simply to illustrate that this group has no particular expertise about bonds. They wouldn't have said they did. Even with this drag of 25 percent of their fund in an area that was not their game, they were in the top percentile of fund management. The Washington Post experience does not cover a terribly long period but it does represent many investment decisions by three managers who were not identified retroactively.

Table 9 is the record of the FMC Corporation fund. I don't manage a dime of it myself but I did, in 1974, influence their decision to select value-oriented managers. Prior to that time they had selected managers much the same way as most larger companies. They now rank number one in the Becker survey of pension funds for their size over the period of time subsequent to this "conversion" to the value approach. Last year they had eight equity managers of any duration beyond a year. Seven of them had a cumulative record better than the S&P. The net difference now between a median performance and the actual performance of the FMC fund over this period is $243 million. FMC attributes this to the mindset given to them about the selection of managers. Those managers are not the managers I would necessarily select but they have the common denominators of selecting securities based on value.

So these are nine records of "coin-flippers" from Graham-and-Doddsville. I haven't selected them with hindsight from among thousands. It's not like I am reciting to you the names of a bunch of lottery winners—people I had never heard of before they won the lottery. I selected these men years ago based upon their framework for investment decision-making. I knew what they had been taught and additionally I had some personal knowledge of their intellect, character, and temperament. It's very important to understand that this group has assumed far less risk than average; note their record in years when the general market was weak. While they differ greatly in style, these investors are, mentally, *always buying the business, not buying the stock.* A few of them sometimes buy whole businesses. Far more often they simply buy small pieces of businesses. Their attitude, whether buying all or a tiny piece of a business, is the same. Some of them hold portfolios with dozens of stocks; others concentrate on a handful. But all exploit the difference between the market price of a business and its intrinsic value.

I'm convinced that there is much inefficiency in the market. These Graham-and-Doddsville investors have successfully exploited gaps between price and value. When the price of a stock can be influenced by a "herd" on Wall Street with prices set at the margin by the most emotional person, or the greediest person, or the most depressed person, it is hard to argue that the market always prices rationally. In fact, market prices are frequently nonsensical.

I would like to say one important thing about risk and reward. Sometimes risk and reward are correlated in a positive fashion. If someone were to say to me, "I have here a six-shooter and I have slipped one cartridge into it. Why don't you just spin it and pull it once? If you survive, I will give you $1 million." I would decline—perhaps stating that $1 million is not enough. Then he might offer me $5 million to pull the trigger twice—now that would be a positive correlation between risk and reward!

The exact opposite is true with value investing. If you buy a dollar bill for 60 cents, it's riskier than if you buy a dollar bill for 40 cents, but the expectation of reward is greater in the latter case. The greater the potential for reward in the value portfolio, the less risk there is.

One quick example: The Washington Post Company in 1973 was selling for $80 million in the market. At the time, that day, you could have sold the assets to any one of ten buyers for not less than $400 million, probably appreciably more. The company owned the *Post*, *Newsweek*, plus several television stations in major markets. Those same properties are worth $2 billion now, so the person who would have paid $400 million would not have been crazy.

Now, if the stock had declined even further to a price that made the valuation $40 million instead of $80 million, its beta would have been greater. And to people that think beta measures risk, the cheaper price would have made it look riskier. This is truly Alice in Wonderland. I have never been able to figure out why it's riskier to buy $400 million worth of properties for $40 million than $80 million. And, as a matter of fact, if you buy a group of such securities and you know anything at all about business valuation, there is essentially no risk in buying $400 million for $80 million, particularly if you do it by buying ten $40 million piles of $8 million each. Since you don't have your hands on the $400 million, you want to be sure you are in with honest and reasonably competent people, but that's not a difficult job.

You also have to have the knowledge to enable you to make a very general estimate about the value of the underlying businesses. But you do not cut it close. That is what Ben Graham meant by having a margin of safety. You don't try and buy businesses worth $83 million for $80 million. You leave yourself an enormous margin. When you build a bridge, you insist it can carry 30,000 pounds, but you only drive 10,000 pound trucks across it. And that same principle works in investing.

In conclusion, some of the more commercially minded among you may wonder why I am writing this article. Adding many converts to the value approach will perforce narrow the spreads between price and value. I can only tell you that the secret has been out for 50 years, ever since Ben Graham and Dave Dodd wrote *Security Analysis*, yet I have seen no trend toward value investing in the 35 years that I've practiced it. There seems to be some perverse human characteristic that likes to make easy things difficult. The academic world, if anything, has actually backed away from the teaching of value investing over the last 30 years.

It's likely to continue that way. Ships will sail around the world but the Flat Earth Society will flourish. There will continue to be wide discrepancies between price and value in the marketplace, and those who read their Graham & Dodd will continue to prosper.

Tables 1–9 follow: [Note: The tables Buffett mentions are in *The Intelligent Investor*, but are not reproduced here. The Sequoia and Munger records are published here.]

If you have a high-speed Internet connection, you may prefer to read this version of the speech (a 1.6 MB .pdf file), which has all of the tables.

Appendix H

Berkshire's Corporate Performance versus the S&P 500

Annual Percentage Change

Year	In Per-Share Book Value of Berkshire (1)	In S&P 500 with Dividends Berkshire (2)	Relative Results (3)
1965	23.8	10.0	13.8
1966	20.3	(11.7)	32.0
1967	11.0	30.9	(19.9)
1968	19.0	11.0	8.0
1969	16.2	(8.4)	24.6
1970	12.0	3.9	8.1
1971	16.4	14.6	1.8
1972	21.7	18.9	2.8

(Continued)

237

Annual Percentage Change *(Continued)*

Year	In Per-Share Book Value of Berkshire (1)	In S&P 500 with Dividends Berkshire (2)	Relative Results (3)
1973	4.7	(14.8)	19.5
1974	5.5	(26.4)	31.9
1975	21.9	37.2	(15.3)
1976	59.3	23.6	35.7
1977	31.9	(7.4)	39.3
1978	24.0	6.4	17.6
1979	35.7	18.2	17.5
1980	19.3	32.3	(13.0)
1981	31.4	(5.0)	36.4
1982	40.0	21.4	18.6
1983	32.3	22.4	9.9
1984	13.6	6.1	7.5
1985	48.2	31.6	16.6
1986	26.1	18.6	7.5
1987	19.5	5.1	14.4
1988	20.1	16.6	3.5
1989	44.4	31.7	12.7
1990	7.4	(3.1)	10.5
1991	39.6	30.5	9.1
1992	20.3	7.6	12.7
1993	14.3	10.1	4.2
1994	13.9	1.31	2.6
1995	43.1	37.6	5.5
1996	31.8	23.0	8.8
1997	34.1	33.4	.7

Annual Percentage Change *(Continued)*

Year	In Per-Share Book Value of Berkshire (1)	In S&P 500 with Dividends Berkshire (2)	Relative Results (3)
1998	48.3	28.6	19.7
1999	.52	1.0	(20.5)
2000	6.5	(9.1)	15.6
2001	(6.2)	(11.9)	5.7
2002	10.0	(22.1)	32.1
2003	21.0	28.7	(7.7)
2004	10.5	10.9	(.4)
2005	6.4	4.9	1.5
2006	18.4	15.8	2.6
2007	11.0	5.5	5.5
2008	(9.6)	(37.0)	27.4
Compounded Annual Gain—1965–2008	8.9%	11.4%	20.3%
Overall Gain—1964–2008	4,276%		
	362,319%		

NOTES: Data are for calendar years with these exceptions: 1965 and 1966, year ended 9/30; 1967, 15 months ended 12/31.

Starting in 1979, accounting rules required insurance companies to value the equity securities they hold at market rather than at the lower of cost or market, which was previously the requirement. In this table, Berkshire's results through 1978 have been restated to conform to the changed rules. In all other respects, the results are calculated using the numbers originally reported.

The S&P 500 numbers are **pre-tax** whereas the Berkshire numbers are **after-tax**. If a corporation such as Berkshire were simply to have owned the S&P 500 and accrued the appropriate taxes, its results would have lagged the S&P 500 in years when that index showed a positive return, but would have exceeded the S&P 500 in years when the index showed a negative return. Over the year, the tax costs would have caused the aggregate lag to be substantial.

Appendix I

Berkshire Hathaway Common Stock

Year-End Stock Prices

Year	A Shares	B Shares
1965	12	
1966	17	
1967	20	
1968	37	
1969	42	
1970	39	
1971	70	
1972	80	
1973	71	
1974	40	
1975	38	
1976	89	

(Continued)

Year-End Stock Prices *(Continued)*

Year	A Shares	B Shares
1977	138	
1978	157	
1979	320	
1980	425	
1981	560	
1982	775	
1983	1,310	
1984	1,275	
1985	2,470	
1986	2,820	
1987	2,950	
1988	4,700	
1989	8,675	
1990	6,675	
1991	9,050	
1992	11,750	
1993	16,325	
1994	20,400	
1995	32,100	
1996	34,100	1,112
1997	46,000	1,539
1998	70,000	2,350
1999	56,100	1,830
2000	71,000	2,354
2001	75,600	2,525
2002	72,750	2,423
2003	84,250	2,815
2004	87,900	2,936
2005	88,620	2,936
2006	109,990	3,666
2007	141,600	4,736
2008	96,600	3,214

Notes

Contents

1. "Owner Related Business Principles," *Berkshire Hathaway Inc. Owner's Manual* (1996).

2. Roger Lowenstein, *Buffett: The Making of an American Capitalist* (New York: Random House, 1995), 111.

3. Warren Buffett, letter to shareholders, Berkshire Hathaway Annual Report (2004), 23.

4. Warren Buffett, letter to shareholders, Berkshire Hathaway Annual Report (1988), 13.

5. Warren Buffett, letter to shareholders, Berkshire Hathaway Annual Report (2004), 4.

6. Warren Buffett, letter to shareholders, Berkshire Hathaway Annual Report (1984), 6.

7. Warren Buffett, "The Security I Like Best," *The Commercial and Financial Chronicle* (December 6, 1951).

8. Warren Buffett, letter to shareholders, Berkshire Hathaway Annual Report (2005), 10.

9. Warren Buffett, letter to shareholders, Berkshire Hathaway Annual Report (2006), 8.

10. Warren Buffett, letter to shareholders, Berkshire Hathaway Annual Report (2006), 19.

11. "In His Own Words—Conversation with Charlie Rose," PBS, May 2, 2004.

12. Roger Lowenstein, *Buffett: The Making of an American Capitalist* (New York: Random House, 1995), 389.

13. Carol J. Loomis, "The Inside Story of Warren Buffett," *Fortune* (April 11, 1968).

14. Warren Buffett, letter to shareholders, Berkshire Hathaway Annual Report (1994), 7.

15. "In His Own Words—Conversation with Charlie Rose," PBS (May 2, 2004).

16. Warren Buffett, letter to shareholders, Berkshire Hathaway Annual Report (1996), 13.

17. "In His Own Words—Conversation with Charlie Rose," PBS (May 2, 2004).

18. Warren Buffett, letter to Shareholders, Berkshire Hathaway Annual Report (1993), 16.

Introduction

1. Warren Buffett, letter to shareholders, Berkshire Hathaway Annual Report (1987), 22.

2. Carol J. Loomis, "Buffett's Big Bet," *Fortune* (June 9, 2008).

3. Carol J. Loomis, "The Inside Story of Warren Buffett," *Fortune* (April 11, 1968).

4. "In His Own Words—Conversation with Charlie Rose," PBS (May 2, 2004).

Chapter 1   Shareholders as Partners

1. "Owner-Related Business Principles," *Berkshire Hathaway Inc. Owner's Manual* (1996).

2. Warren Buffett, letter to shareholders, Berkshire Hathaway Annual Report (2002), 21.

3. "Owner-Related Business Principles," *Berkshire Hathaway Inc. Owner's Manual* (1996).

4. Warren Buffett, letter to shareholders, Berkshire Hathaway Annual Report (1993), 19.

5. Warren Buffett, letter to shareholders, Berkshire Hathaway Annual Report (1994), 2.

6. Warren Buffett, letter to shareholders, Berkshire Hathaway Annual Report (1996), 2.

Chapter 2   Corporate Culture

1. Charles T. Munger, *Poor Charlie's Almanack: The Wit and Wisdom of Charles T. Munger*, ed. Peter D. Kaufman (Virginia Beach, VA: Donning Company Publishers, 2005).

2. Warren Buffett, Berkshire Hathaway memo to managers (July 23, 2008).

3. "In His Own Words—Conversation with Charlie Rose," PBS (May 2, 2004).

4. Warren Buffett, letter to shareholders, Berkshire Hathaway Annual Report (2008), 7.

5. Warren Buffett, letter to shareholders, Berkshire Hathaway Annual Report (2003), 3.

6. Warren Buffett, letter to shareholders, Berkshire Hathaway Annual Report (1998), 7.

7. Warren Buffett, letter to shareholders, Berkshire Hathaway Annual Report (2000), 7.

8. "Ask Warren," CNBC Squawk Box Program (March 3, 2008).

9. *Warren Buffett: Woodstock for Capitalists*, DVD, produced and directed by Ian Darling.

10. Warren Buffett, letter to shareholders, Berkshire Hathaway Annual Report (1991), 10.

11. Warren Buffett, letter to shareholders, Berkshire Hathaway Annual Report (2005), 6.

12. Warren Buffett, Berkshire Hathaway memo to managers (July 23, 2008).

13. Charles T. Munger, *Poor Charlie's Almanack: The Wit and Wisdom of Charles T. Munger*, ed. Peter D Kaufman (Virginia Beach, VA: Donning Company Publishers, 2005).

14. Warren Buffett, letter to shareholders, Berkshire Hathaway Annual Report, (1990), Appendix B.

Chapter 3   Corporate Governance

1. Warren Buffett, letter to shareholders, Berkshire Hathaway Annual Report (1993), 17.

2. Warren Buffett, letter to shareholders, Berkshire Hathaway Annual Report (2003), 9.

3. Warren Buffett, letter to shareholders, Berkshire Hathaway Annual Report (2002), 16.

4. Warren Buffett, letter to shareholders, Berkshire Hathaway Annual Report (2002,) 17.

5. Warren Buffett, letter to shareholders, Berkshire Hathaway Annual Report (2002), 18.

6. Warren Buffett, letter to shareholders, Berkshire Hathaway Annual Report (2004), 23.

7. Warren Buffett, letter to shareholders, Berkshire Hathaway Annual Report (2005), 21.

8. Warren Buffett, letter to shareholders, Berkshire Hathaway Annual Report (2006), 18.

9. Warren Buffett, letter to shareholders, Berkshire Hathaway Annual Report (2003), 10.

10. Warren Buffett, letter to shareholders, Berkshire Hathaway Annual Report (2004), 22.

11. Warren Buffett, letter to shareholders, Berkshire Hathaway Annual Report (2002), 18.

12. Warren Buffett, letter to shareholders, Berkshire Hathaway Annual Report (2002), 19.

Chapter 4   Berkshire Managers

1. Warren Buffett, letter to shareholders, Berkshire Hathaway Annual Report (1987), 5.

2. "In His Own Words—Conversation with Charlie Rose," PBS (May 2, 2004).

3. Warren Buffett, letter to shareholders, Berkshire Hathaway Annual Report (1986), 2.

4. Warren Buffett, letter to shareholders, Berkshire Hathaway Annual Report (1986), 2.

5. Warren Buffett, letter to shareholders, Berkshire Hathaway Annual Report (2002), 4.

6. Warren Buffett, letter to shareholders, Berkshire Hathaway Annual Report (1986), 1.

7. Warren Buffett, letter to shareholders, Berkshire Hathaway Annual Report (1995), 5.

8. Warren Buffett, letter to shareholders, Berkshire Hathaway Annual Report (2006), 7.

9. "In His Own Words—Conversation with Charlie Rose," PBS (May 2, 2004).

10. "Ask Warren," CNBC Squawk Box Program (March 3, 2008).

11. Warren Buffett, letter to shareholders, Berkshire Hathaway Annual Report (1986), 2.

12. Warren Buffett, letter to shareholders, Berkshire Hathaway Annual Report (1999), 5.

Chapter 5   Communication

1. "Owner-Related Business Principles," *Berkshire Hathaway Inc. Owner's Manual* (1996).

2. *Warren Buffett, Woodstock for Capitalists*, DVD, produced and directed by Ian Darling.

3. Warren Buffett, letter to shareholders, Berkshire Hathaway Annual Report (2000), 17.

4. Warren Buffett, letter to shareholders, Berkshire Hathaway Annual Report (1979), 11.

5. Charles T. Munger, *Poor Charlie's Almanack: The Wit and Wisdom of Charles T. Munger*, ed. Peter D Kaufman (Virginia Beach, VA: Donning Company Publishers, 2005), 90.

6. Warren Buffett, letter to shareholders, Berkshire Hathaway Annual Report (1987), 1.

7. Warren Buffett, letter to shareholders, Berkshire Hathaway Annual Report (2000), 11.

8. Warren Buffett, letter to shareholders, Berkshire Hathaway Annual Report (2000), 19.

9. Warren Buffett, letter to shareholders, Berkshire Hathaway Annual Report (2000), 18.

10. Warren Buffett, letter to shareholders, Berkshire Hathaway Annual Report (1979), 11.

11. Warren Buffett, letter to shareholders, Berkshire Hathaway Annual Report (2002), 3.

12. Warren Buffett, letter to shareholders, Berkshire Hathaway Annual Report (2002), 21.

13. "Owner-Related Business Principles," *Berkshire Hathaway Inc. Owner's Manual* (1996).

14. Warren Buffett, letter to shareholders, Berkshire Hathaway Annual Report (2004), 4.

15. Warren Buffett, letter to shareholders, Berkshire Hathaway Annual Report (1984), 3.

16. Warren Buffett, letter to shareholders, Berkshire Hathaway Annual Report (1995), 19.

17. Warren Buffett, letter to shareholders, Berkshire Hathaway Annual Report (2006), 24.

18. Warren Buffett, letter to shareholders, Berkshire Hathaway Annual Report (1990), 20.

19. Warren Buffett, letter to shareholders, Berkshire Hathaway Annual Report (1991), 19.

20. "In His Own Words—Coversation with Charlie Rose," PBS (May 2, 2004).

Chapter 6   Acquisition of Nebraska Furniture Mart

1. Warren Buffett, letter to shareholders, Berkshire Hathaway Annual Report (1984), 6.

2. Warren Buffett, letter to shareholders, Berkshire Hathaway Annual Report (1983), 4.

3. "In His Own Words—Conversation with Charlie Rose," PBS (May 2, 2004).

4. Warren Buffett, letter to shareholders, Berkshire Hathaway Annual Report (1983), 3.

5. Warren Buffett, letter to shareholders, Berkshire Hathaway Annual Report (1984), 5.

6. Warren Buffett, letter to shareholders, Berkshire Hathaway Annual Report (1986), 6.

7. Warren Buffett, letter to shareholders, Berkshire Hathaway Annual Report (1987), 5.

8. Warren Buffett, letter to shareholders, Berkshire Hathaway Annual Report (1988), 25.

9. Warren Buffett, letter to shareholders, Berkshire Hathaway Annual Report (1992), 19.

10. Warren Buffett, letter to shareholders, Berkshire Hathaway Annual Report (1984), 6.

11. Warren Buffett, letter to shareholders, Berkshire Hathaway Annual Report (1992), 19.

12. Warren Buffett, letter to shareholders, Berkshire Hathaway Annual Report (2003), 19.

Chapter 7   Acquisition of GEICO

1. "In His Own Words—Conversation with Charlie Rose," PBS (May 2, 2004).

2. "In His Own Words—Conversation with Charlie Rose," PBS (May 2, 2004).

3. Warren Buffett, letter to shareholders, Berkshire Hathaway Annual Report (1995), 5.

4. Warren Buffett, letter to shareholders, Berkshire Hathaway Annual Report (1998), 7.

Chapter 8   Acquisition of General Reinsurance

1. Warren Buffett, letter to shareholders, Berkshire Hathaway Annual Report (2002), 21.

2. Warren Buffett, letter to shareholders, Berkshire Hathaway Annual Report (2002), 8.

3. Warren Buffett, letter to shareholders, Berkshire Hathaway Annual Report (2003), 12.

4. Warren Buffett, letter to shareholders, Berkshire Hathaway Annual Report (2003), 15.

5. Warren Buffett, letter to shareholders, Berkshire Hathaway Annual Report (2003), 15.

6. Warren Buffett, letter to shareholders, Berkshire Hathaway Annual Report (2004), 11.

7. Warren Buffett, letter to shareholders, Berkshire Hathaway Annual Report (2005), 10.

8. Warren Buffett, letter to shareholders, Berkshire Hathaway Annual Report (2006), 14.

9. Warren Buffett, letter to shareholders, Berkshire Hathaway Annual Report (2008), 16.

10. Warren Buffett, letter to shareholders, Berkshire Hathaway Annual Report (2002), 13.

Chapter 9   The Assessment and Management of Risk

1. Warren Buffett, letter to shareholders, Berkshire Hathaway Annual Report (2003), 21.

2. Warren Buffett, letter to shareholders, Berkshire Hathaway Annual Report (2001), 7.

3. Warren Buffett, letter to shareholders, Berkshire Hathaway Annual Report (1996), 5.

4. Warren Buffett, letter to shareholders, Berkshire Hathaway Annual Report (1996), 6.

5. Warren Buffett, letter to shareholders, Berkshire Hathaway Annual Report (2001), 9.

6. Warren Buffett, letter to shareholders, Berkshire Hathaway Annual Report (2002), 10.

7. Warren Buffett, letter to shareholders, Berkshire Hathaway Annual Report (2004), 10.

8. Warren Buffett, letter to shareholders, Berkshire Hathaway Annual Report (2005), 7.

9. Warren Buffett, letter to shareholders, Berkshire Hathaway Annual Report (2006), 8.

10. Warren Buffett, letter to shareholders, Berkshire Hathaway Annual Report (2003), 21.

Chapter 10   Executive Compensation

1. Warren Buffett, letter to shareholders, Berkshire Hathaway Annual Report (2002), 18.

2. Warren Buffett, letter to shareholders, Berkshire Hathaway Annual Report (2006), 19.

3. Warren Buffett, letter to shareholders, Berkshire Hathaway Annual Report (2005), 17.

4. Warren Buffett, letter to shareholders, Berkshire Hathaway Annual Report (2006), 19.

5. Warren Buffett, letter to shareholders, Berkshire Hathaway Annual Report (1999), 8.

6. Warren Buffett, letter to shareholders, Berkshire Hathaway Annual Report (1994), 8.

7. Warren Buffett, letter to shareholders, Berkshire Hathaway Annual Report (1985), 13.

8. Warren Buffett, letter to shareholders, Berkshire Hathaway Annual Report (2003), 7.

9. Warren Buffett, letter to shareholders, Berkshire Hathaway Annual Report (2005), 16.

10. Warren Buffett, letter to shareholders, Berkshire Hathaway Annual Report (1985), 13.

Chapter 11   Time Management

1. "The World According to 'Poor Charlie,'" *Kiplinger Magazine* (December, 2005).

2. "In His Own Words—Conversation with Charlie Rose," PBS (May 2, 2004).

3. Ibid.

4. Janet Lowe, *Warren Buffett Speaks: Wit and Wisdom from the World's Greatest Investor* (Hoboken, NJ: John Wiley & Sons, 2007), 95.

5. Ibid.

6. Janet Lowe, *Damn Right! Behind the Scenes with Berkshire Hathaway Billionaire Charlie Munger* (New York: John Wiley & Sons, 2000), 239.

7. Roger Lowenstein, *Buffett: The Making of an American Capitalist* (New York: Random House, 1995), 276.

8. Janet Lowe, *Warren Buffett Speaks: Wit and Wisdom from the World's Greatest Investor* (Hoboken, NJ: John Wiley & Sons, 2007), 97.

Chapter 12   How to Manage a Crisis

1. Carol J. Loomis, "Warren Buffett's Wild Ride at Solomon," *Fortune* (October 27, 1997).

2. Ibid.

3. Roger Lowenstein, *Buffett: The Making of an American Capitalist* (New York: Random House, 1995), 390.

4. Ibid, 397.

5. Ibid, 395.

6. Roger Lowenstein, *Buffett: The Making of an American Capitalist* (New York: Random House, 1995), 395.

7. Janet Lowe, *Damn Right!: Behind the Scenes with Berkshire Hathaway Billionaire Charlie Munger* (New York: John Wiley & Sons, 2000), 195.

8. Ibid.

9. Roger Lowenstein, *Buffett: The Making of an American Capitalist* (New York: Random House, 1995), 408.

10. Warren Buffett, letter to shareholders, Berkshire Hathaway Annual Report (1991), 1.

11. Warren Buffett, Letter and Report to the Shareholders of Solomon, Third Quarter (1991).

12. Warren Buffett, letter to shareholders, Berkshire Hathaway Annual Report (1992), 3.

13. Warren Buffett, letter to shareholders, Berkshire Hathaway Annual Report (1997), 15.

14. Warren Buffett, letter to shareholders, Berkshire Hathaway Annual Report (1997), 16.

15. Janet Lowe, *Damn Right!: Behind the Scenes with Berkshire Hathaway Billionaire Charlie Munger* (New York: John Wiley & Sons, 2000).

16. Ibid.

17. Ibid.

18. Ibid.

19. Warren Buffett, Berkshire Hathaway memo to managers (July 23, 2008).

Chapter 13   Management Principles and Practices

1. Warren Buffett, letter to shareholders, Berkshire Hathaway Annual Report (2005), 14.

2. Warren Buffett, letter to shareholders, Berkshire Hathaway Annual Report (1998), 7.

3. Warren Buffett, letter to shareholders, Berkshire Hathaway Annual Report (1983), 11.

4. Warren Buffett, letter to shareholders, Berkshire Hathaway Annual Report (2008), 14.

5. Warren Buffett, letter to shareholders, Berkshire Hathaway Annual Report (1979), 2.

6. Warren Buffett, letter to shareholders, Berkshire Hathaway Annual Report (1985), 10.

7. Warren Buffett, letter to shareholders, Berkshire Hathaway Annual Report (2007), 6–8.

8. Berkshire Hathaway Annual Meeting (2007).

9. Warren Buffett, letter to shareholders, Berkshire Hathaway Annual Report (1987), 16.

10. Warren Buffett, letter to shareholders, Berkshire Hathaway Annual Report (1994), 7.

11. Warren Buffett, letter to shareholders, Berkshire Hathaway Annual Report (1984), 19.

12. Warren Buffett, letter to shareholders, Berkshire Hathaway Annual Report (1991), 5.

13. Warren Buffett, letter to shareholders, Berkshire Hathaway Annual Report (1987), 4.

14. Warren Buffett, letter to shareholders, Berkshire Hathaway Annual Report (2005), 14.

15. Warren Buffett, letter to shareholders, Berkshire Hathaway Annual Report (1992), 4.

16. Warren Buffett, letter to shareholders, Berkshire Hathaway Annual Report (1987), 24.

17. Warren Buffett, letter to shareholders, Berkshire Hathaway Annual Report (1991), 10.

18. Warren Buffett, letter to shareholders, Berkshire Hathaway Annual Report (1995), 3.

19. Warren Buffett, letter to shareholders, Berkshire Hathaway Annual Report (1990), 9.

20. Warren Buffett, letter to shareholders, Berkshire Hathaway Annual Report (1985), 9.

21. Warren Buffett, letter to shareholders, Berkshire Hathaway Annual Report (2005), 5.

22. Warren Buffett, letter to shareholders, Berkshire Hathaway Annual Report (1992), 1.

23. Warren Buffett, letter to shareholders, Berkshire Hathaway Annual Report (1995), 3.

24. Warren Buffett, letter to shareholders, Berkshire Hathaway Annual Report (1999), 10.

25. Warren Buffett, letter to shareholders, Berkshire Hathaway Annual Report (1995), 2.

26. Warren Buffett, letter to shareholders, Berkshire Hathaway Annual Report (1999), 13.

27. Warren Buffett, letter to shareholders, Berkshire Hathaway Annual Report (1994), 6.

28. Warren Buffett, letter to shareholders, Berkshire Hathaway Annual Report (2005), 4.

29. Warren Buffett, letter to shareholders, Berkshire Hathaway Annual Report (2005), 6.

30. Warren Buffett, letter to shareholders, Berkshire Hathaway Annual Report (1979), 13.

31. Warren Buffett, letter to shareholders, Berkshire Hathaway Annual Report (1999), 5.

32. Warren Buffett, letter to shareholders, Berkshire Hathaway Annual Report (2005), 11.

33. Warren Buffett, letter to shareholders, Berkshire Hathaway Annual Report (1987), 6.

34. Warren Buffett, letter to shareholders, Berkshire Hathaway Annual Report (1995), 12.

35. Warren Buffett, letter to shareholders, Berkshire Hathaway Annual Report (1990), 9.

36. Warren Buffett, letter to shareholders, Berkshire Hathaway Annual Report (1996), 4.

37. Warren Buffett, letter to shareholders, Berkshire Hathaway Annual Report (2002), 4.

38. Warren Buffett, letter to shareholders, Berkshire Hathaway Annual Report (2004), 8.

39. Warren Buffett, letter to shareholders, Berkshire Hathaway Annual Report (1994), 6.

40. Warren Buffett, letter to shareholders, Berkshire Hathaway Annual Report (2007), 13.

41. Warren Buffett, letter to shareholders, Berkshire Hathaway Annual Report (1988), 6.

42. Warren Buffett, letter to shareholders, Berkshire Hathaway Annual Report (2006), 17.

43. Warren Buffett, letter to shareholders, Berkshire Hathaway Annual Report (2005), 20.

44. "Owner-Related Business Principles," Berkshire Hathaway Inc. Owners Manual (1996).

45. Warren Buffett, letter to shareholders, Berkshire Hathaway Annual Report (2003), 17.

46. Warren Buffett, letter to shareholders, Berkshire Hathaway Annual Report (1992), 22.

47. Warren Buffett, letter to shareholders, Berkshire Hathaway Annual Report (1987), 23.

48. Warren Buffett, letter to shareholders, Berkshire Hathaway Annual Report (1980), 14.

49. Warren Buffett, letter to shareholders, Berkshire Hathaway Annual Report (2002), 12.

50. Warren Buffett, letter to shareholders, Berkshire Hathaway Annual Report (1996), 12.

51. Warren Buffett, letter to shareholders, Berkshire Hathaway Annual Report (1978), 8.

52. Warren Buffett, letter to shareholders, Berkshire Hathaway Annual Report (2004), 5.

53. Warren Buffett, letter to shareholders, Berkshire Hathaway Annual Report (1992), 20.

54. Warren Buffett, letter to shareholders, Berkshire Hathaway Annual Report (2006), 19.

55. Warren Buffett, letter to shareholders, Berkshire Hathaway Annual Report (2000), 4.

56. Warren Buffett, letter to shareholders, Berkshire Hathaway Annual Report (1983), 14.

57. Warren Buffett, letter to shareholders, Berkshire Hathaway Annual Report (2003), 1.

58. Warren Buffett, letter to shareholders, Berkshire Hathaway Annual Report (1983), 15.

59. Warren Buffett, letter to shareholders, Berkshire Hathaway Annual Report (1979), 12.

60. Warren Buffett, letter to shareholders, Berkshire Hathaway Annual Report (1999), 16.

61. Warren Buffett, letter to shareholders, Berkshire Hathaway Annual Report (1988), 22.

62. Warren Buffett, letter to shareholders, Berkshire Hathaway Annual Report (1999), 17.

Chapter 14 Executive Behavior

1. Warren Buffett, letter to shareholders, Berkshire Hathaway Annual Report (2002), 21.

2. Warren Buffett, letter to shareholders, Berkshire Hathaway Annual Report (2001), 3.

3. Warren Buffett, letter to shareholders, Berkshire Hathaway Annual Report (1984), 18.

4. Warren Buffett, letter to shareholders, Berkshire Hathaway Annual Report (1999), 10.

5. Warren Buffett, letter to shareholders, Berkshire Hathaway Annual Report (2006), 19.

6. Warren Buffett, letter to shareholders, Berkshire Hathaway Annual Report (1988), 13.

7. Warren Buffett, letter to shareholders, Berkshire Hathaway Annual Report (1998), 14.

8. Warren Buffett, letter to shareholders, Berkshire Hathaway Annual Report (1996), 12.

9. "An Exclusive Conversation with Warren Buffet," Interview with Charlie Rose, (May 10, 2007).

10. Warren Buffett, letter to shareholders, Berkshire Hathaway Annual Report (1994), 7.

11. Warren Buffett, letter to shareholders, Berkshire Hathaway Annual Report (1984), 17.

12. Warren Buffett, letter to shareholders, Berkshire Hathaway Annual Report (2000), 18.

13. Warren Buffett, letter to shareholders, Berkshire Hathaway Annual Report (1989), 21.

Chapter 15   Mistakes I've Made

1. Warren Buffett, letter to shareholders, Berkshire Hathaway Annual Report (2000), 10.

2. Warren Buffett, letter to shareholders, Berkshire Hathaway Annual Report (1989), 22.

3. Warren Buffett, letter to shareholders, Berkshire Hathaway Annual Report (2000), 10.

4. Warren Buffett, letter to shareholders, Berkshire Hathaway Annual Report (2000), 13.

5. Warren Buffett, letter to shareholders, Berkshire Hathaway Annual Report (2003), 15.

6. Warren Buffett, letter to shareholders, Berkshire Hathaway Annual Report (1991), 14.

7. Warren Buffett, letter to shareholders, Berkshire Hathaway Annual Report (2007), 8.

8. Warren Buffett, letter to shareholders, Berkshire Hathaway Annual Report (1997), 13.

9. Warren Buffett, letter to shareholders, Berkshire Hathaway Annual Report (1996), 13.

10. Warren Buffett, letter to shareholders, Berkshire Hathaway Annual Report (1997), 16.

11. "In His Own Words—Conversation with Charlie Rose," PBS (May 2, 2004).

Chapter 16   Personal Investing

1. Warren Buffett, letter to shareholders, Berkshire Hathaway Annual Report (1992), 12.

2. Warren Buffett, letter to shareholders, Berkshire Hathaway Annual Report (1996), 12.

3. Warren Buffett, letter to shareholders, Berkshire Hathaway Annual Report (1993), 13.

4. Warren Buffett, letter to shareholders, Berkshire Hathaway Annual Report (2000), 13.

5. Warren Buffett, letter to shareholders, Berkshire Hathaway Annual Report (2000), 14.

6. Warren Buffett, letter to shareholders, Berkshire Hathaway Annual Report (1992), 2.

7. Warren Buffett, letter to shareholders, Berkshire Hathaway Annual Report (1985), 3.

8. Warren Buffett, letter to shareholders, Berkshire Hathaway Annual Report (1986), 15.

9. Warren Buffett, letter to shareholders, Berkshire Hathaway Annual Report (1997), 4.

10. Warren Buffett, letter to shareholders, Berkshire Hathaway Annual Report (1997), 5.

11. "In His Own Words—Conversation with Charlie Rose," PBS (May 2, 2004).

12. Warren Buffett, "The Superinvestors of Graham-and-Doddsville" (edited transcript of speech given at Columbia University, New York, 1984).

Chapter 17   Buffett, the Teacher

1. Jim Rasmussen, "Billionaire Talks Strategy with Students," *Omaha Herald* (January 2, 1994): 173.

2. In His Own Words—Conversation with Charlie Rose," PBS (May 2, 2004).

3. Warren Buffett, Berkshire Hathaway annual meeting (2007).

4. Cynthia H. Milligan, "Warren, A Conversation with Dean Cynthia H. Milligan," *Nebraska Business* (Fall 2001), 2.

5. Warren Buffett (speech before University of Florida MBA students, September 4, 2006).

6. Warren Buffett, letter to shareholders, Berkshire Hathaway Annual Report (2000), 11.

7. Warren Buffett, letter to shareholders, Berkshire Hathaway Annual Report (2004), 21.

Chapter 18   Humor and Stories

1. Warren Buffett, letter to shareholders, Berkshire Hathaway Annual Report (2001), 4.

2. Warren Buffett, letter to shareholders, Berkshire Hathaway Annual Report (2007), 3.

3. Warren Buffett, letter to shareholders, Berkshire Hathaway Annual Report (2005), 14.

4. Warren Buffett, letter to shareholders, Berkshire Hathaway Annual Report (1990), 1.

5. Warren Buffett, letter to shareholders, Berkshire Hathaway Annual Report (2005), 7.

6. Warren Buffett, letter to shareholders, Berkshire Hathaway Annual Report (1987), 4.

7. Warren Buffett, letter to shareholders, Berkshire Hathaway Annual Report (2006), 6.

8. Warren Buffett, letter to shareholders, Berkshire Hathaway Annual Report (2005), 4.

9. Warren Buffett, letter to shareholders, Berkshire Hathaway Annual Report (2004), 22.

10. Warren Buffett, letter to shareholders, Berkshire Hathaway Annual Report (2002), 4.

11. Warren Buffett, letter to shareholders, Berkshire Hathaway Annual Report (2007), 20.

12. Warren Buffett, letter to shareholders, Berkshire Hathaway Annual Report (1989), 19.

13. Warren Buffett, letter to shareholders, Berkshire Hathaway Annual Report (1997), 19.

14. Warren Buffett, letter to shareholders, Berkshire Hathaway Annual Report (1995), 1.

15. Warren Buffett, letter to shareholders, Berkshire Hathaway Annual Report (1992), 9.

16. Warren Buffett, letter to shareholders, Berkshire Hathaway Annual Report (1989), 26.

17. Janet Lowe, *Warren Buffett Speaks: Wit and Wisdom from the World's Greatest Investor* (Hoboken, NJ: John Wiley & Sons, 2007), 15.

18. Warren Buffett, letter to shareholders, Berkshire Hathaway Annual Report (1992), 17.

About the Author

Richard J. Connors is a Registered Investment Advisor and owner of Connors Investment Management Company in St. Louis, Missouri. Beginning in 2006, he has presented a class on Warren Buffett at the Washington University in St. Louis Lifelong Learning Institute. He is a graduate of the University of Notre Dame Business School and the St. Louis University School of Law.